Construct 2 Game Development by Example

Learn how to make games for multiple platforms with Construct 2

John Bura

[PACKT] PUBLISHING

BIRMINGHAM - MUMBAI

Construct 2 Game Development by Example

First published: June 2014

Production reference: 1180614

Published by Packt Publishing Ltd.
Livery Place
35 Livery Street
Birmingham B3 2PB, UK.

ISBN 978-1-84969-806-1

`www.packtpub.com`

Cover image by Asher Wishkerman (`wishkerman@hotmail.com`)

Credits

Author
John Bura

Reviewers
Albert Chen
D.M. Noyé
Keefer Sery

Commissioning Editor
Pramila Balan

Acquisition Editors
Pramila Balan
Sam Wood

Content Development Editor
Poonam Jain

Technical Editors
Pratik More
Ritika Singh
Rohit Kumar Singh

Copy Editors
Roshni Banerjee
Adithi Shetty

Project Coordinator
Amey Sawant

Proofreaders
Paul Hindle
Joanna McMahon

Indexer
Hemangini Bari

Production Coordinator
Shantanu Zagade

Cover Work
Shantanu Zagade

About the Author

John Bura has been programming games since 1997 and teaching since 2002. He is the owner of the game development studio Mammoth Interactive. This company produces games for Xbox 360, iPhone, iPad, Android, HTML5, ad-games, and others. Mammoth Interactive recently sold a game to Nickelodeon! He has been contracted by many companies to provide game design, audio, programming, level design, and project management. To this day, he has contributed to 40 commercial games. Several of the games he has produced have risen to number one in Apple's App Store. In his spare time, he likes playing ultimate frisbee, cycling, and working out.

About the Reviewers

Albert Chen is Assistant Professor in the Game Design and Development program at Cogswell Polytechnical College in Sunnyvale, CA. He has led students in developing serious games using game engines for The Boeing Company, NeuroSky, and Ericsson. His team won the Boeing Performance Excellence Award in 2008.

Prior to joining Cogswell in 2007, he was a professional game developer for over 12 years, working at EA, LucasArts, Factor 5, and The 3DO Company. He has a Bachelor of Arts degree in International Relations from UC Davis and a Master of Arts degree in Entrepreneurship and Innovation from Cogswell Polytechnical College.

I would like to thank my family for their love and support: Joy, Kayli, Brandon, and my mother, Sin-Hing Chen.

D.M. Noyé (Dwandell M. Noyé) is a successful entrepreneur, conceptual designer, and technical consultant with extensive experience working on major commercial projects with a number of large corporations as well as independent ventures spanning several fields, from music and literary arts to video games.

I'd like to thank Packt Publishing for believing in my expertise and giving me the opportunity to share it on this great project. I'd also like to thank the entire Scirra Construct community for the deep knowledge base they've built over a number of years, allowing me to acquire the forward-thinking skill of event-based programming.

Keefer Sery is currently a Game Art and Production major at Drexel University, expecting to graduate in 2015. He is also a freelancer for Digitas Health. His most notable work in Construct 2 was a segment of the research and development for Evolutionary Guidance Media's *Cyberhero League*. The project went on to become a winning entry in the World Future Society's BetaLaunch competition.

I would like to thank my grandmother, Janet Mitchener, for giving me the opportunity to attend school, and Dr. Dana Klisanen for giving me my first break in the industry.

www.PacktPub.com

Support files, eBooks, discount offers, and more

You might want to visit www.PacktPub.com for support files and downloads related to your book.

Did you know that Packt offers eBook versions of every book published, with PDF and ePub files available? You can upgrade to the eBook version at www.PacktPub.com and as a print book customer, you are entitled to a discount on the eBook copy. Get in touch with us at service@packtpub.com for more details.

At www.PacktPub.com, you can also read a collection of free technical articles, sign up for a range of free newsletters and receive exclusive discounts and offers on Packt books and eBooks.

http://PacktLib.PacktPub.com

Do you need instant solutions to your IT questions? PacktLib is Packt's online digital book library. Here, you can access, read and search across Packt's entire library of books.

Why subscribe?

- Fully searchable across every book published by Packt
- Copy and paste, print and bookmark content
- On demand and accessible via web browser

Free access for Packt account holders

If you have an account with Packt at www.PacktPub.com, you can use this to access PacktLib today and view nine entirely free books. Simply use your login credentials for immediate access.

Table of Contents

Preface

Games have always been my passion. Creativity and production have always been on my mind. I love talking about production and I hope you enjoy reading about how to make games. This book will give beginners a first-hand knowledge of how to make games in Construct 2. I made my first game in 1997 when I was attending university.

In this book, you will learn how to make several games and learn the secrets of game development. After reading this book, you should have several playable games to build a foundation and move forward. It is important that you actually make the games instead of just reading the book. Game development and entrepreneurship is not a spectator sport. The best developers actually release their games instead of just thinking about making games.

This book is laid out so that anybody can pick it up and make a game. It is also recommended that you go through the chapters in order. This book is best suited towards beginners and people who have never made a game before. Construct 2 is a visual programming language. This means that you don't have to hand code every single detail. Because of this, most of the logic is presented in images. The book is written this way because people who like visual programming languages love images.

Before we continue, let me introduce myself. My name is John Bura and I have been programming since 1997 and teaching since 2002. I have released several games for console and mobile platforms. You can check out my website at `www.mammothinteractive.com`. I hope you get a lot out of this book. This book is designed for beginners who have never programmed before. If you have done some programming, you will be amazed at how easy game development is in Construct 2.

What this book covers

Chapter 1, Getting Started with Construct 2, is an introduction to the book. You can learn about HTML5 games, Construct 2, and general game design in this chapter.

Chapter 2, Inputs and Controls, teaches you how to implement inputs and controls in Construct 2. Inputs and controls are the first and most important part of game design.

Chapter 3, Variables and Arrays, shows you how to store data in variables and arrays.

Chapter 4, Game Mechanics, covers the mechanics of a game, which are extremely important to learn and understand in order to make a great game. In this chapter, you will learn how to implement them.

Chapter 5, Making a Simple Shooter, covers shooters, which is one of the most popular game genres out there. You will learn the mechanics of making a simple shooter in this chapter.

Chapter 6, Making a Tower Defense Game, teaches you how to make one of the most popular and addictive game genres.

Chapter 7, Making a Puzzle Physics Game, teaches you how to incorporate physics and puzzle elements into a game in Construct 2.

Chapter 8, Exporting Your Game, covers how to export your game. People need to play your game. Construct 2 has many different areas to which you can export your game.

Appendix, Where to Go from Here, wraps up everything you have learned in the book. There are also tips on how to start your own game studio.

What you need for this book

For this book, you will need Construct 2. In order to get Construct 2, you need to go to `www.scirra.com` and download it. Construct 2 only works on a PC right now. You will also need a PC to run Construct 2.

Who this book is for

This book is meant for complete beginners. I assume that the people reading this will know nothing about computers or game development. If you are an experienced developer or you are knowledgeable in coding, this book might be too basic for you.

Conventions

In this book, you will find a number of styles of text that distinguish between different kinds of information. Here are some examples of these styles, and an explanation of their meaning.

Code words in text, database table names, folder names, filenames, file extensions, pathnames, dummy URLs, user input, and Twitter handles are shown as follows: "This is called an `if` statement, and all it does is check for a condition to be true."

A block of code is set as follows:

```
GameObject.Speed = 10;
GameObject.Move.Right;
```

New terms and **important words** are shown in bold. Words that you see on the screen, in menus or dialog boxes for example, appear in the text like this: "To add an event, all you have to do is click on the **Add event** button."

Warnings or important notes appear in a box like this.

Tips and tricks appear like this.

Reader feedback

Feedback from our readers is always welcome. Let us know what you think about this book—what you liked or may have disliked. Reader feedback is important for us to develop titles that you really get the most out of.

To send us general feedback, simply send an e-mail to `feedback@packtpub.com`, and mention the book title via the subject of your message.

If there is a topic that you have expertise in and you are interested in either writing or contributing to a book, see our author guide on `www.packtpub.com/authors`.

Customer support

Now that you are the proud owner of a Packt book, we have a number of things to help you to get the most from your purchase.

Errata

Although we have taken every care to ensure the accuracy of our content, mistakes do happen. If you find a mistake in one of our books—maybe a mistake in the text or the code—we would be grateful if you would report this to us. By doing so, you can save other readers from frustration and help us improve subsequent versions of this book. If you find any errata, please report them by visiting `http://www.packtpub.com/submit-errata`, selecting your book, clicking on the **errata submission form** link, and entering the details of your errata. Once your errata are verified, your submission will be accepted and the errata will be uploaded on our website, or added to any list of existing errata, under the Errata section of that title. Any existing errata can be viewed by selecting your title from `http://www.packtpub.com/support`.

Piracy

Piracy of copyright material on the Internet is an ongoing problem across all media. At Packt, we take the protection of our copyright and licenses very seriously. If you come across any illegal copies of our works, in any form, on the Internet, please provide us with the location address or website name immediately so that we can pursue a remedy.

Please contact us at `copyright@packtpub.com` with a link to the suspected pirated material.

We appreciate your help in protecting our authors, and our ability to bring you valuable content.

Questions

You can contact us at `questions@packtpub.com` if you are having a problem with any aspect of the book, and we will do our best to address it.

1
Getting Started with Construct 2

Game development is very similar to making music, writing books, making movies, and pretty much every other creative process. As a creator, you might have an idea that you want people to enjoy. You have to find the tools and the time necessary to make your ideas a reality. If you don't make your idea a reality, people will not get to enjoy your creation. It only makes sense that you choose the right tools for the right job.

With lots of options in terms of how to develop your game and with what engine, it is easy to become lost. Let's take a moment to see what we really want in a game engine. A game engine should have the following attributes:

- It should be very user friendly
- It should have a lot of export options
- It should be fairly inexpensive
- It should be able to make your creation a reality

Let's have a small introduction to Construct 2. Construct 2 is one of the best non-programming engines around. I have made a ton of games on it.

So, what makes **Construct 2 (C2)** so awesome? The first reason is that it develops games using HTML5. HTML5 is the new version of HTML, and the best part about this is that you can play these HTML5 games right in your browser. The Web has a ton of infrastructure around it, and HTML5 games tap into that infrastructure. HTML5 games can be played almost anywhere, which makes exporting a real charm. While HTML5 is still under development, browser support gets better by the day.

In this chapter, we will cover the following topics:

- Downloading and installing Construct 2
- Coding in Construct 2

Downloading and installing Construct 2

Downloading and installing Construct 2 is pretty easy. You need to have a computer if you want to use Construct 2. You cannot run this on a Mac. You need to perform the following steps to download and install Construct 2:

1. Go to `http://www.scirra.com`.
2. Click on the **Download** button, as shown in the following screenshot:

3. Once you've downloaded it, follow the instructions and the installation should be simple.

What do the numbers mean?

The numbers refer to the version of Construct 2 you are using (`https://www.scirra.com/construct2/releases`). This is simply just Scirra's way of versioning the software. There are stable releases and beta releases. Scirra releases a beta version first to work out all of the bugs then they release a stable version. You should use the stable release as the beta releases might be a bit unstable. On that note, I always download the beta releases and I have never had a problem. However, it is advisable to use the stable releases.

Coding in Construct 2

For all of our visual programming examples, we will be typing them in pseudo-code for easier understanding. This code will not work, but it will give you an idea about the concepts of programming. So, let's use an example of moving something to the right. The code might look something like the following line of code:

```
GameObject.Move.Right;
```

This works, but we haven't set up a speed for the object. Right now, either the default speed will be the speed of the object and the object will move too fast for the human eye to see, or the compiler might get an error. If you misspell a word or make some kind of syntax error, the game might not run. So, we might have to update our code as follows:

```
GameObject.Speed = 10;
GameObject.Move.Right;
```

Notice how there is a semicolon at the end of each line. The semicolon tells the computer to read the next line. However, if you look at the code, we haven't told the computer to check for a button being pressed. If we add that code, it might be something similar to the following code:

```
if (RightArrow.Pressed) {
GameObject.Speed = 10;
GameObject.Move.Right;
}
```

As per the preceding line of code, if the right arrow is pressed then the `GameObject` will move to the right. This is called an `if` statement, and all it does is check for a condition to be true. In this case, if the right arrow is pressed then the `GameObject` will move to the right; however, if the right arrow is not pressed then nothing will happen. Now, let's add the logic for the left arrow being pressed. The code is as follows:

```
if (RightArrow.Pressed) {
GameObject.Speed = 10;
GameObject.Move.Right;
}
if (LeftArrow.Pressed) {
GameObject.Speed = 10;
GameObject.Move.Left;
}
```

We should mention at this point that there are only two lines of code in these `if` statements, but there can be many more. Imagine how gigantic the code base is for some of the games you play. Those games are much more complex. Sometimes, the logic for the right arrow being pressed can be more than a page of logic. Let's add some code that will make the `GameObject` move in four directions. The code is as follows:

```
if (RightArrow.Pressed) {
GameObject.Speed = 10;
GameObject.Move.Right;
}
if (LeftArrow.Pressed) {
GameObject.Speed = 10;
GameObject.Move.Left;
}
if (UpArrow.Pressed) {
GameObject.Speed = 10;
GameObject.Move.Up;
}
if (DownArrow.Pressed) {
GameObject.Speed = 10;
GameObject.Move.Down;
}
```

This is a lot of code and we are not even making a complex game. So far, our game just has a `GameObject` moving up, down, left, and right. We have no projectiles, no antagonists, and no artificial intelligence. So, why a code like this? Well, it's only recently that non-coding languages have been around. If you have ever played a game, it was painstakingly coded. We should also point out that the preceding code is an abbreviated version to make it simpler. Depending on the language, moving something across the screen might take many more lines of code.

Working with visual programming languages

Visual programming languages do exactly the same thing that regular programming languages do, except that all of the logic is placed visually. This is more efficient for several reasons:

- You can layout information in different areas
- Logic that would take multiple lines of code can be in one dialog box
- You can visually see that your game is coming together

At this point, we should also mention that, in most game development environments, you have to do most of the work by typing commands. Having an editor where you visually assemble your game, even if it is just the level design, wasn't always the case. One of the best features of a visual programming language is that you can see everything and test everything much more easily than traditional game development environments.

Layout and event sheets

In Construct 2, we have two main areas in which we work. The first area is called the layout, which is a visual representation of what the game will look like when a player plays it. In this area, we can perform the following actions:

- Drop in all of our game objects so that we can arrange them the way we like
- Set the look of the game
- Add the **heads-up display** (**HUD**) and other **Graphic User Interface** (**GUI**) elements

The following screenshot shows the layout with some game objects on it:

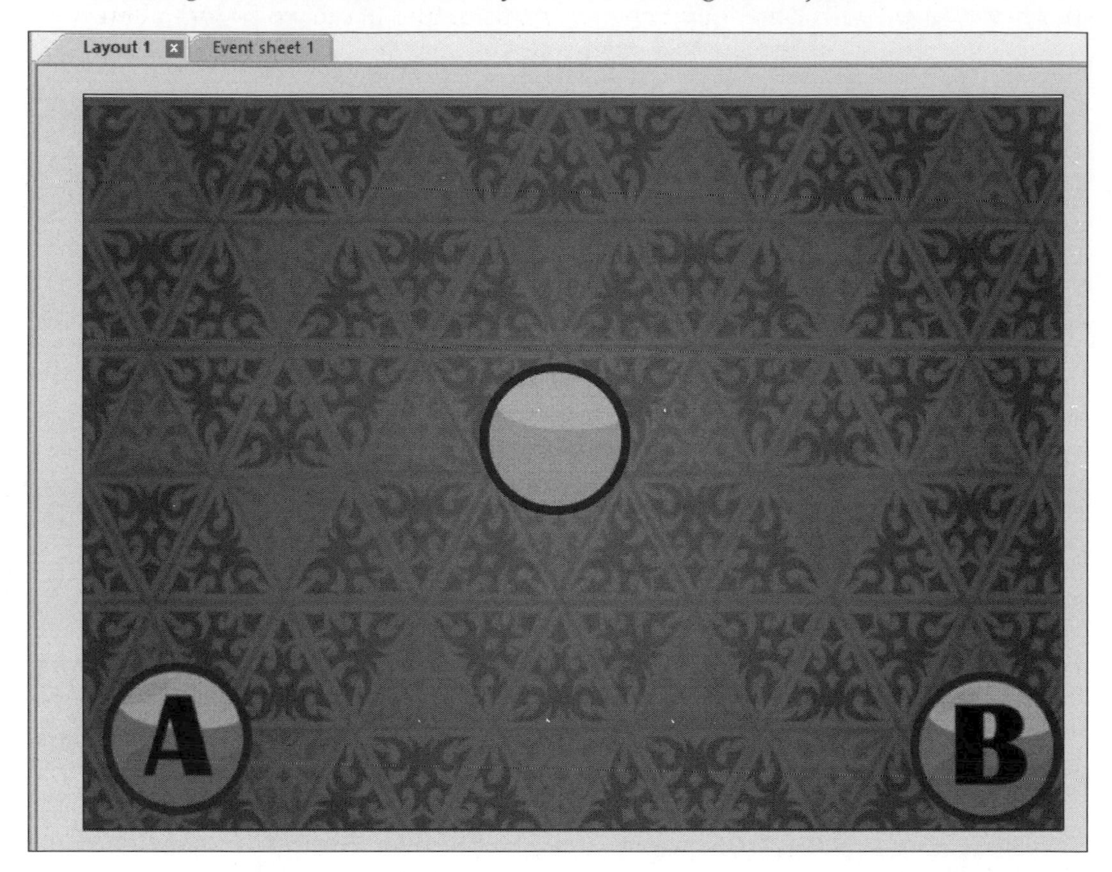

Each game object is a sprite. A sprite can have an image, an animation (multiple images), and a game logic attached to it. Your event sheet will look like the following screenshot:

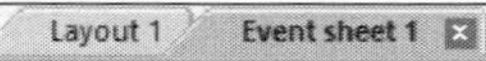

The second area is the event sheet. An event sheet is where the game logic goes. This is where we would "code" the game in other environments (see the preceding image).

If we want to add some logic so that the game characters will move left and right, this is where we will add it. Right now, there is nothing in our event sheet; however, we can go and add something to demonstrate how we will "code" in the game logic.

To add an event, all you have to do is click on the **Add event** button. Another way of adding an event is to just double-click on the area underneath the **Event sheet 1** tab, as shown in the following screenshot:

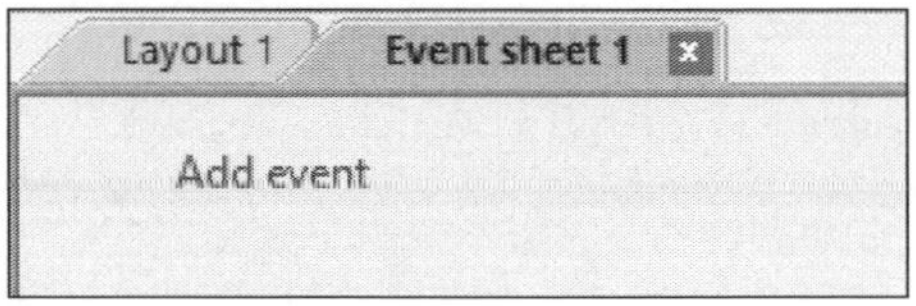

The **Add event** dialog box will provide you with all of the possible game objects and commands you can use in your game.

Sprites

As you can see in the **Layout1** window, all the game objects in the game are here. You will also see a system icon. This icon brings up the internal commands and functional commands that you can use.

If we want to select the sprite to move forward, we can simply select the sprite and give it a command. Remember, in other environments, you would have to type that in. If we want to make the sprite move left with the **A** button, we can simply select the **A** button and add some logic that would make the sprite move left, as shown in the following screenshot:

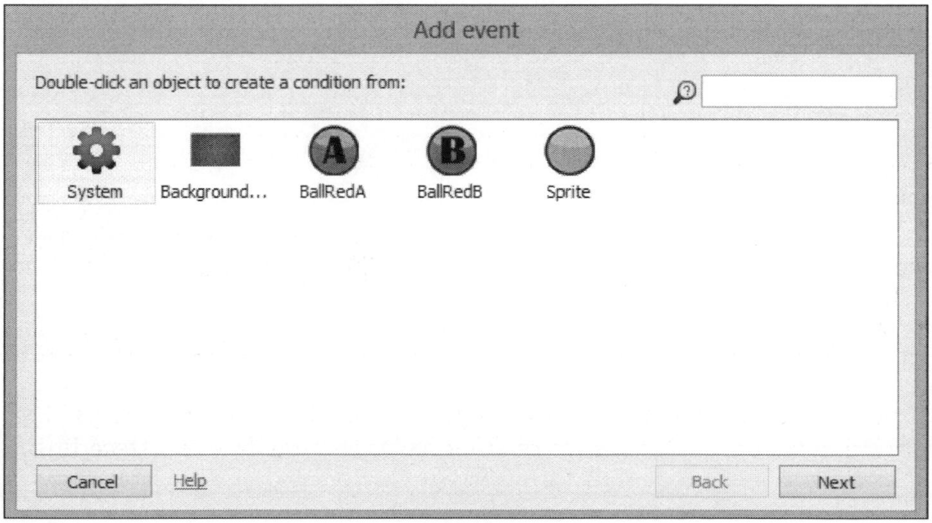

You will also notice that all of the game objects are properly named. It is very important to name all of your game objects appropriately. When your game has a few hundred game objects, it will become much easier to manage if your game objects are named properly.

Let's go ahead and select the sprite by double-clicking on it. Once you do this, you will be able to see a bunch of conditions. These conditions must be met before we give an action to perform. In the same way as the `if` statement we looked at a few pages ago, we need to make sure a condition is true; only then we can go ahead and add an action. The **Add event** window should look like the following screenshot:

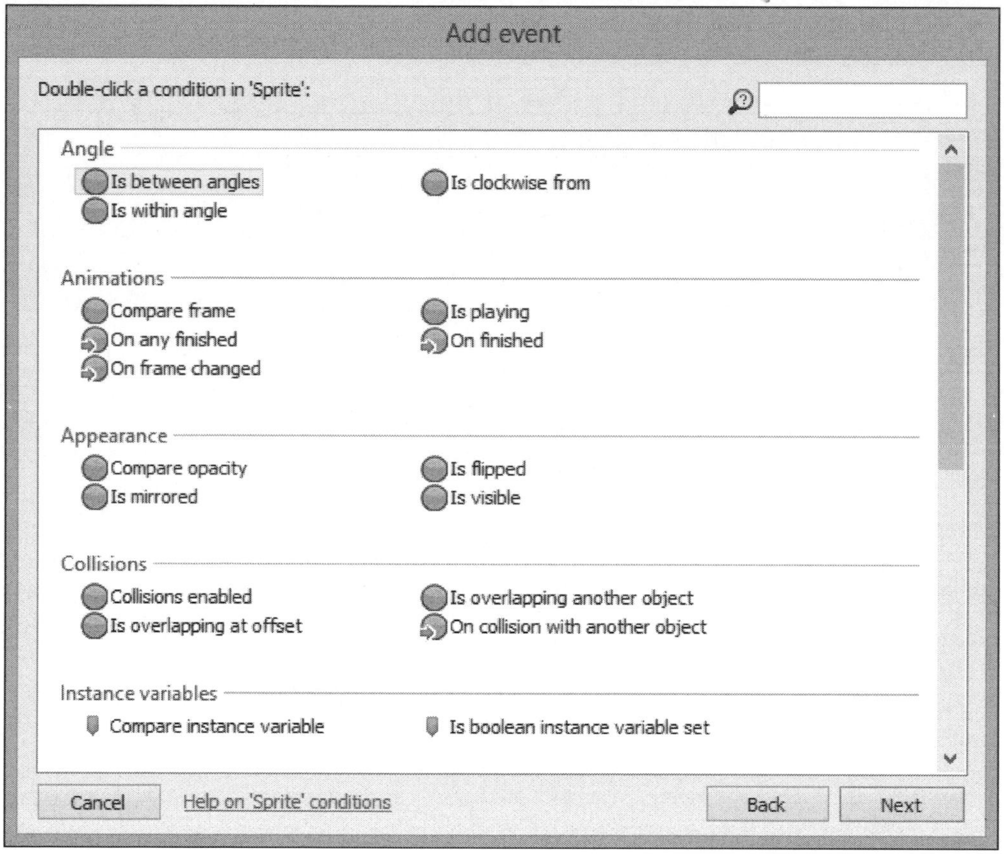

Now, let's scroll down and select **Is on-screen** as shown in the following screenshot:

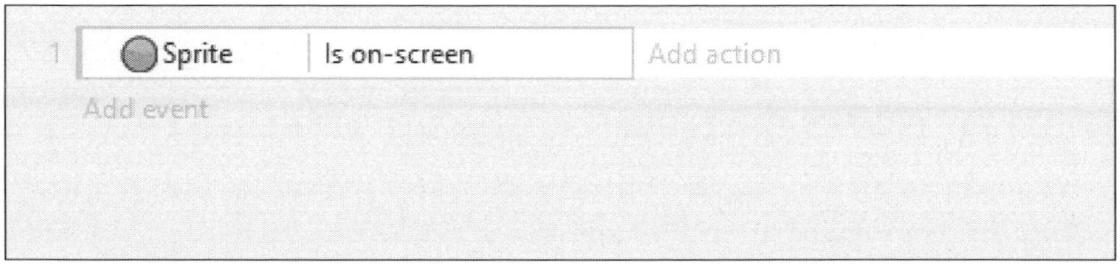

As you can see, once you select **Is on-screen**, the onscreen condition is added to the event sheet. You can also see that you can add an action and another event. We want the sprite to do something before we move on.

If you click on **Add action**, you will get a similar dialog box but with actions instead of conditions. Let's go ahead and click on the **Sprite** element and the following screen will pop up:

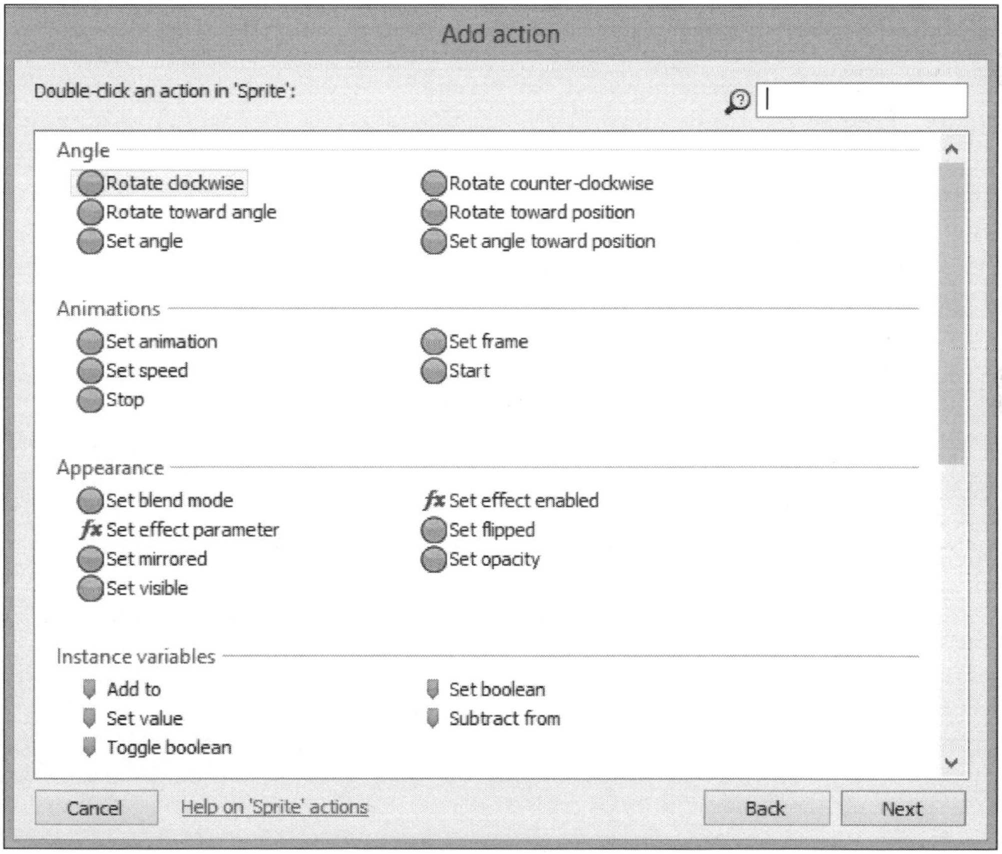

You will see actions that you can add to the sprite, as shown in the preceding screenshot. Take a moment to look at all of the actions and you can see how versatile Construct 2 really is.

Once you have finished looking, go ahead and click on **Rotate clockwise**. This will make the sprite rotate. You can enter in any number in the **Degrees** textbox:

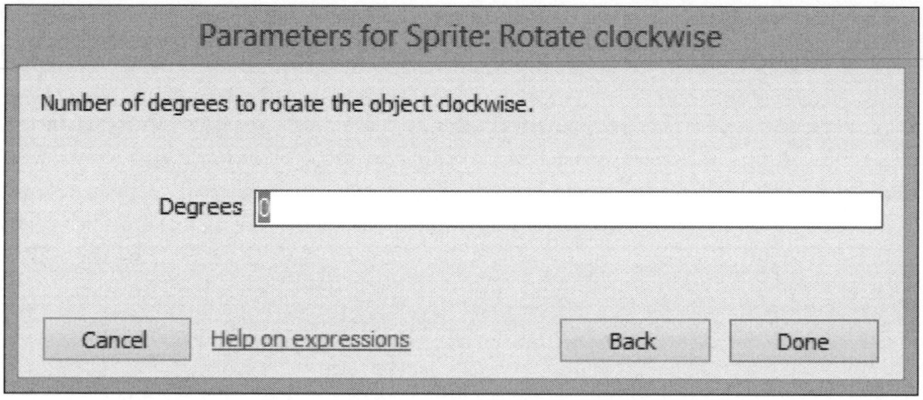

Let's look at what we are telling the computer to do. While the condition of the sprite is onscreen, the action will be to rotate the sprite. If we were to run the game, the sprite will rotate. This may seem like it is really simple, but imagine if you had to code all of that by typing in commands. It would take a very long time. What we have just shown you is the power of visual programming languages. They take out most of the work needed to develop games. Instead, you can focus on creativity and design versus technicality.

Summary

In this chapter, we learned about Construct 2 and how it works. More importantly, we learned how and why Construct 2 is an amazing engine to work with and why it can save us time. Construct 2 has a visual programming language. We set up a small example in this chapter and we saw that a visual programming language is easy to follow.

In the next chapter, we are going to talk about inputs and controls. Inputs and controls are one of the most important parts of game design. Have you ever played a game with amazing graphics and amazing action but the controls don't work properly? Bad controls ruin games from the hobby level to the AAA level. Luckily, Construct 2 has some fantastic controls already set up and the engine is so versatile that you can add robust controls of your own.

2
Inputs and Controls

Inputs and controls are really important for game design. Games are interactive by nature, and designers need to plan out and test controls in order to make an effective game.

In this chapter, we will learn about the following topics:

- Keyboard inputs
- Rotating the angle
- Mouse inputs
- Game loop
- Touch control inputs

Getting started with inputs and controls

Software works with human interaction. The most basic activity of any computer interface is a user providing information and the computer reacting to that information. In other programming languages, one of the most basic concepts you learn is the function. The basic premise of a function is to work with inputs.

The way the user inputs information is actually really important. Imagine a simple calculator application that has really nice buttons and works exactly the way you expect it to. Now, imagine a calculator application where the buttons were in a different order than the usual one. The application would be much harder to use. Obviously, you want the application and the user experience to be as good and as easy as possible. Applications such as games have a purpose, and the software and hardware should not interfere.

Let's move this concept to games. Let's imagine a platform game, which is a game where you run and jump onto platforms. For our example, we will be making the game for a computer. Touch devices have different inputs, which we will discuss shortly. In this platformer game, the player will have to run and jump. In order to do that, we need to have specific controls that the player can understand. There are various ways to implement controls, but the controls need to be easy to understand. In the case of classic game genres, they cannot be different from what the player is expecting.

Inputs to a game are really important. First of all, they make the computer software work; but more importantly, they make the game what it is. Without good input controls, a game doesn't live up to its potential and all of the time you spend on mechanics and art is wasted. It is good to spend a lot of time to make sure the controls and the inputs in the game are well thought out. Whether you are making a simple indie game or an AAA game, controls are vital for the success of the game.

So, how do we think about controls in Construct 2? Well, the first thing you need to think about is for which platform are you making the game. Mobile games are very different from computer games. You have to approach the entire input design differently. Certain genres work on certain platforms, and these same genres might not work on other platforms. Imagine if you made a real-time strategy game such as Starcraft for the iPhone—it wouldn't work. This game can fundamentally not be on the iPhone because of the mechanics and the inputs. Knowing the limitations of your inputs is vital to making a good game. Construct 2 offers a lot of options for inputs, and the currently offered inputs are as follows:

- Keyboard inputs
- Mouse inputs
- Touch (mobile) inputs
- Gamepad (XBOX 360 Gamepad) inputs

Adding inputs is not an easy task in any game environment. Usually, the developer has to write a lot of code to make it work. Luckily, Construct 2 takes most of that out of the equation because most of the code is written in the backend and all you have to do is add the visual blocks.

Keyboard inputs

Keyboard inputs simply involve the keyboard. There are many ways to use the keyboard. You can use the number pad, you can use the arrow keys, and you can even use the main keys itself. It is always important to know that not every keyboard has a number pad, so make sure the design takes this into account.

Let's add keyboard functionality. In order to work with this, we need to add at least one game object to Construct 2. Simply drag an image from your desktop to Construct 2. Your game should look something like the following screenshot:

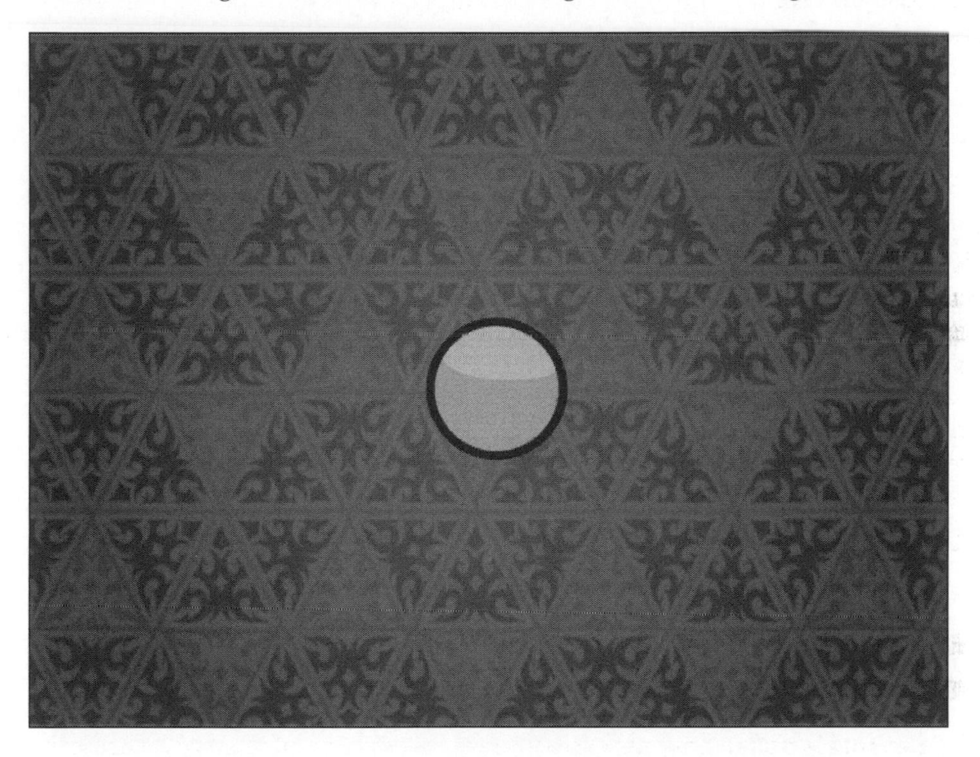

We now have a game object to work with. In order to add any kind of controller functionality, you have to first add the functionality manually. Keyboard control does not come preloaded in a new Construct 2 project.

Inserting a new keyboard object

If you want to add the keyboard or any input functionality, double-click anywhere other than the game objects. You should get the **Insert New Object** window as shown in the following screenshot:

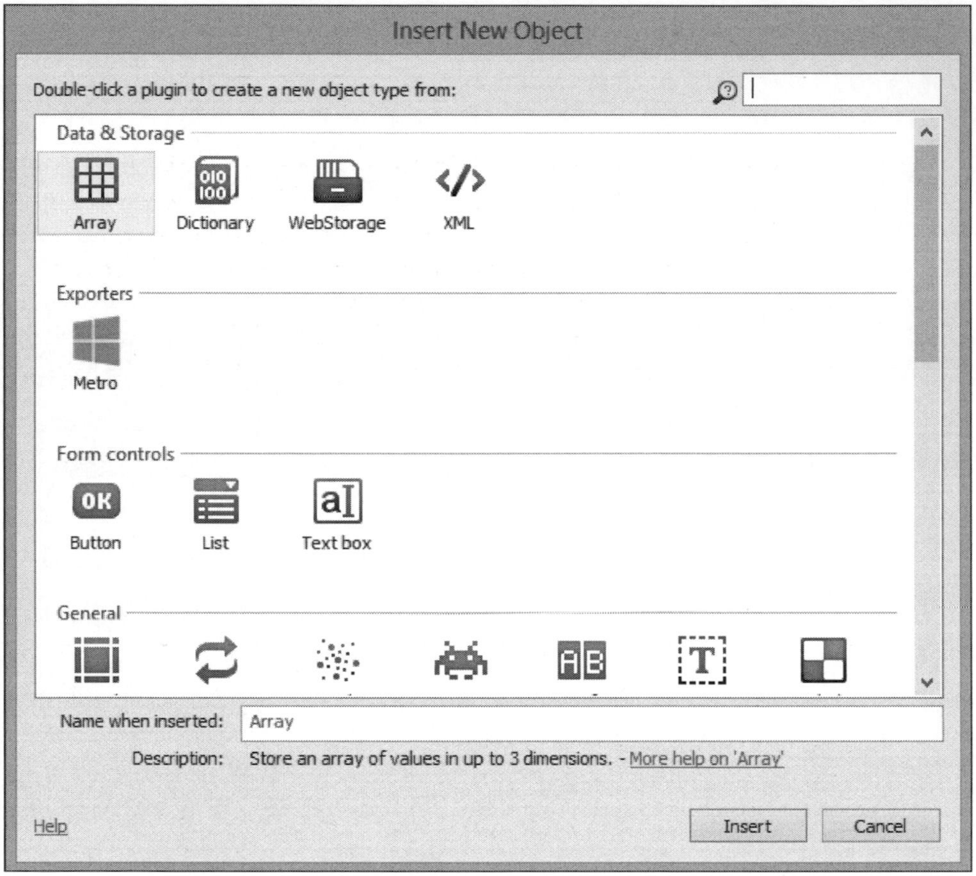

In the **Insert New Object** window, you can add a whole bunch of new objects. If you want to add more functionality, this is where we can add them.

The reason for this comes from the roots of software development. Generally, in order to add more functionality, you have to add more libraries and more functions. If you don't need these libraries or functions, there is no point having them in your project. They could cause conflicts or they could use up too much memory. You should always have just enough objects in your game to make it work. Keep in mind, however, that having too many objects is just as bad as having too few. Luckily in Construct 2, most of the problems with adding objects have been taken out of the equation.

Scroll down on the page and double-click on the **Keyboard** icon to add it to Construct 2's functionality, as shown in the following screenshot:

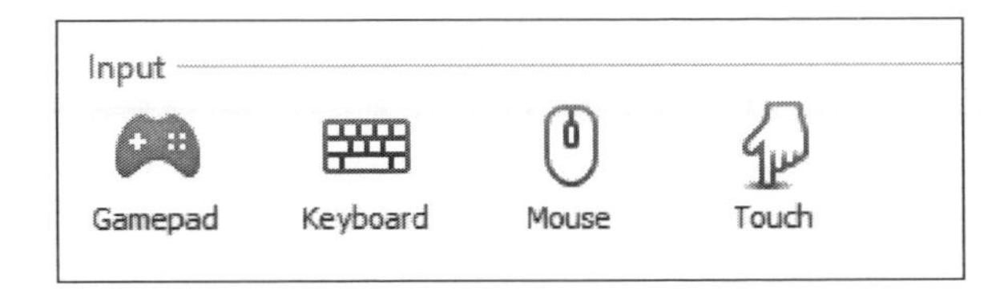

Adding functionality to the keyboard object

Let's start by adding some functionality to the **Keyboard** object. We need to open our event sheet to add some functionality to the object we have placed on the screen. In order to do that, double-click anywhere on the event sheet. You should see the **Keyboard** icon appear, as shown in the following screenshot. If you didn't add the keyboard functionality, this icon would not be there. Go ahead and double-click on the **Keyboard** icon.

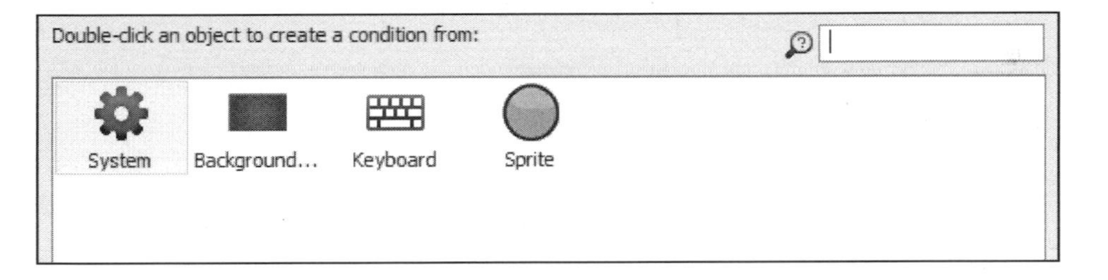

Once you double-click on the **Keyboard** icon, the **Add event** window should pop up. This is shown in the following screenshot:

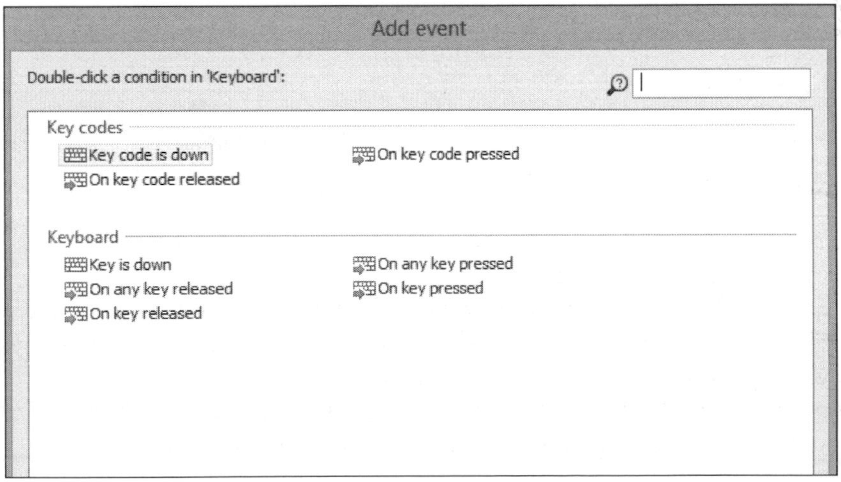

Remember that events in a game are possible outcomes. In this case, we are going to select **On key pressed**.

Setting the keyboard key

Now, we are going to add an action. In this case, the question is, "Is a certain key pressed?" If yes, then the object will move up. Once you click **On key pressed**, you should get the **Parameters for Keyboard: On key pressed** window shown in the following screenshot:

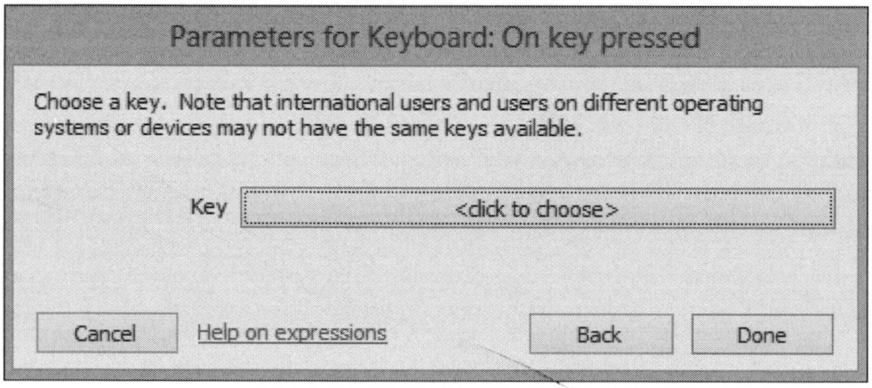

Go ahead and select **<click to choose>**. You should get the dialog box shown in the following screenshot:

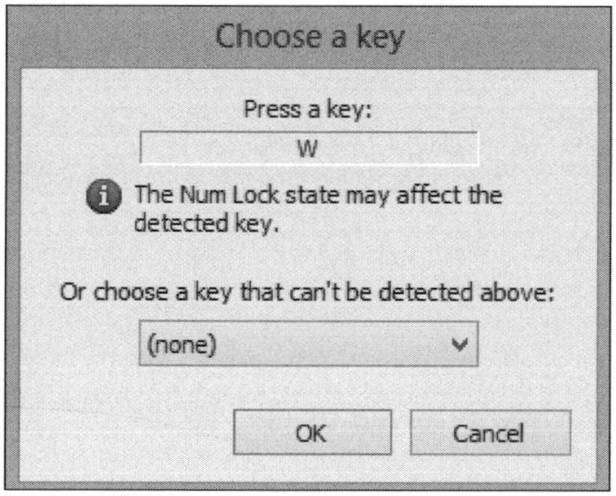

In the **Choose a key** window, you can simply press the key you want. This feature speeds up the workflow quite a bit. If you need to choose another key, for example, the return key, you can use the drop-down box. Once you have the key you want, press **OK** and click on **Done**. You should get something like the following screenshot:

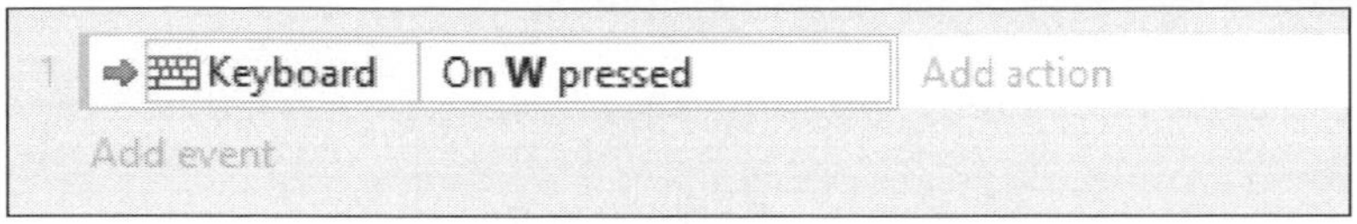

This is the event or the "question" that is being asked: "Is the *W* key pressed?"

Controlling the sprite with the keyboard

We can now add a variety of options, but what we really want to do is make the sprite move in a direction. In order to do that, we need to click on **Add action**. Double-click on the sprite and you should get the following window:

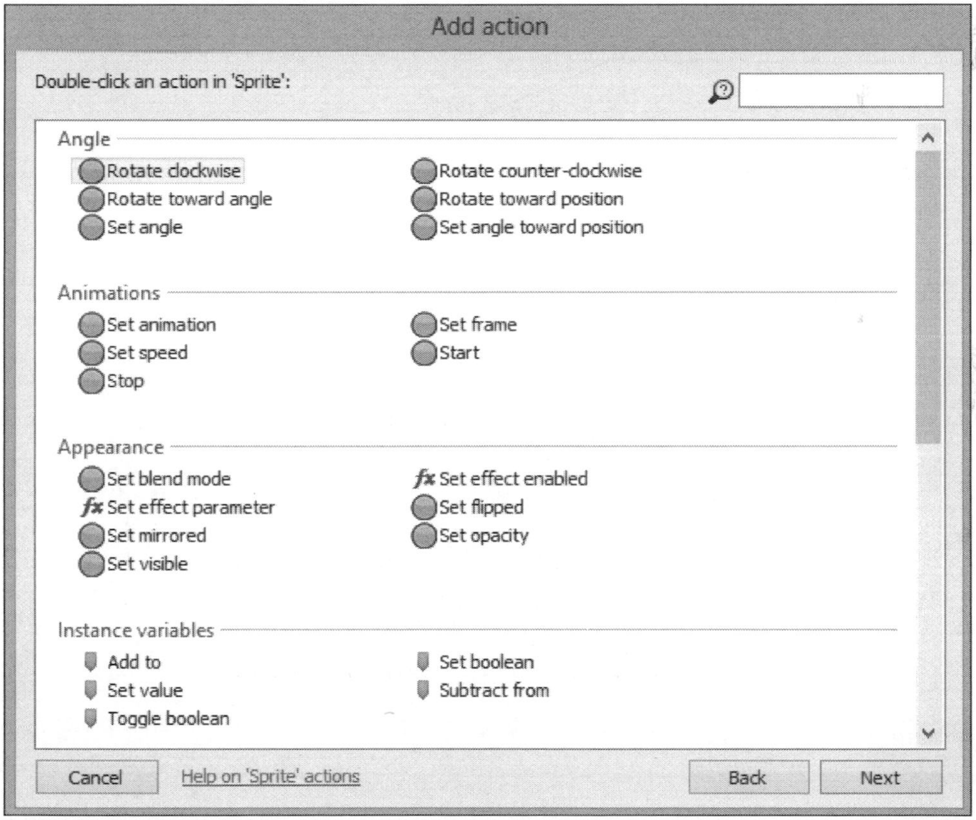

Setting up the direction of the sprite's movement

In the **Add action** window, we can see all of the possible actions we can add for a sprite. In this situation, we want the sprite to move up when the user presses the *W* key. Scroll down until you see **Size & Position** and double-click on **Move at angle** as shown in the following screenshot:

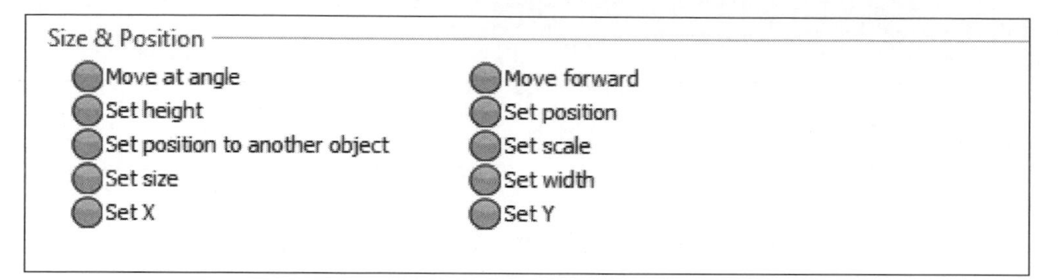

Once you have done that, it should bring up the **Parameters for Sprite: Move at angle** window shown in the following screenshot:

This window will tell the sprite to move at a certain angle and at a certain distance. The angle `0` is the direct right of the sprite. Angle `180` is the direct left of the sprite. Angle `90` is straight down from the sprite and angle `270` is straight up. We want to move the sprite straight up, so type in `270` where it says **Angle** and press **Done**. Once you do that, you should see the following on the screen:

Setting keys for other directions

We have two options to set up commands to move in the other three directions. The first option is to manually do everything all over again, and the second option is to simply copy-and-paste the action. In order to copy-and-paste, you need to click on the purple bar below an event, press *Ctrl* + *C* to copy, and then press *Ctrl* + *V* to paste. Do this three more times so that we have four events in total, as shown in the following screenshot:

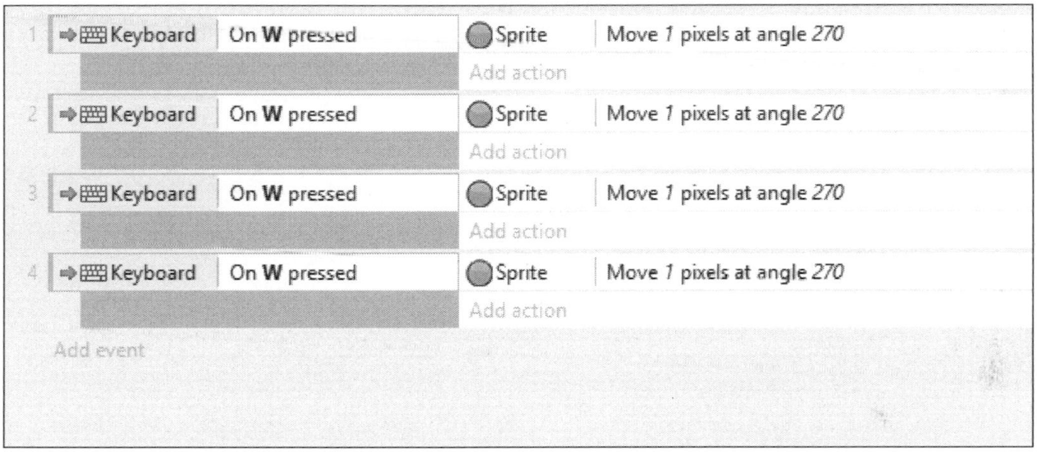

We need to change the keys that are being pressed and the angles that they correspond to. Change the keys by double-clicking on them. They should be in this order: *W* (up), *A* (left), *S* (down), and *D* (right). Then, change the angles by double-clicking them. Change them to `180`, `90`, and `0`. When you're done, our event list should look like this:

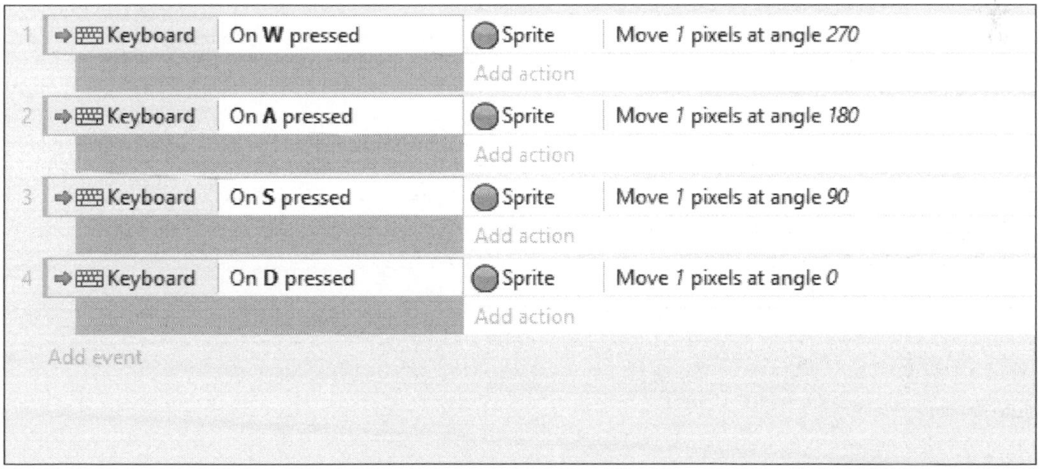

Testing the keyboard controls

Go ahead and run the game by pressing *F5*. This will then test run the game, and you can push *W*, *A*, *S*, and *D* to see the object move around. We now have a game with WASD controls that are easy to understand for most players.

Making the sprite move constantly

Right now, the sprite just moves one pixel in each direction. If you hold any of the WASD keys down, the sprite still moves only one pixel. Let's change the appropriate line of code so that when we hold the key down, the sprite will constantly move. The steps are as follows:

1. Right-click on the **Keyboard** event and select **Replace condition**, as shown in the following screenshot:

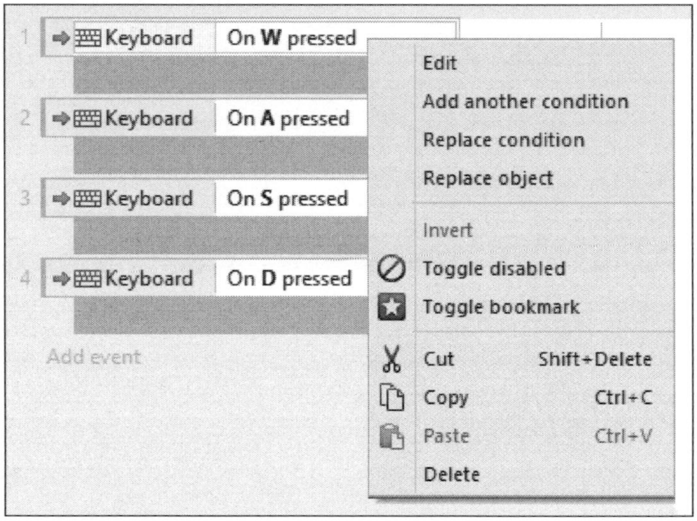

2. You should then get the **Replace condition** window shown in the following screenshot:

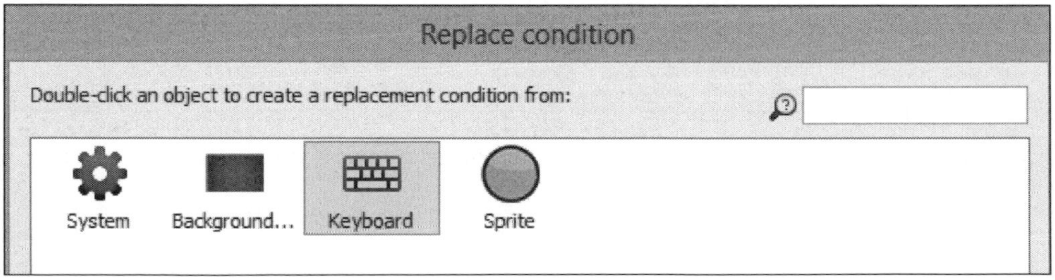

3. The process is very similar to what we have done before. Go ahead and select **Keyboard**.

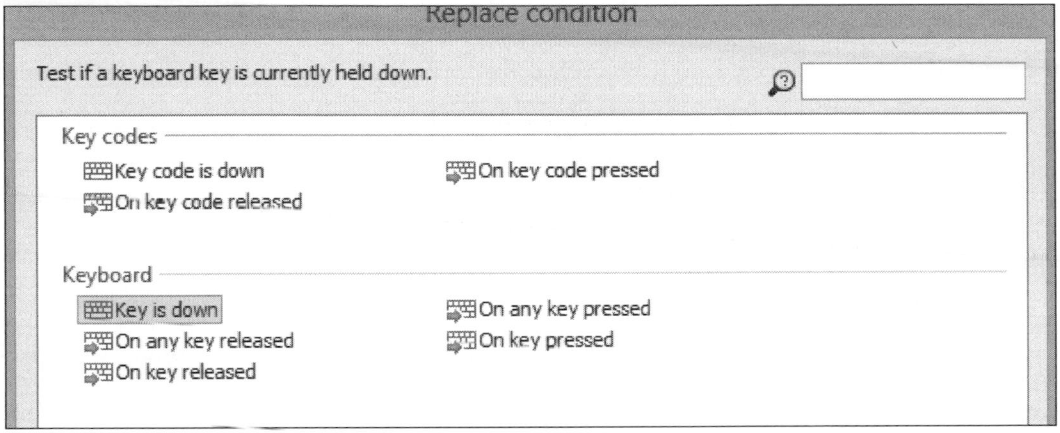

4. Now, select **Key is down**.
5. Then, repeat the process to set a keyboard key. Select *W* where *W* was before, and so on.

   Once you have done that, the event list should look like the following screenshot:

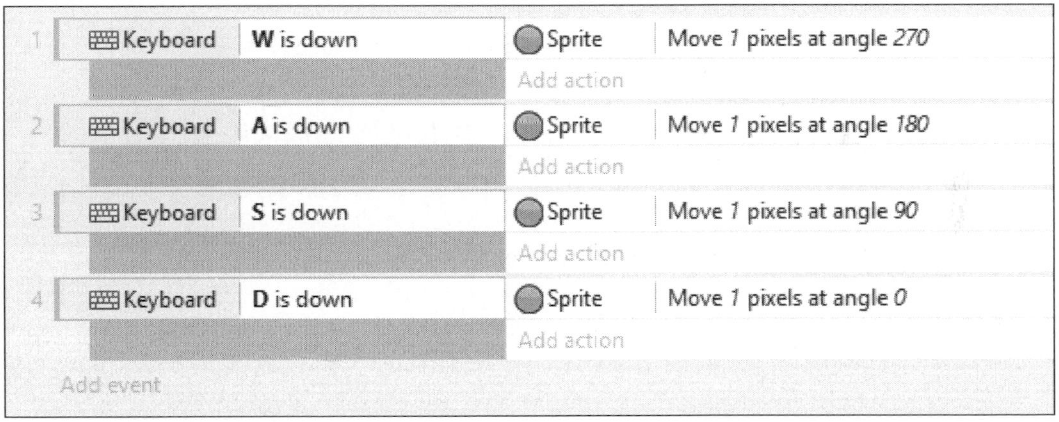

You can see that there is only a subtle difference. However, run the game by pressing *F5* and you can see that there is quite a bit of improvement to the controls. They are now much smoother. Running the game will give you a preview as to how the game will look when a player plays it.

Changing the sprite's speed

If you want to change the speed with which the sprite moves, double-click on the sprite and set it to move more than `1` pixel in the **Parameters for Sprite** window.

Keeping the sprite onscreen

You will notice that the sprite will move offscreen. In order to keep it onscreen, perform the following steps:

1. Select the sprite and select **Behaviors** in the left-hand side panel, as shown in the following screenshot:

2. Once you click on **Behaviors**, click on the plus icon in the **Sprite: Behaviors** window. This is what the window should look like:

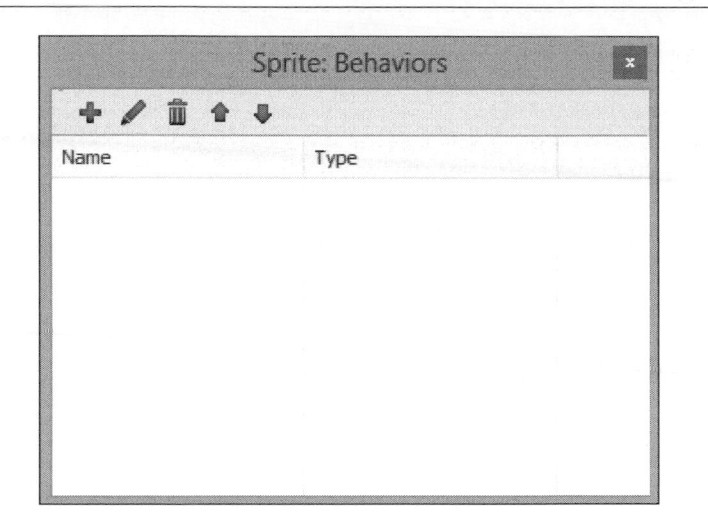

3. Now, you should get the **Add behavior** window. We will be talking about this window throughout the book. For now, just select **Bound to layout**, as shown in the following screenshot:

Add behavior
Double-click a behavior to add:
Attributes
Jump-thru
No Save
Persist
Solid
General
Anchor
Bound to layout
Destroy outside layout
Drag & Drop
Fade
Flash
Text
Image Effects & Text On ...
Line Of Sight
Pin
Scroll To
Timer
Wrap
Stop an object leaving the layout.
Help
Add
Cancel

Now, your sprite will not move off the screen! It's as simple as that.

Mouse inputs

Mouse inputs are important when it comes to any kind of computer game. In other environments, this will take a lot of coding, and trial and error to call the mouse. Luckily, we can use the mouse with great ease in Construct 2.

Adding mouse functionality

The first thing we have to do is add the mouse functionality to the project. Double-click in the layout background and double-click on the **Mouse** icon.

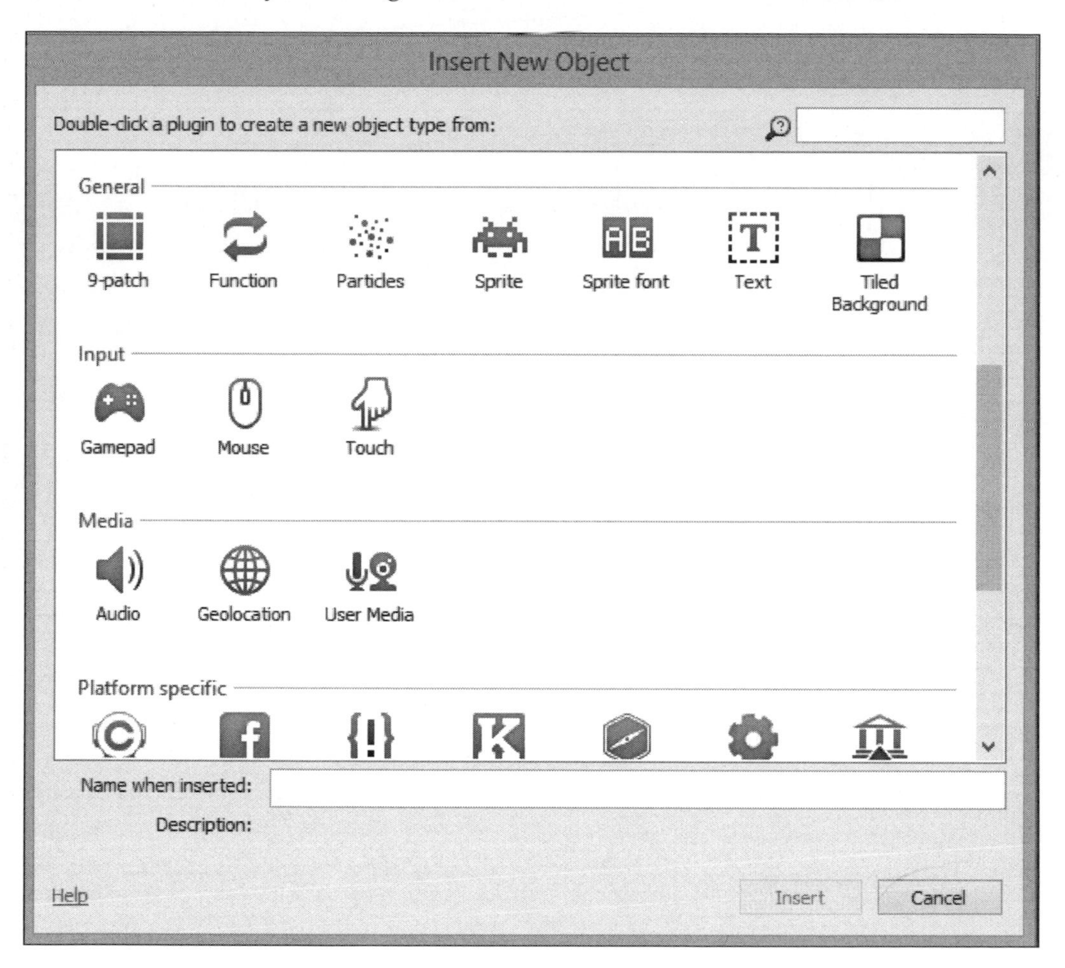

This will add the mouse functionality to the project.

What we need to do next is to attach some of the mouse functions to the sprite. Open up the event sheet and click on **Add event**.

What we are going to do is rotate the object to the mouse location. Go ahead and choose **System**, as shown in the following screenshot:

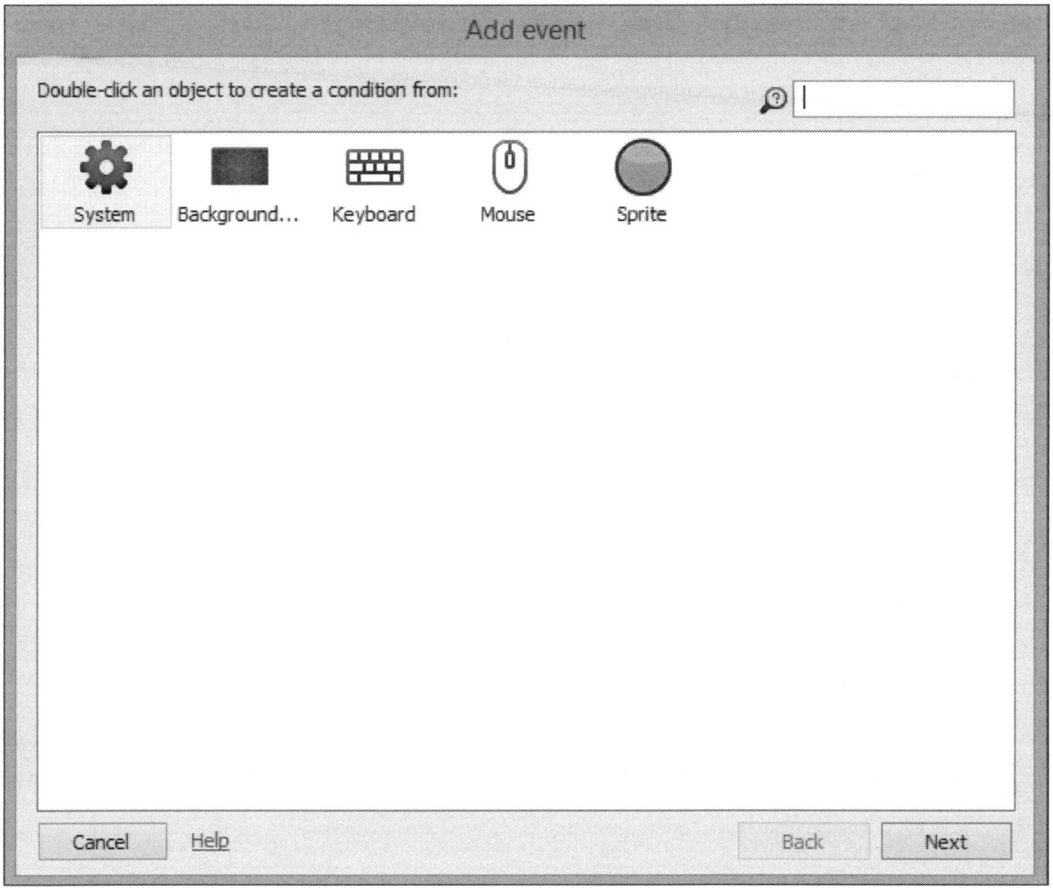

Setting up the Every tick command

In the **Add event** window, we need to access the **Every tick** command.

In every game, there is something called game loop. This is a loop that constantly updates information. When we put code or logic in the game loop, it constantly checks to see whether it is true. Logic includes elements such as controls, collisions, scores, and virtually all other portions of a game. In other programming environments, the game loop is extremely important and accessing it can be very different depending on the environment.

We need to access the **Every tick** function because we need to constantly check where the mouse is. While the mouse moves around the screen, the computer will check to see its location. If we didn't use the **Every tick** function or the game loop, the sprite will only rotate once instead of constantly. You usually use the **Every tick** function for functions that require constant attention. For most other functions that need to be called once, you can use other functions. So, let's go ahead and click on **Every tick**.

#	Object	Condition	Object	Action
1	Keyboard	**W** is down	Sprite	Move *1* pixels at angle *270*
			Add action	
2	Keyboard	**A** is down	Sprite	Move *1* pixels at angle *180*
			Add action	
3	Keyboard	**S** is down	Sprite	Move *1* pixels at angle *90*
			Add action	
4	Keyboard	**D** is down	Sprite	Move *1* pixels at angle *0*
			Add action	
5	System	Every tick	Add action	

Add event

Rotating the sprite to the mouse location

Now that we have added the **Every tick** event, we need to add an action. This action is going to rotate the sprite to the mouse position. In order to do this, click on **Add event**. You should get the following window:

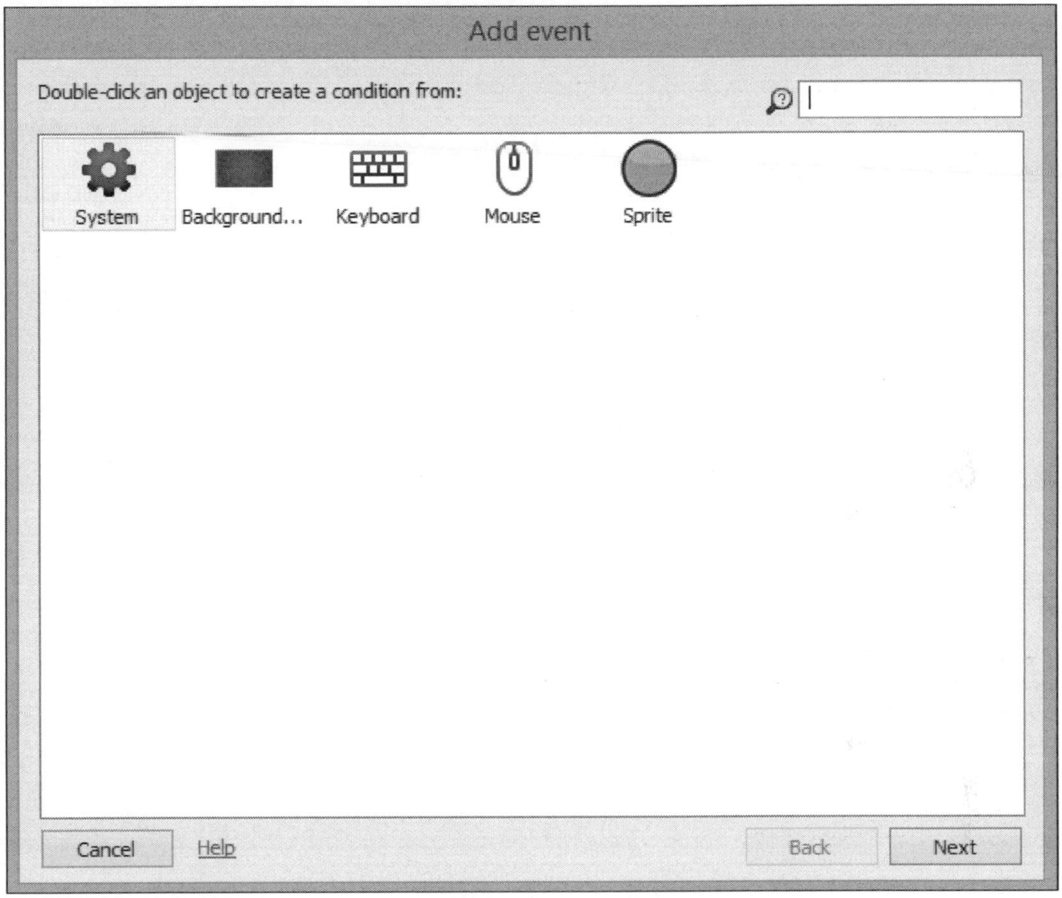

This time, we are going to select **Sprite**. If we want to rotate the sprite, we have to access the sprite via the **Add action** window. We can't just use the mouse function to rotate the sprite.

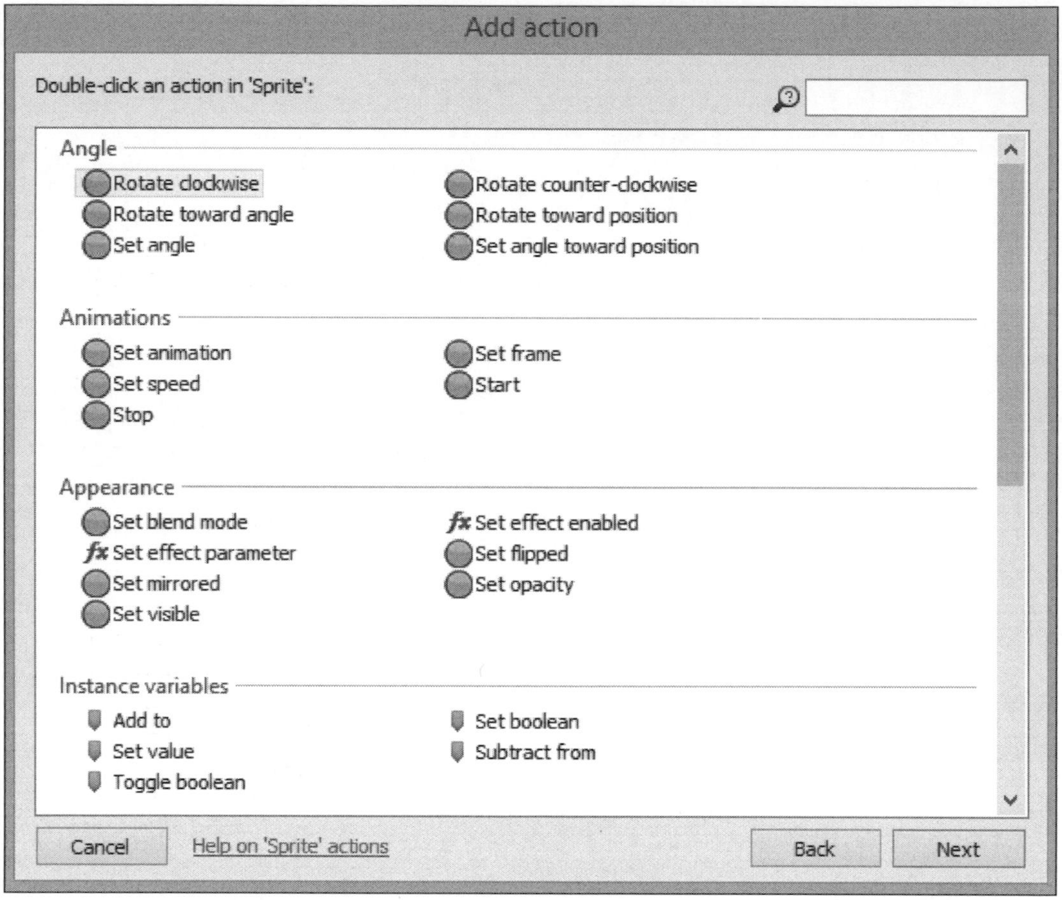

Add action

Double-click an action in 'Sprite':

Angle

Rotate clockwise
Rotate counter-clockwise
Rotate toward angle
Rotate toward position
Set angle
Set angle toward position

Animations

Set animation
Set frame
Set speed
Start
Stop

Appearance

Set blend mode
Set effect enabled
Set effect parameter
Set flipped
Set mirrored
Set opacity
Set visible

Instance variables

Add to
Set boolean
Set value
Subtract from
Toggle boolean

Cancel
Help on 'Sprite' actions
Back
Next

In the **Add action** window shown in the preceding screenshot, we can see that there are a lot of options to rotate the sprite. For this particular example, we are going to select **Set angle toward position**. This will open up the **Parameters for Sprite: Set angle toward position** dialog box, as shown in the following screenshot:

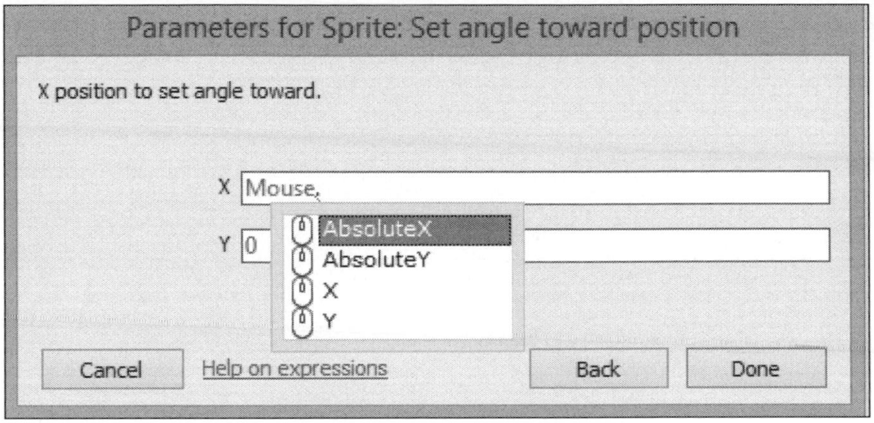

In the preceding window, you will see two options: **X** and **Y**. What you need to do is type in the word `Mouse` and then insert a period. As you can see, you have several different options; select **X** and **Y** for the respective option, not **Absolute X** and **Absolute Y**. Once you are finished, it should look like the following screenshot:

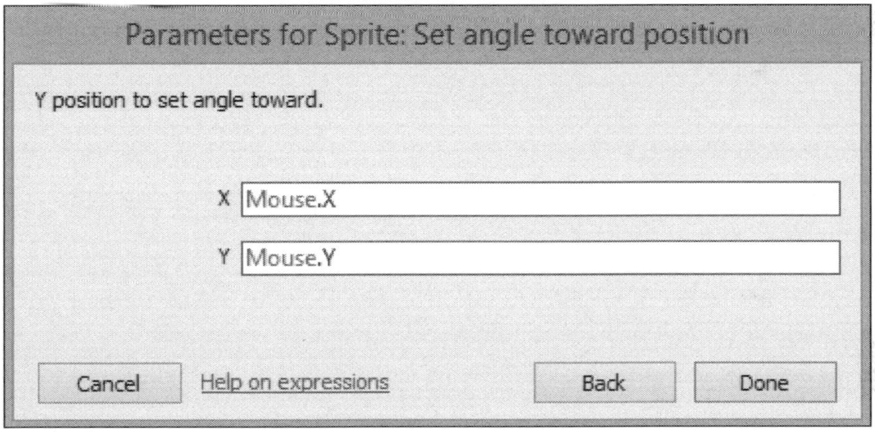

Then, press **Done** and your event sheet should look like the following screenshot:

You can go ahead and try this out. As you can see, the object will rotate to the mouse clicks.

Facing the sprite towards the mouse point

A common problem that arises when you make a sprite rotate to the mouse location is that the graphic seems to be off. This means that the object might be sideways or backwards and the object isn't facing the mouse correctly. Well, there is a simple reason for this. The code works perfectly; it's just that the graphic has not been put into Construct 2 correctly. If you click on the object, you can see where the object will be rotated to.

As you can see in the following screenshot, there is a little line pointing to the right. This line will always face the mouse.

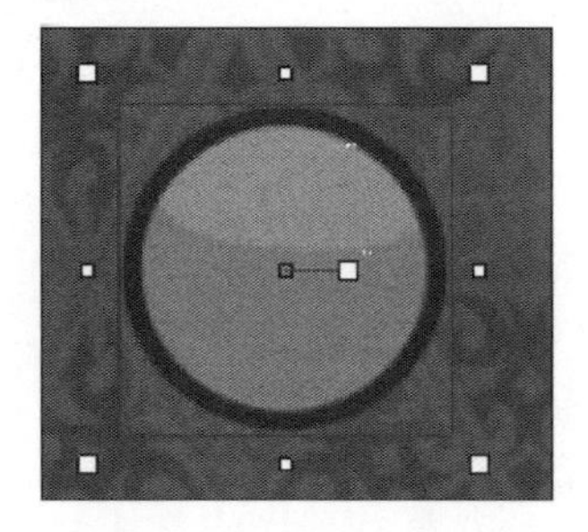

If we want to rotate the graphic, we can do it in Construct 2; just double-click on the sprite. This will bring up the sprite editor, where we can change the rotation, collision, and many more sprite properties. It is shown in the following screenshot:

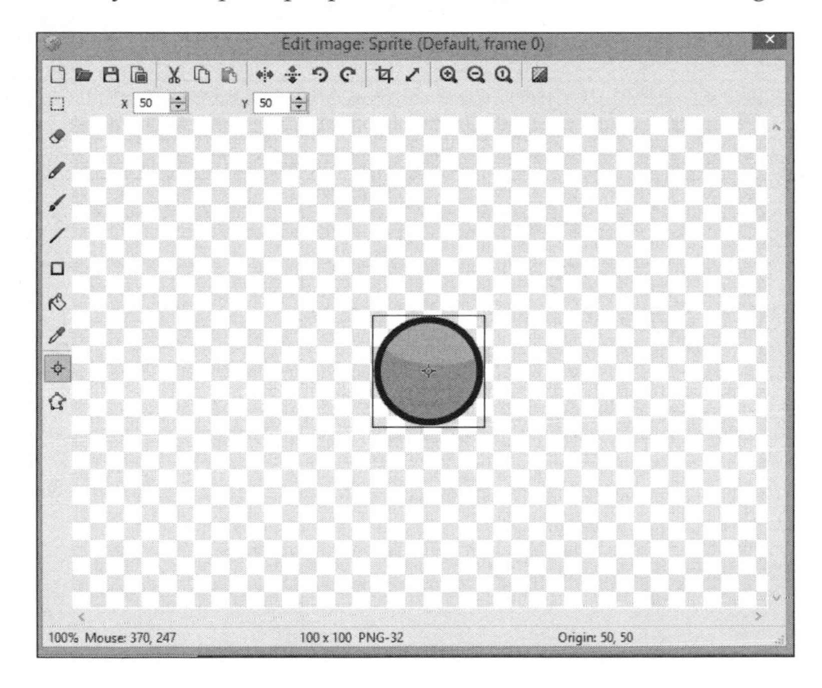

Go ahead and click on the icon for rotation; it is at the top and shows a curved arrow around a circle. Rotate your game object to make it face towards the right. This should change your game object to the right rotation.

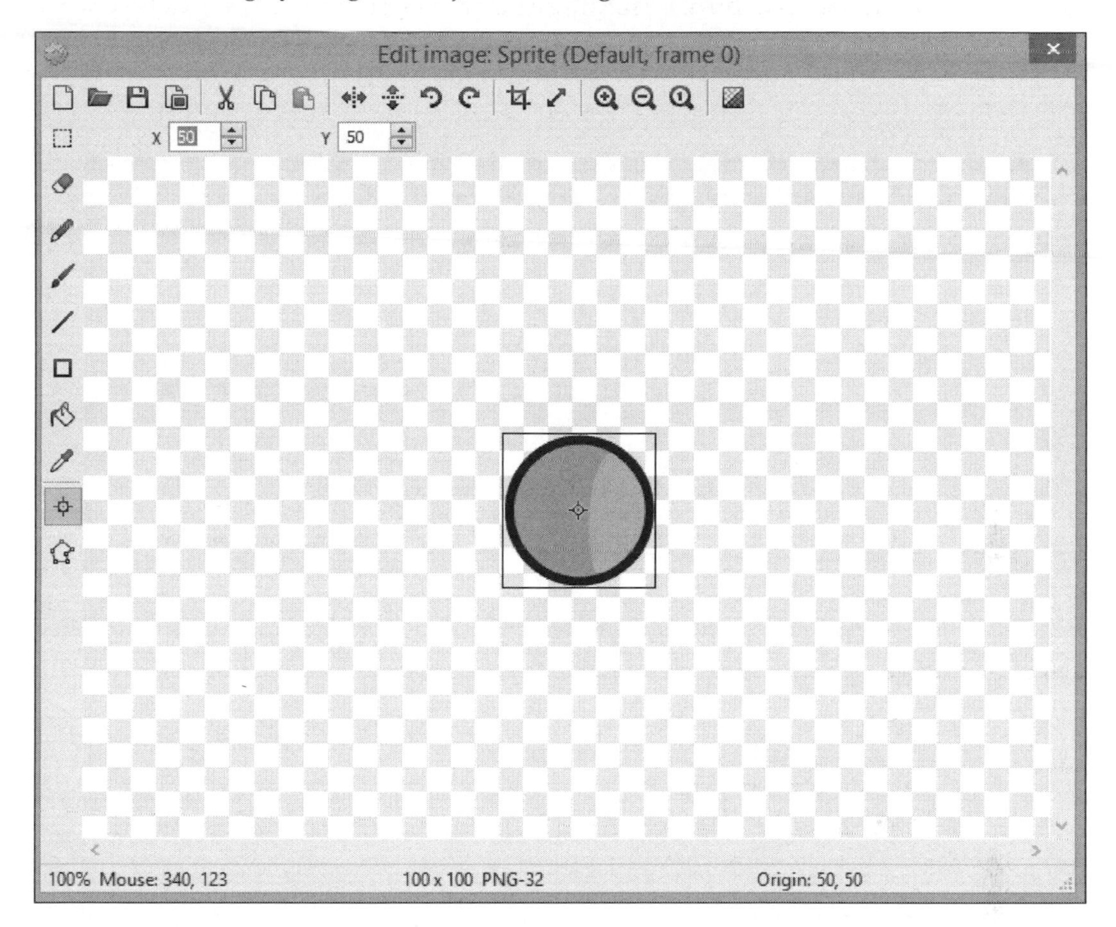

In the preceding screenshot, we can see that the object is now rotated the correct way. If you run the game, you can see this in action.

Touch control inputs

Touch controls are vital for mobile games. They are really important since a lot of HTML5 games run very well on mobile devices, while Flash does not. Open up a new Construct 2 file and add a sprite. Then, double-click on the layout background to get the **Insert New Object** window. Here, add the **Touch** functionality. This is shown in the following screenshot:

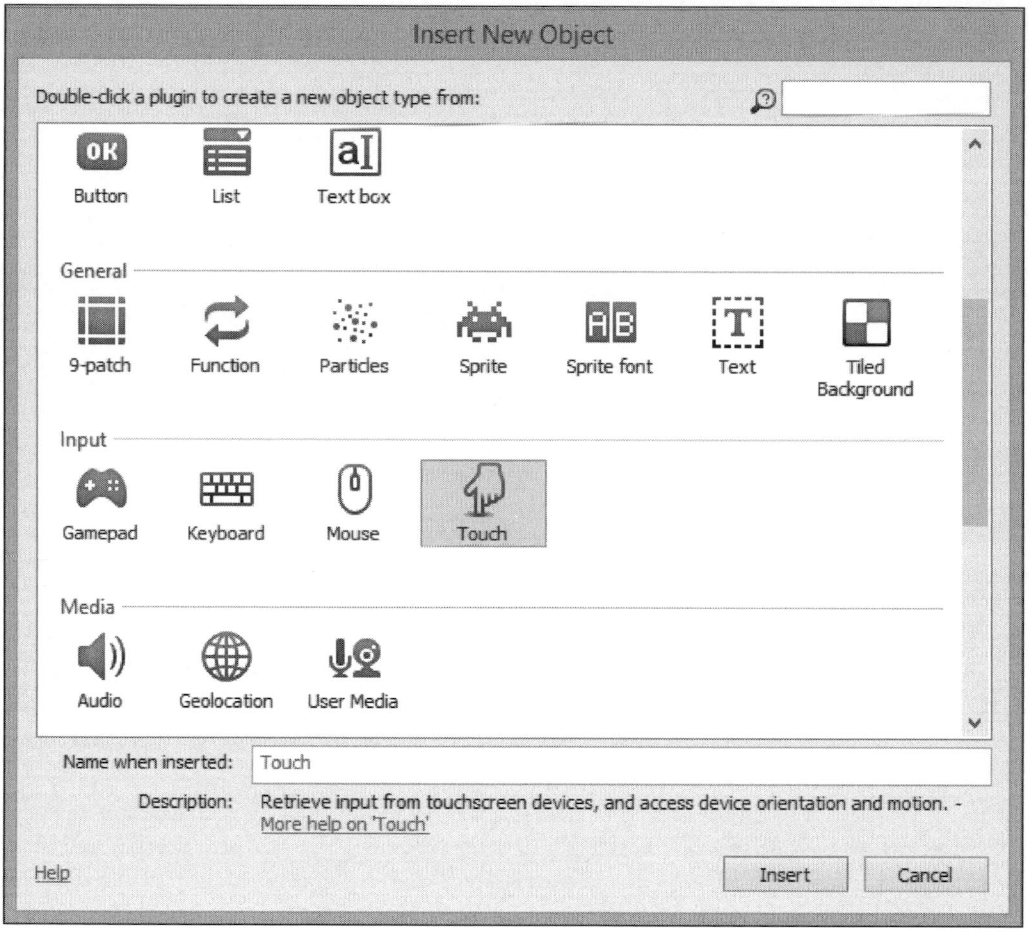

Once you have added the touch functionality, hop over to the event sheet and add the `touch` event. This is shown in the following screenshot:

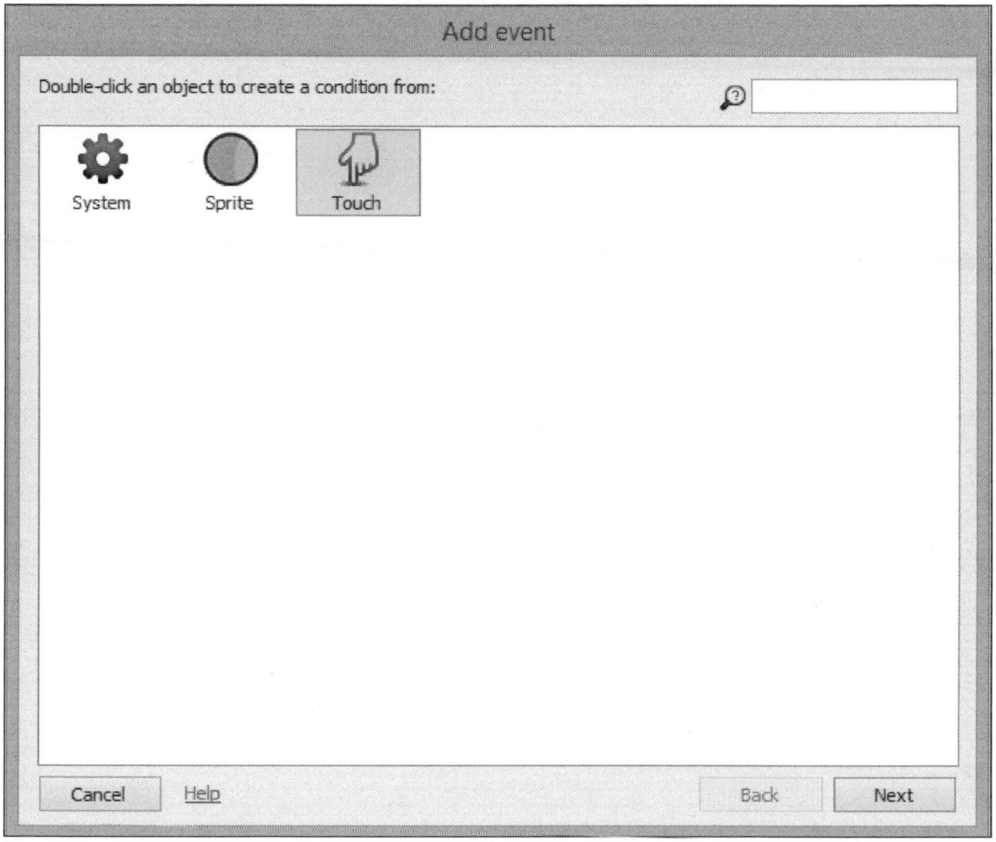

Double-clicking on the **Touch** event icon directs you to get the **Add event** page.

Once you have done this, go ahead and select **On any touch end** as shown in the following screenshot:

Click on **Done**. Your event sheet should look like the following screenshot:

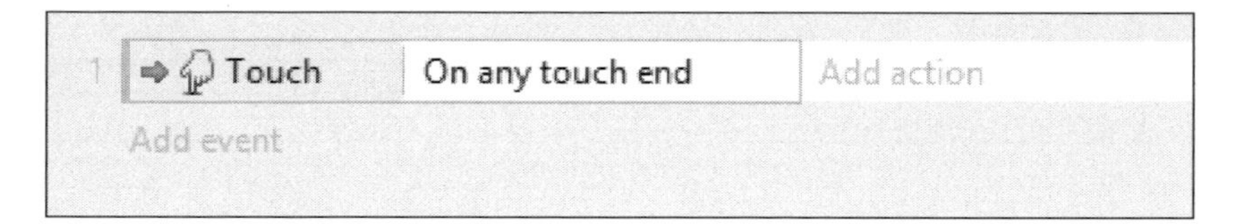

Now, add an action and click on **Sprite** in the **Add action** window, as shown in the following screenshot:

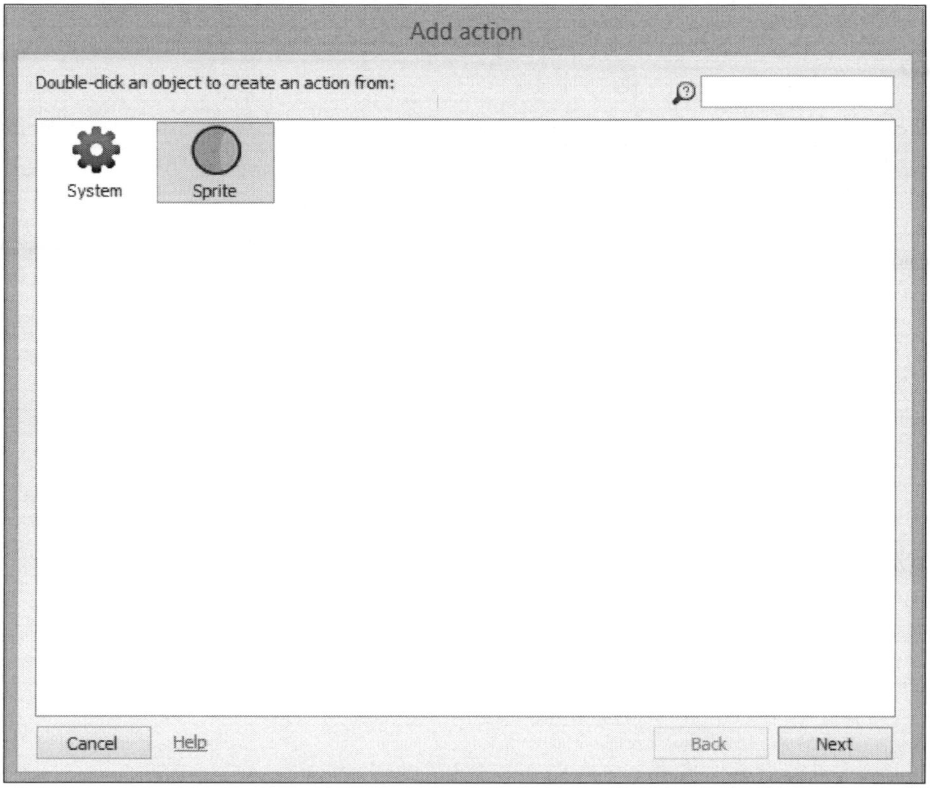

On the next **Add Action** window, scroll down and select **Set position** under the **Size & Position** list. This is shown in the following screenshot:

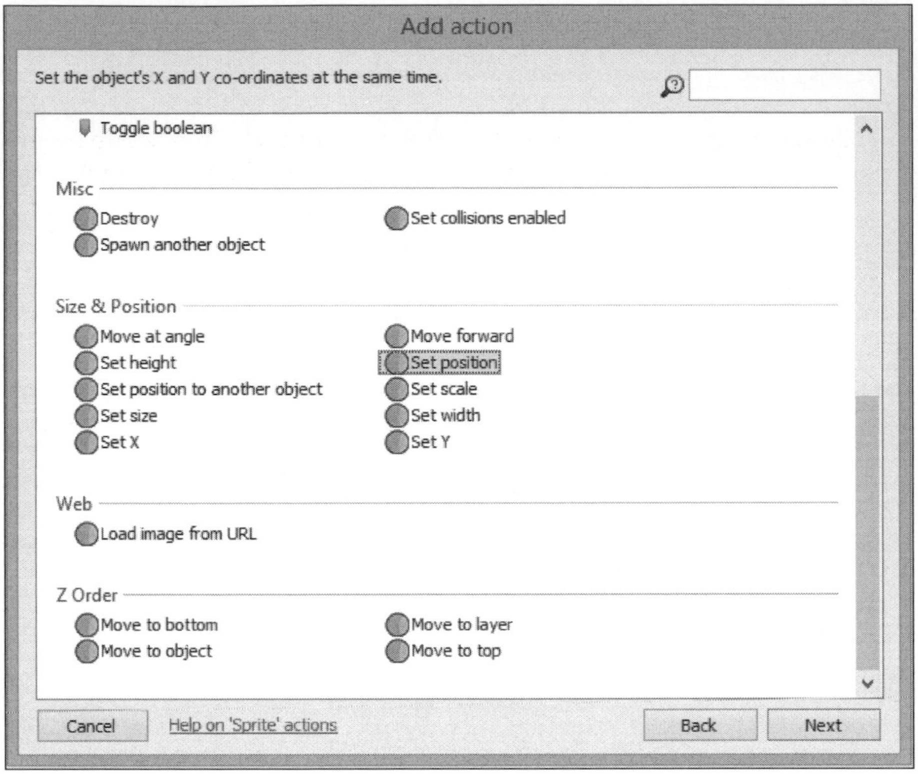

In the **Parameters for Sprite: Set position** window, which is shown in the following screenshot, set the position to `Touch.X` and `Touch.Y` in the same way as you set the mouse position. This will move the sprites' X and Y position to where you touch.

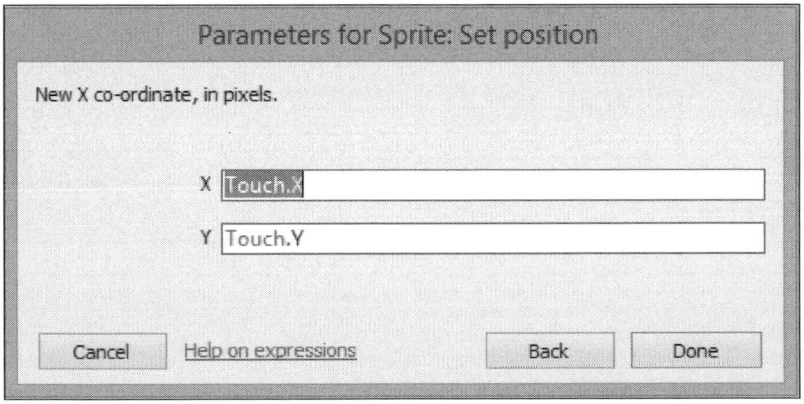

Go ahead and run the game; even if you are on a computer. The mouse button and the touch commands are synced for testing and a mouse click will simulate a touch. If you do not have a mouse-intensive game, we suggest you just use the touch command.

Summary

In this chapter, we learned how to use the keyboard and how to use the mouse. In addition, we explored some of the other functionalities that Construct 2 has to offer, such as keyboard inputs and rotating to an angle. We have also introduced the idea of the game loop and how Construct 2 accesses it. We also covered the touch control.

In the next chapter, we will cover variables to add more complexity to our games.

3

Variables and Arrays

Variables and arrays are essential to computer programming and game design. Without them, games would not work and would not be fun to play.

In this chapter, we will cover the following topics:

- What are variables?
- Why are variables so important?
- Different kinds of variables in Construct 2
- Learning about arrays

Introducing variables

Computer programming is based on mathematical principles. After all, the first computer was made to actually calculate equations, and it was only later that applications (as we know them) were developed. You have probably heard of variables in science and math classes. In computers, these variables are necessary to make applications and they are very important in games. Even a small indie game might have hundreds of variables.

Variables are places where you can store small amounts of data. This data can be a name, a number, a date, a game object, or it can even store true or false information. Variables are essential to games because they can store items such as the following:

- Score
- Player name
- Game objects
- Mouse position
- Keyboard input

In order to store data, you have to store data in the right kind of variables. We can think of variables as boxes, and what you put in these boxes depends on what type of box it is.

In most native programming languages, you have to declare a variable and its type.

Number variables

Let's go over some of the major types of variables. The first type is **number variables**. These variables store numbers and not letters. That means, if you tried to put a name in, let's say `"John Bura"`, then the app simply won't work.

Integer variables

There are numerous different types of number variables. **Integer variables**, called `Int` variables, can be positive or negative whole numbers—you cannot have a decimal at all. So, you could put -1 as an integer variable but not 1.2.

Real variables

Real variables can be positive or negative, and they can be decimal numbers. A real variable can be 1.0, -40.4, or 100.1, for instance.

There are other kinds of number variables as well. They are used in more specific situations. For the most part, integer and real variables are the ones you need to know—make sure you don't get them mixed up. If you were to run an app with this kind of mismatch, chances are it won't work.

String variables

There is another kind of variable that is really important. This type of variable is called a **string variable**. String variables are variables that comprise letters or words. This means that if you want to record a character's name, then you will have to use a string variable. In most programming languages, string variables have to be in quotes, for example, `"John Bura"`. The quote marks tell the computer that the characters within are actually strings that the computer can use.

When you put a number `1` into a string, is it a real number 1 or is it just a fake number? It's a fake number because strings are not numbers—they are strings. Even though the string shows the number 1, it isn't actually the number 1. Strings are meant to display characters, and numbers are meant to do math. Strings are not meant to do math—they just hold characters. If you tried to do math with a string, it wouldn't work (except in JavaScript, which we will talk about shortly).

Strings shouldn't be used for calculations—they are meant to hold and display characters. If we have a string `"1"`, it will be recorded as a character rather than an integer that can be used for calculations.

Boolean variables

The last main type of variable that we need to talk about is **Boolean variables**. Boolean variables are either true or false, and they are very important when it comes to games. They are used where there can only be two options. The following are some examples of Boolean variables:

- `isAlive`
- `isShooting`
- `isInAppPurchaseCompleted`
- `isConnectedToInternet`

Most of these variables start off with the word `is`. This is usually done to signify that the variable that we are using is a Boolean. When you make games, you tend to use a lot of Boolean variables because there are so many *states* that game objects can be in. Often, these states have only two options, and the best thing to do is use a Boolean.

Sometimes, you need to use an integer instead of a Boolean. Usually, `0` equals false and `1` equals true. We will cover using these variables in Construct 2 later in the chapter.

Other variables

When it comes to game production, there are a lot of specific variables that differ from environment to environment. Sometimes, there are `GameObject` variables, and there can also be a whole bunch of more specific variables.

Declaring variables

If you want to store any kind of data in variables, you have to declare them first. In the backend of Construct 2, there are a lot of variables that are already declared for you. This means that Construct 2 takes out the work of declaring variables. The variables that are taken care of for you include the following:

- Keyboard
- Mouse position
- Mouse angle
- Type of web browser

Writing variables in code

When we use Construct 2, a lot of the backend busywork has already been done for us. So, how do we declare variables in code? Usually, variables are declared at the top of the coding document, as shown in the following code:

```
Int score;
Real timescale = 1.2;
Bool isDead;
Bool isShooting = false;
String name = "John Bura";
```

Let's take a look at all of them. The type of variable is listed first. In this case, we have the `Int`, `Real`, `Bool` (Boolean), and `String` variables. Next, we have the name of the variable. If you look carefully, you can see that certain variables have an `=` (equals sign) and some do not. When we have a variable with an equals sign, we initialize it. This means that we set the information in the variable right away. Sometimes, you need to do this and at other times, you do not. For example, a score does not need to be initialized because we are going to change the score as the game progresses.

As you already know, you can initialize a Boolean variable to either true or false—these are the only two states a Boolean variable can be in. You will also notice that there are quotes around the string variable.

Let's take a look at some examples that won't work:

```
Int score = -1.2;
Bool isDead = "false";
String name = John Bura;
```

There is something wrong with all these examples. First of all, the `Int` variable cannot be a decimal. Second, the `Bool` variable has quotes around it. Lastly, the `String` variable has no quotes. In most environments, this will cause the program to not work. However, in HTML5 or JavaScript, the variable is changed to fit the situation.

Variables in JavaScript

Construct 2 exports to HTML5, and this means that a lot of the functionality in the game is written in JavaScript. In JavaScript, the type of variable is not defined until you initialize it. While this makes programming in JavaScript much easier, it has its pros and cons. The biggest con is that sometimes you forget which variables are of what type, which leads to unexpected results when you run the app.

Examining JavaScript code

JavaScript is a very popular web language. It is much easier to code in than most other programming languages.

Let's take a look at some examples of JavaScript code.

```
var score;
var timescale = 1.2;
var name = "John Bura";
var playerName;
```

You will notice that all of the variables are simply called `var` instead of `Int`, `Bool`, `String`, or `Real`. This means that, until you initialize the variable, `var` can be whatever you want it to be.

So in this case, `score` is not a number—it is simply a variable. However, `timescale` is a number variable because we have initialized it as such with the `=` sign. Similarly, `var name` is a string because we initialized it, while `var playerName` is simply a variable. Their nature doesn't become set until they are initialized. JavaScript has become popular because you can have less precise code and still make it work.

Now, in JavaScript, there is something that doesn't happen in most environments—you can mix and match variables. I strongly advise not doing this. As a programmer who started with integer and string values, I highly suggest you keep your variables organized. If you mix and match variables and simply don't care, you will have a hard time releasing your game—and releasing is important.

Since Construct 2 is exported in JavaScript, it is important to have a basic understanding of how it works. It is also important to know what kinds of variables are present because, even in JavaScript, you have to use different kinds of variables.

Variables in Construct 2

Like most things in Construct 2, variables are really simple. Even though adding variables is fairly straightforward in other languages, Construct 2 makes it easy.

Adding a variable

Adding variables in games is really important. Without variables, you cannot store any data. This will make the game almost nonfunctional, and it limits you to small games.

To add a variable, go to your event sheet and right-click on it. This should bring up a cascading menu. Clicking on the **Add event** icon will let you add a variable:

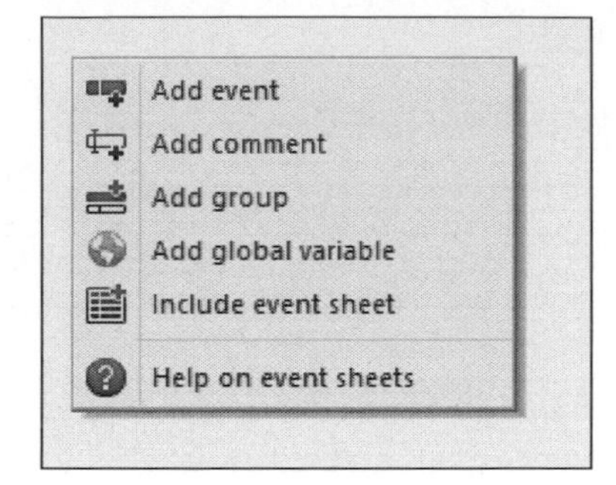

There are two types of variables in Construct 2: **global** and **local** variables. Variables can be *seen* in different places. Global variables will be *seen* throughout the entire game. Local variables you want only to be seen by a game object or a function.

Creating a global variable

Right-click on the event sheet and you can add a global variable. Go ahead and click on **Add global variable**.

As you can see in the preceding screenshot, there are four fields. You can name your variable something memorable and that makes sense. Naming your variable appropriately will make the development process much smoother. Variable names such as `score`, `numberOfShots`, and `powerUpLevel` are recommended. You cannot have spaces in your variables—the computer will not allow you to have spaces.

[One thing that I strongly advise is that you do not capitalize the first word; instead, capitalize the other words in the variable. This will make it easier for you or anybody else to read it.]

As you can also see here, you have two option types—either **Number** or **Text**. This can either be `Real` or `String`. The **Initial value** field is where you can initialize variables. Construct 2 automatically initializes this field for you; however, if you want to have a number or a name, you can put it here. Remember, if you make a text variable, you cannot do calculations with it; you can only calculate with numeric variables.

The **Description** box is optional, but make sure that you always input something in there; it will save you a lot of trouble down the road. All this does is put a little reminder about what the variable does.

[When your game has more than 200 variables, you are going to wish you had put the descriptions in. In addition, if you come back to your game at a later time, you might forget what these variables do. Reminders are great and I highly recommend using them.]

Creating a score variable

Let's make a `Score` variable that keeps track of the score. Again, variables store data. We need to set up a `Score` variable to store the score data. Whenever you need to store a small amount of information, you need to make a variable. The addition of a new global variable should look like the following screenshot:

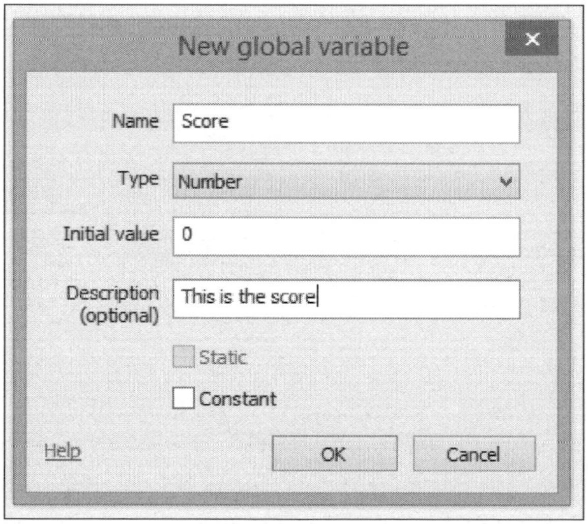

Once you have something that looks like this, you can go ahead and click on **OK**.

Global number Score = 0 This is the score
Add event

In the preceding screenshot, you can see what the `Score` variable looks like in Construct 2. You can see that it is at the top of the event sheet—and it will stay at the top of the event sheet, just like the variables in other programming languages.

Adding a variable to a sprite

Let's add a local variable. Add a sprite to the game and select it. You will see that, in the **Properties** window on the left-hand side, there is something called **Instance variables**. These are local variables, which means that this game object is the only game object that uses these variables. Usually, these instance variables are variables such as health, shields, and other stats; each game object's variables will be different.

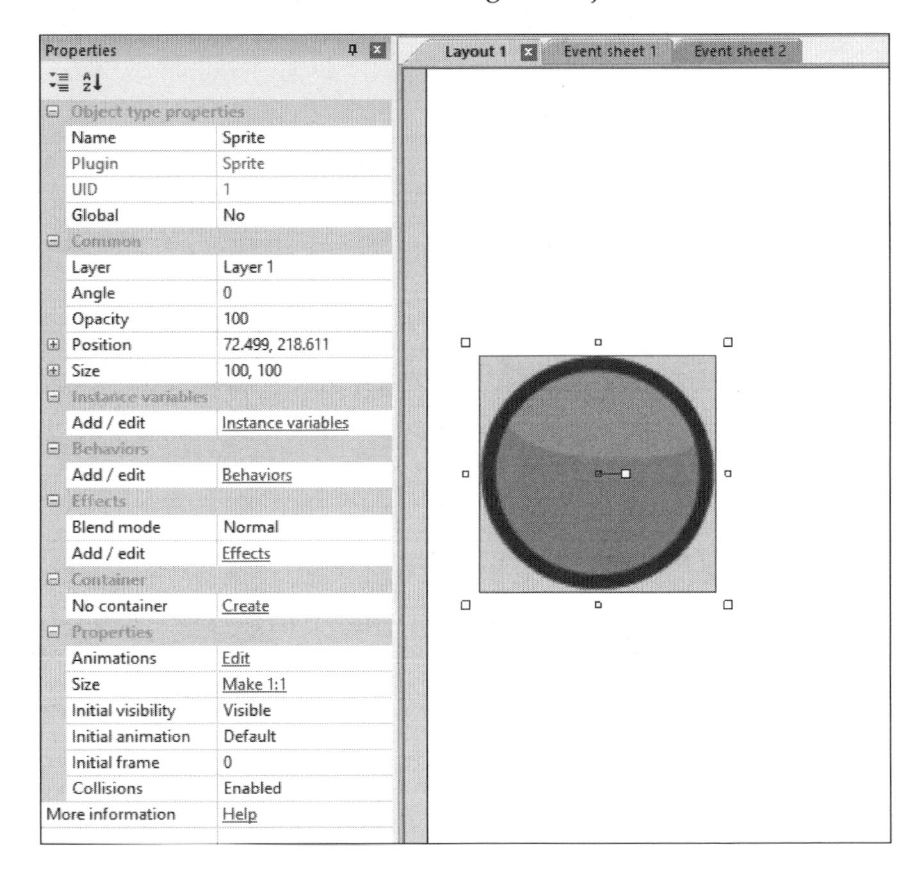

Go ahead and click on **Instance variables**. You should come up with a dialog box like the one shown in following screenshot:

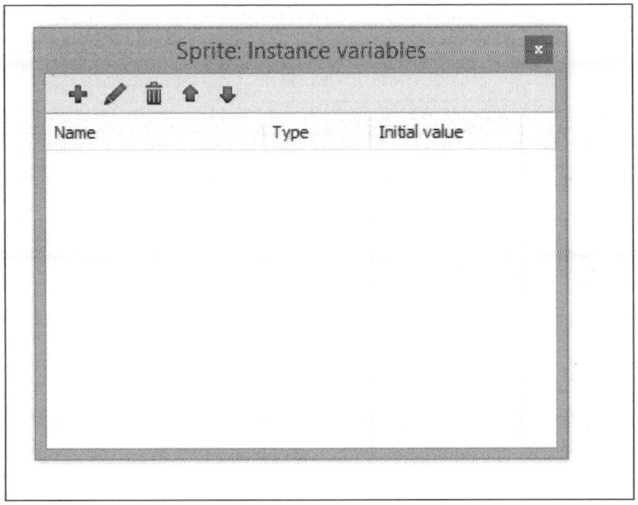

Click on the plus sign (+) to add a variable. The **New instance variable** window will appear, as shown in the following screenshot:

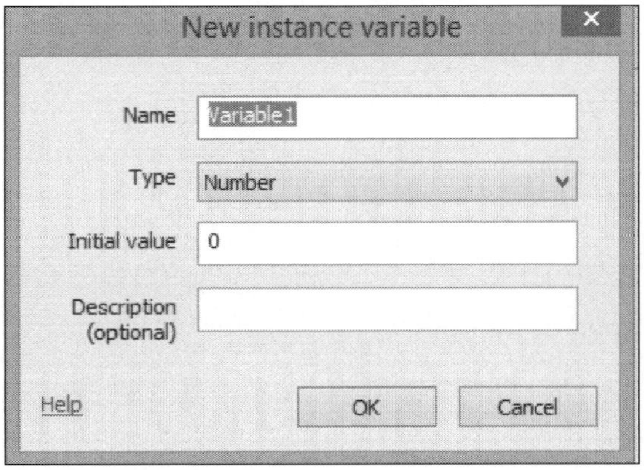

Here, you can see that the dialog box is similar to the one for global variables. The only difference is that you can now add a Boolean variable as well. For the most part, all of these options are the same. I again highly recommend that you put a description whenever possible.

Creating a health variable

Let's go and create a `health` variable and give it an **Initial value** of `100` in the previous window. We can name variables whatever we want. We could even name it "banana" if we really wanted to. Instead, we give the variables names that can help us easily understand the data that the variable holds. By setting up the `health` variable, we now have a container for the health number. This way, we can add events that add to or subtract from the health value. We can even set up the game logic to move to a "game over" screen if the health is below zero. **Game logic** is simply the logic needed to make a game. It can also be called **programming**. Notice how `health` isn't capitalized. This is because local variables are usually not capitalized. While there is no direct rule that states this, most programmers tend to make global variables uppercase and local variables lowercase. The reason for this is that when you look at the screen, you will know which one is a global variable and which one is a local variable. Different programmers have different paradigms. So, if you are working with other programmers, make sure you know what they like and don't like in terms of naming variables. The addition of a new instance variable looks something like the following screenshot:

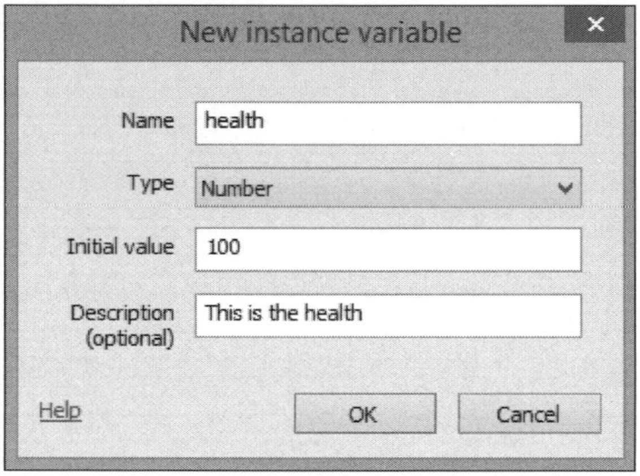

Once you have something like the preceding screenshot, you can click on **OK**.

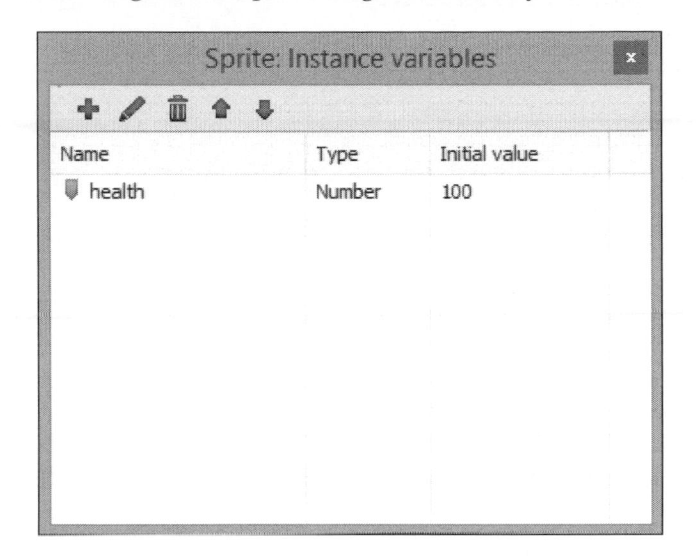

Now you have an instance variable!

Introducing arrays

Arrays are really powerful when it comes to game design. Essentially, an **array** is a grid of data. We can fill up this grid with any kind of information that we want. In the past, arrays were used quite heavily as the technology was limited, and even today arrays are still used and are still very useful. Here is a visual representation of an array:

(data)	(data)	(data)	(data)
(data)	(data)	(data)	(data)

An array is a table of data. You have probably seen this in a spreadsheet program. We can store multiple items of data in arrays. This differs from variables because we can now add large amounts, of data.

We can use arrays for the following purposes:

- To save multiple points of data
- To store game object information
- To use a tile map
- To create *save* states that save large amounts of information
- To create a data set that will help us save time during development

Adding an array in Construct 2

How do we add an array in Construct 2? The first thing you need to do is add the array object. Once we do that, we can access all of the array features. We can also set up as many different arrays as we want. Double-click on the background of the layout and click on **Array**, as shown in the following screenshot:

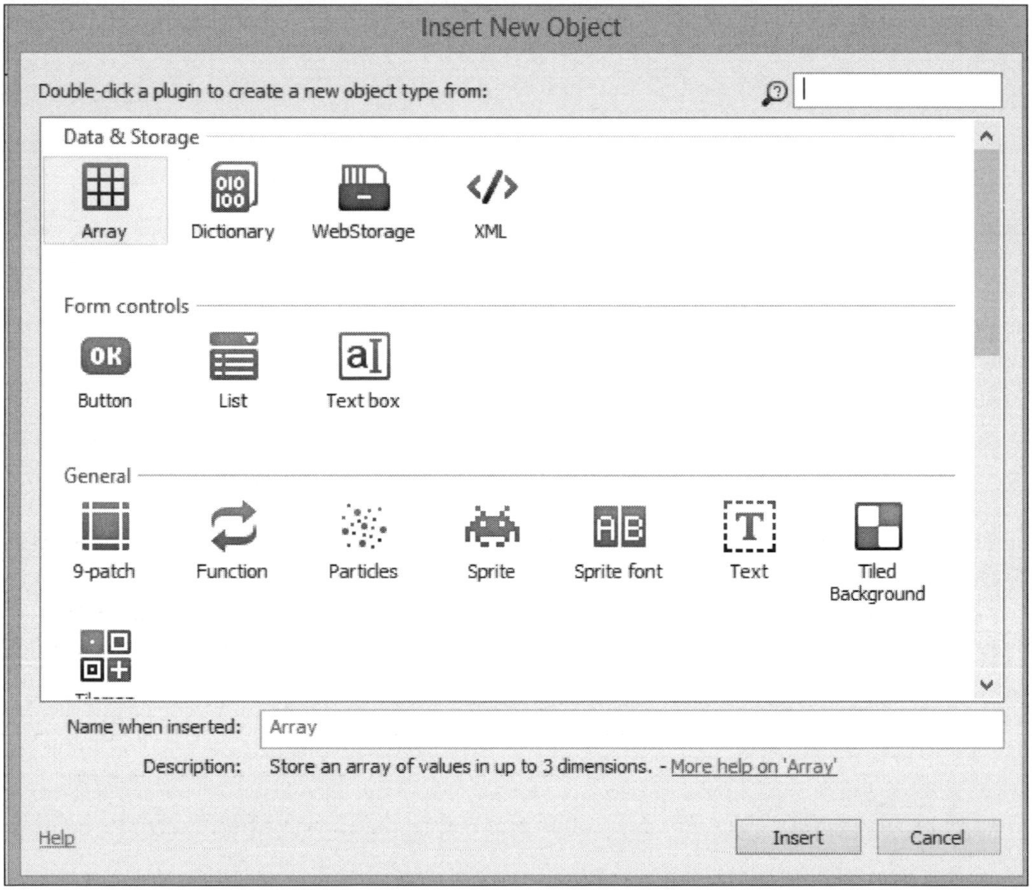

Checking an array's properties

Once you have done this, you can see that the object type is called an array. This is like adding a sprite. You can have multiple sprites in one game and you can have multiple arrays in one game. If you wish to add more than one array, simply double-click on the background and add another one. If you want to change the name of the array, you simply need to select it, press the *F2* key, and then rename it. Click on the array on the right-hand side and look to the left to see the properties, as shown in the following screenshot:

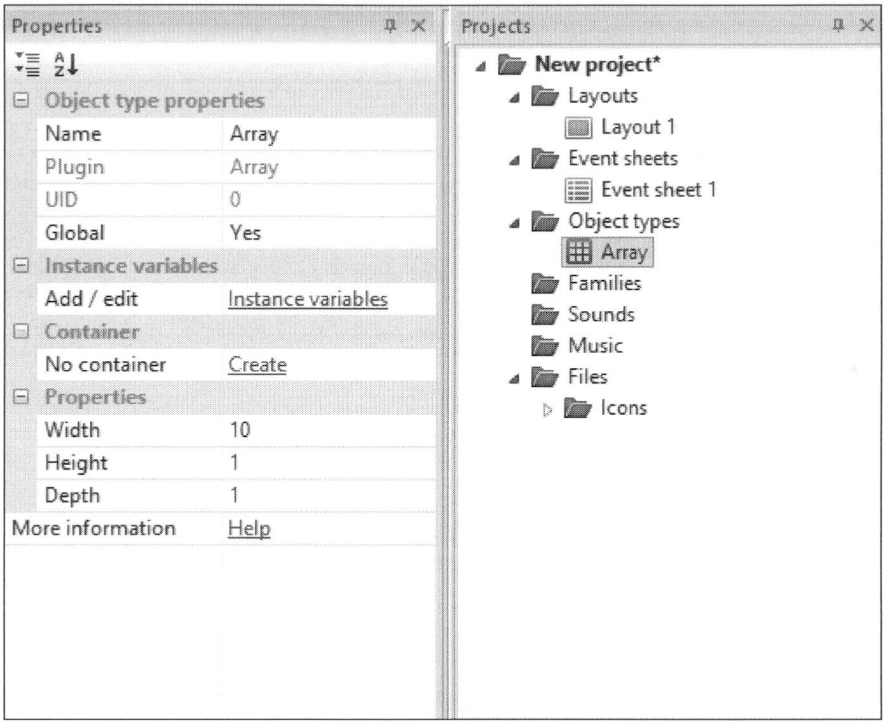

You can see the properties of the array in the preceding screenshot. It has a width, a height, and a depth. What this means is that arrays can be one-dimensional, two-dimensional, or three-dimensional. Currently, we have a one-dimensional array. This means that it only has a width. In this case, the array will be a single row and looks like the following table:

It has a width of 10 cells with a height of one cell and a depth of one cell.

For the most part, it is recommended that you start with easy arrays. Most starting developers can get confused with complexity. It is always better to make development simple.

One thing about arrays is that the base of an array starts at 0. This means that the cells are numbered as shown in the following screenshot:

0	1	2	3	4	5	6	7	8	9

This may look weird at first, but in computing, the start of a sequence of numbers is generally 0 instead of 1. In this case, there are still 10 boxes or cells in which we can put data.

Let's go to the event sheet and add an array event. You can add multiple array events, as shown in the following screenshot:

Add event

Double-click a condition in 'Array':

Array
Compare at X
Compare at XY
Compare at XYZ
Contains value
Is empty

For Each
Compare current value
For each element

Instance variables
Compare instance variable
Is boolean instance variable set
Pick highest/lowest

Misc
On created
On destroyed
Pick by unique ID

Cancel | Help on 'Array' conditions | Back | Next

Setting data and adding variables

It should be noted that you can add an instance or local variables to the array as well. For the most part, this is not usually done; but in certain circumstances, such as when assigning different arrays to different objects, this can be useful.

One of the most important tasks you need to do with arrays is to set and search for data. Let's go ahead and set the first cell to number `9`. Click on **Add action** and set **X** to `0` and **Value** to `9`, as shown in the following screenshot:

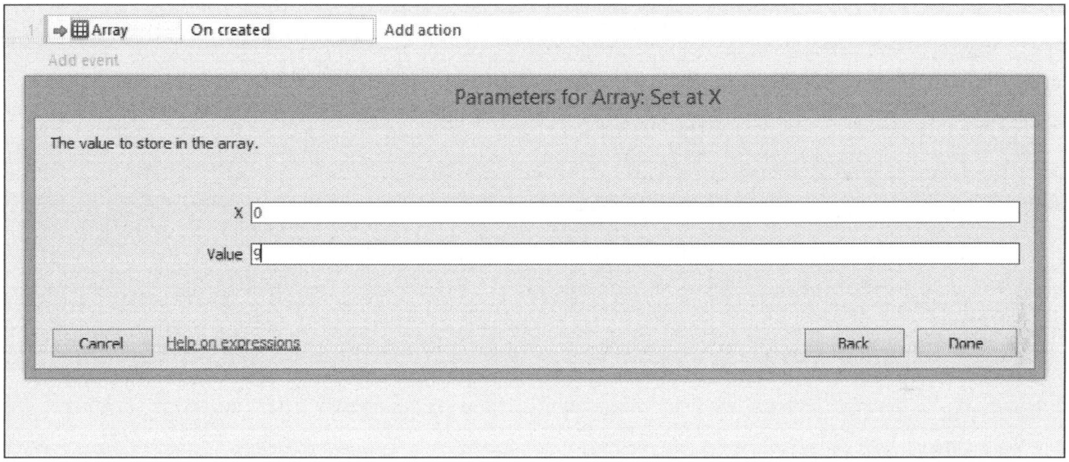

Once you have done that, click on **Done**. Your project should look something like the following screenshot:

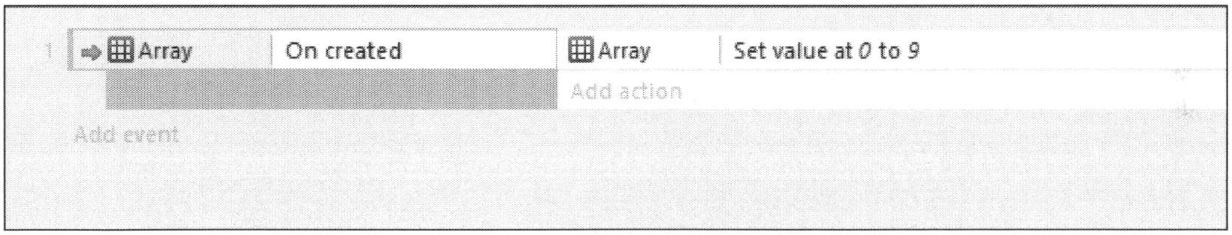

This means that the first cell is set to a value of `9`. Remember that 0 is, in fact, the first cell and that cell 1 is the second cell. The array should look like this:

9	0	0	0	0	0	0	0	0	0

The other cells are zero because we have not yet set them.

Checking an array for data

Now that we know how to set an array, how do we check the array for data? In this case, we will check to see whether the first cell is equal to 9. Double-click on the layout and click on **Array**. Once you have done this, you can click on **Compare at X**, as shown in the following screenshot. This will compare the X values of the array.

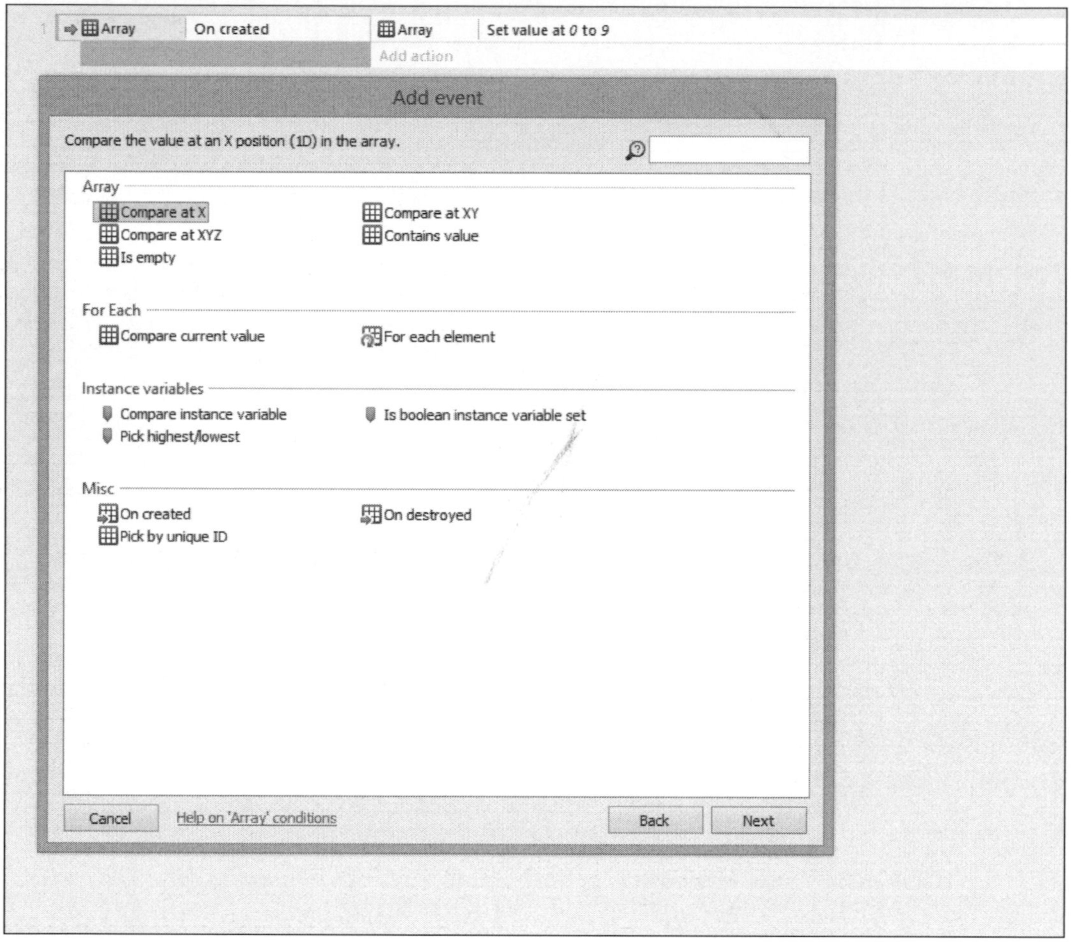

Once you are in the **Add event** window, you can check whatever value you want. In this case, we want to check the first cell and then check the value, which is `9`. We just set this in the last event, so let's keep it consistent. This is shown in the following screenshot:

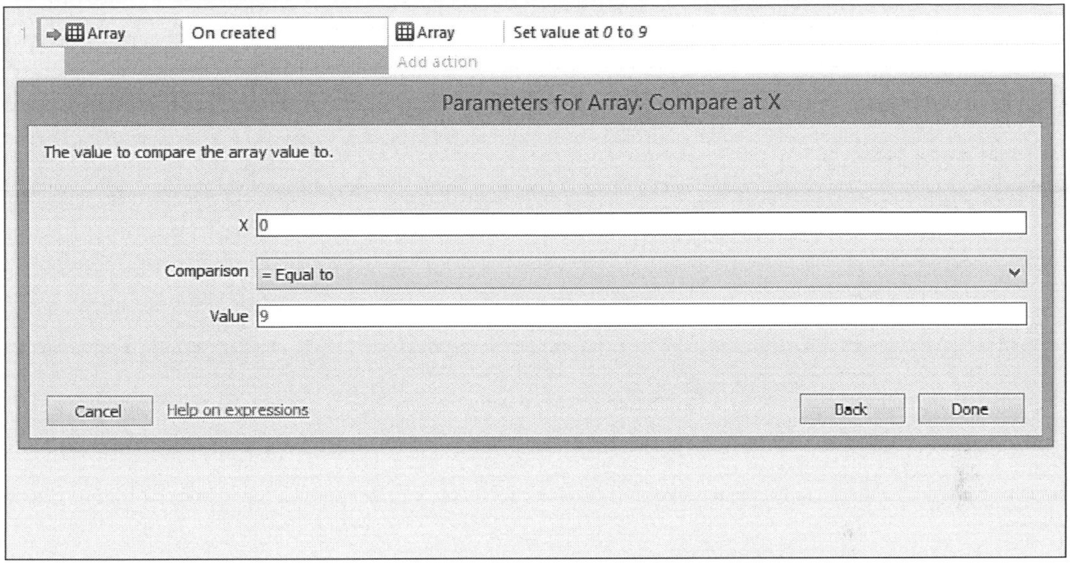

Once you have added this action, you can add any action you want for your game.

Now, you know a little bit about arrays. When you are starting out, it is recommended that you use variables because they are easier to work with. Once your programs become more complex, start adding arrays. It is generally recommended that you start working with one-dimensional arrays, and once you are comfortable using them, move on to two-dimensional arrays. You will be using three-dimensional arrays in rare cases.

Here are some visual examples of arrays that you can use in your games. You can use them to define properties for many game objects:

Game object	Hit Points	Shields	Damage	Speed
Ship A	100	100	50	5
Ship B	200	50	40	3
Ship C	50	50	30	10

You can use this array to define different attributes for characters. In this case, an array can be made for each character on the fly. Lots of **role-playing games (RPG)** do this. Here is an example of such a table:

Character	Hit Points	Armor	Weapon	Magic	Shield
Protagonist	100	50	10	5	3

Summary

In this chapter, we learned how to add global and local variables. Adding variables is a really important in-game feature. Often, you will have hundreds of variables even for a simple game. If you are making a game, get used to making and setting lots of variables. The best part is that Construct 2 makes handling variables really easy.

In the next chapter, we will learn about game mechanics. Game mechanics are the essential backbone to user interactivity.

4 Game Mechanics

Game mechanics are how a game works and how a game feels. You probably already know and have experienced game mechanics if you have played games. What you probably don't know is how to add them to a game engine.

In this chapter, we will cover the following topics:

- How to add game mechanics to Construct 2
- What are game mechanics?
- Adding game mechanics to a sprite

Introducing game mechanics

You probably already know about game mechanics after playing games, but you probably don't know they are game mechanics, as a game designer will refer to them and use them. Game mechanics are simply the rules of the game that allow gameplay. More simply, they build the interactivity in a game to make it playable. Game mechanics can be really simple or they can be really complex. Let's take a look at a few simple game mechanics:

- Running
- Jumping
- Score keeping
- Shooting
- Lives
- Health
- Physics

Game mechanics are used to make a game playable. They can be simple. For example, a player can run and jump, but there are several ways in which we can tweak running and jumping. How fast does the player run? How high does the player jump? How many times can the player jump?

All of these variables equate to a certain kind of gameplay. It is your job as a game designer to figure out what combination works out best for your game. If you want an action-packed game, you can use really fast movements. If you are trying to evoke a more elaborately thought out game, perhaps small and slower movements are best.

> Whenever you put game mechanics in your game, you can evoke an emotion. Experienced game designers can have events in games that evoke rage, jealously, and helplessness. It's up to you to play around with game mechanics and see how you feel about them. Whenever you put game mechanics in, you give the player a certain sensation. This sensation could be blasting your way through space and then making an escape with your spacecraft, or trying to collect enough apples to feed your pets. The mechanics that you lay down, lays the foundation for the sensation the gamer plays.

Apart from the essential game mechanics of running, shooting, and so on, there are many more complex game mechanics. Achievements give the sensation of accomplishment, the same kind of feeling you get when you work at improving yourself. Combos are used when you take two actions and combine them to get something greater and again create a sensation of skill accomplishment. Usually, these kinds of game mechanics reward the player. A sound effect or more points are very common rewards. Rewards, in themselves, are game mechanics. There are many different kinds of rewards, such as scores, power-ups, extra lives and more. With each mechanics, you have to tailor the reward for your target audience.

Game mechanics in Construct 2

Construct 2 allows you to either customize your own mechanics, or you can use the readymade ones that come with the software. You can even code your own custom behaviors with JavaScript, if you want to. This option is more advanced, but as very few non-programming engines will allow you to do so, it's a useful feature.

Setting up a game mechanics project

So, where do we start? Let's open up a new project and save it as `game mechanics`. Go ahead and add a sprite to the project as well. We will be using this sprite for many game mechanics. Your project should look like the one shown in the following screenshot:

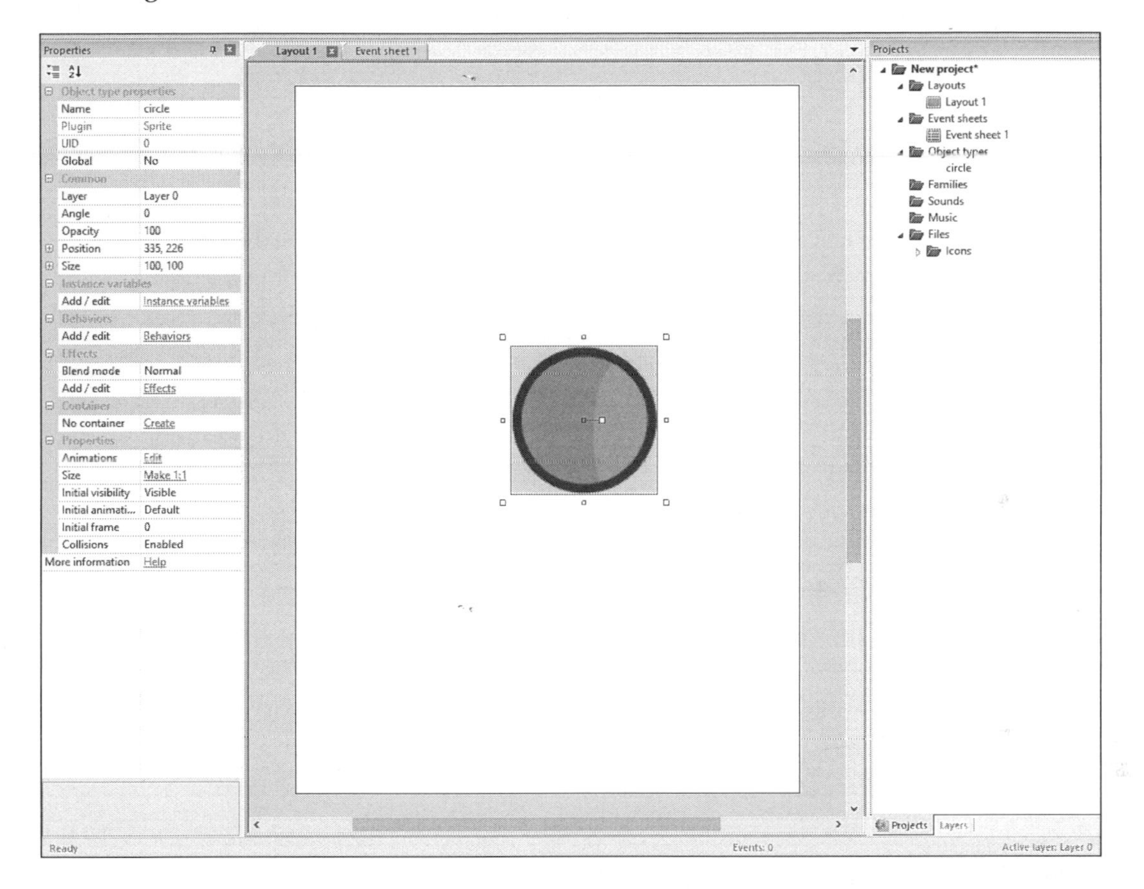

We now have a sprite that we can play around with to add game mechanics. Let's start off with the readymade game mechanics and after that we will move on to custom game mechanics.

Adding a game mechanics behavior to a sprite

Without game mechanics, sprites are just images. In order to make them interactive in your game, you have to add mechanics to them.

Click on **Behaviors** on the left-hand side in the **Properties** window pane. You should get a window that looks like the following screenshot:

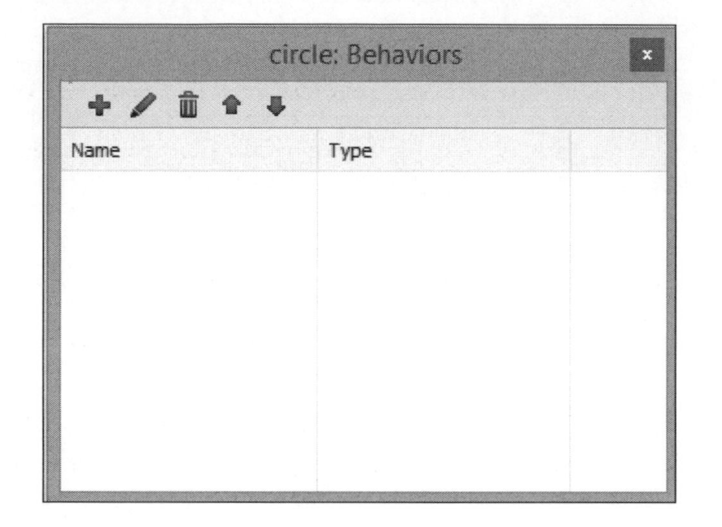

In the **Behaviors** window, click on the plus sign. The **Add behavior** window will appear, as shown in the following screenshot:

Here, you can see a lot of behaviors that you can add. Not all of these are game mechanics, but a lot of them are. In Construct 2, we can add behaviors to the sprite. Most of these are game mechanics.

At this point, I should mention that you can easily add certain readymade behaviors here, but you can also customize each behavior in the event sheets, if you want to. Some designers tend to do this because they want complete control over everything that happens in their game.

Giving a sprite 8Direction movement

Making a moving sprite is important for most games. Construct 2 has a fantastic behavior that easily adds the moving game mechanics to your sprite/player.

Go ahead and scroll the behaviors list, you should reach the **8Direction** behavior. Select that and you should see it appear in your sprite's **Behaviors** window.

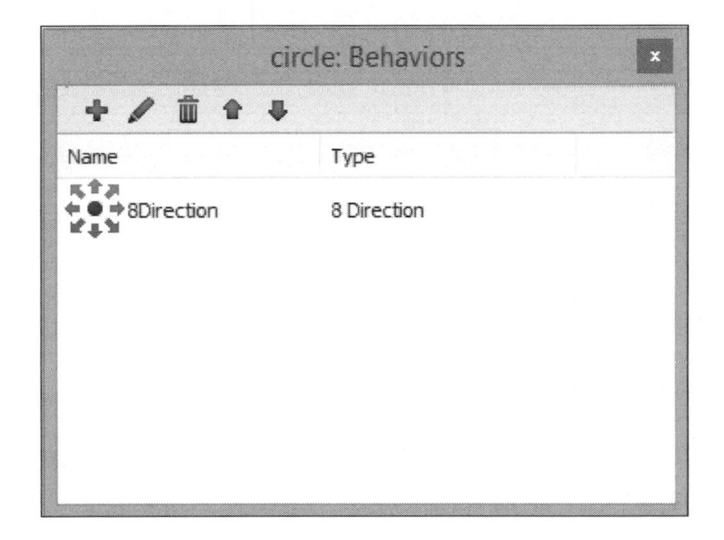

Editing the properties of a behavior

Some of the behaviors have properties, and some do not. Behavior properties exist to make changes to the behavior if necessary. For example, if you want your player to move faster, you can go edit the **Behaviors** property. When you give an object a behavior, you have added extra functionality to that object and can now edit more properties in the event list as a result. In the following screenshot, you can see some of the properties that you can edit in the layout editor:

Behaviors	
8Direction	
Max speed	200
Accelerati...	600
Decelerati...	500
Directions	8 directions
Set angle	360 degree (smo...
Default co...	Yes
Initial state	Enabled

Just because your game has running, jumping, and shooting mechanics, it doesn't automatically make it fun to play. It is the relationship between the mechanics, the player, the target audience, and the graphics that makes a game fun to play.

Let's take a look at all of these properties and how they affect the game play.

Creating a speed power-up

Let's take a look at the first one, **Max speed**. If you run the game, you will see that the player moves around the game in eight directions. **Max speed** is the maximum amount of speed of this movement.

Let's imagine for a moment that we want to add a power-up to the game. This power-up will make the player move twice as fast for a small period of time.

Inserting the power-up object

The first thing we need to do is add another **Gameobject** to the screen. When we collide with this game object, we will activate the power-up mechanic.

Adding a collision event

Right now, when we collide with the power-up box, nothing happens. That's because we have to add the mechanics for it.

1. Go to the event sheet and click **Add event** to bring up the **Add event** window, which is shown in the following screenshot:

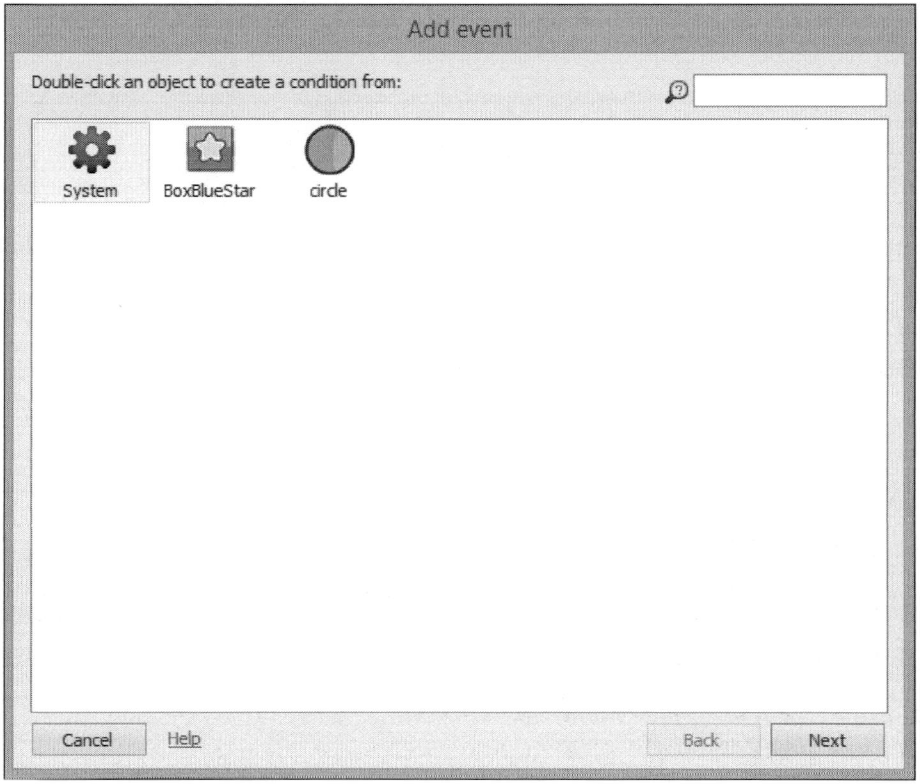

2. Go ahead and click on **circle** or whatever you have named your sprite. This should bring up the **Add event** dialog box for the circle, which should look like the following screenshot:

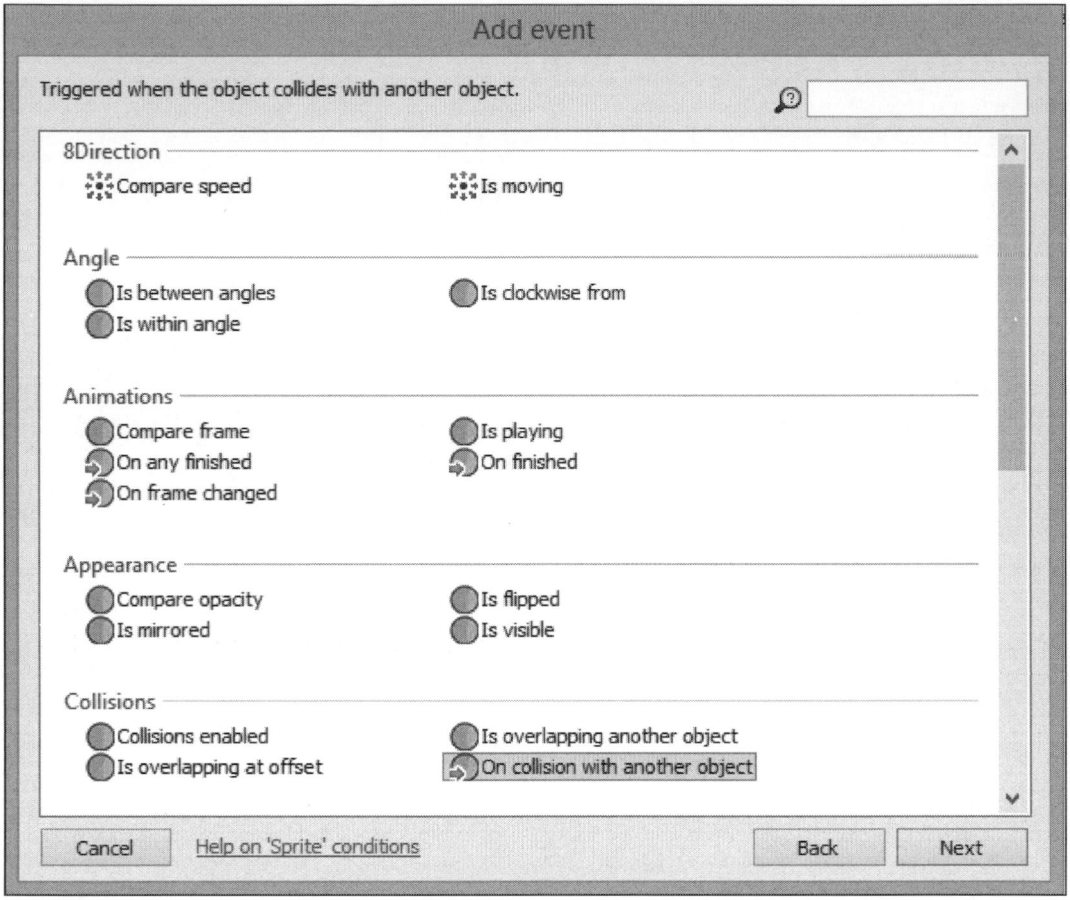

3. Click on **On collision with another object**. When the player collides with a specific object (the box), an action will happen.
4. Once you select this, the **Pick an object** window should pop up. Select the **BoxBlueStar**, or whatever you have called your power-up object, as shown in the following screenshot:

5. After selecting **BoxBlueStar** in the **Pick an object** window, the following window should appear:

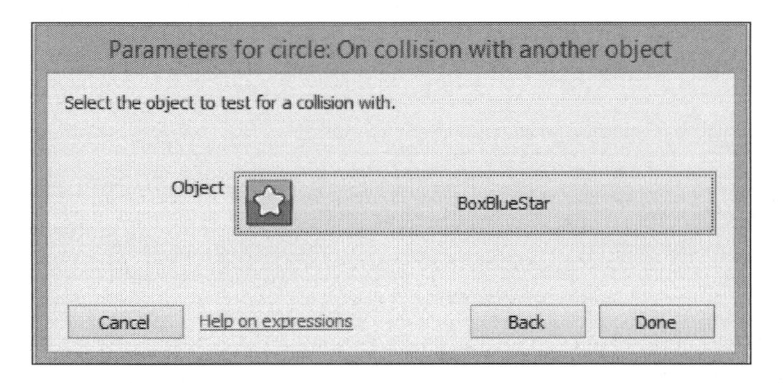

6. Click on **Done** and the event sheet should look like the following screenshot:

Destroying the power-up on collision

Now, we need to add a few actions. The first action is going to be destroying the box. If we don't do this, the box will not be destroyed and it will look weird to the player. Add an action and click on the power-up box.

Go ahead and click on **BoxBlueStar**.

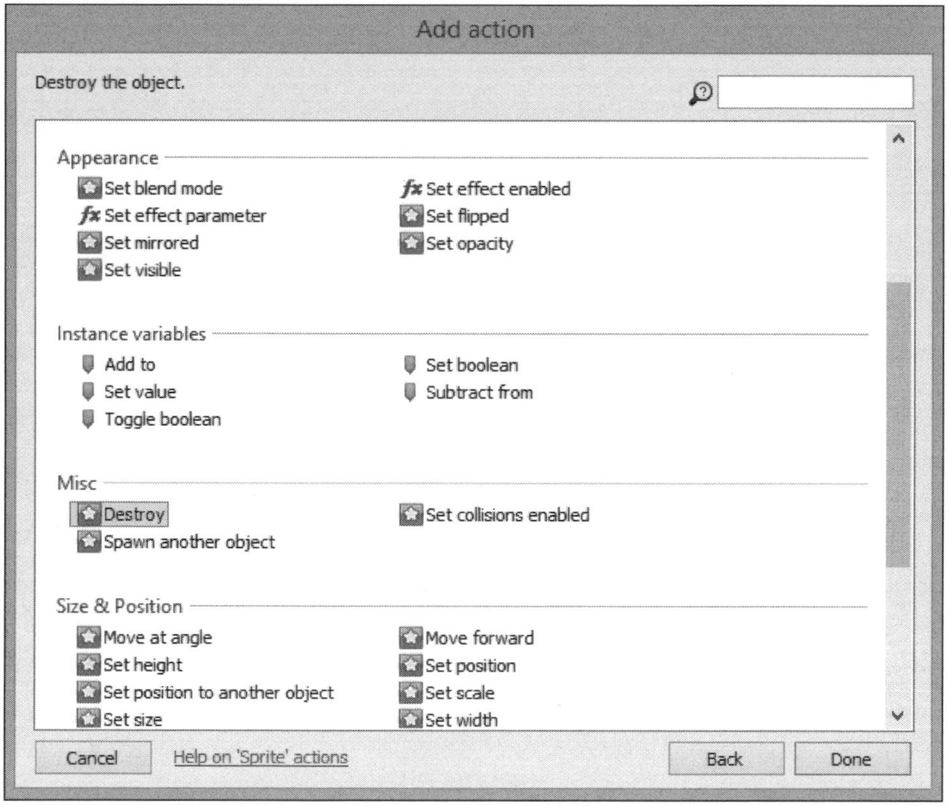

Click on **Destroy**, and your event sheet should look like the following screenshot:

Run the game and test to see whether the box does indeed get destroyed.

Increasing the player sprite's speed

We are almost finished. The next thing we need to do is change the settings so that the player speed is doubled for a short period of time. This is actually really simple to achieve! Add an action, select the player sprite, and click on **Next**.

Go ahead and select the circle. You should see a window similar to the following screenshot pop up:

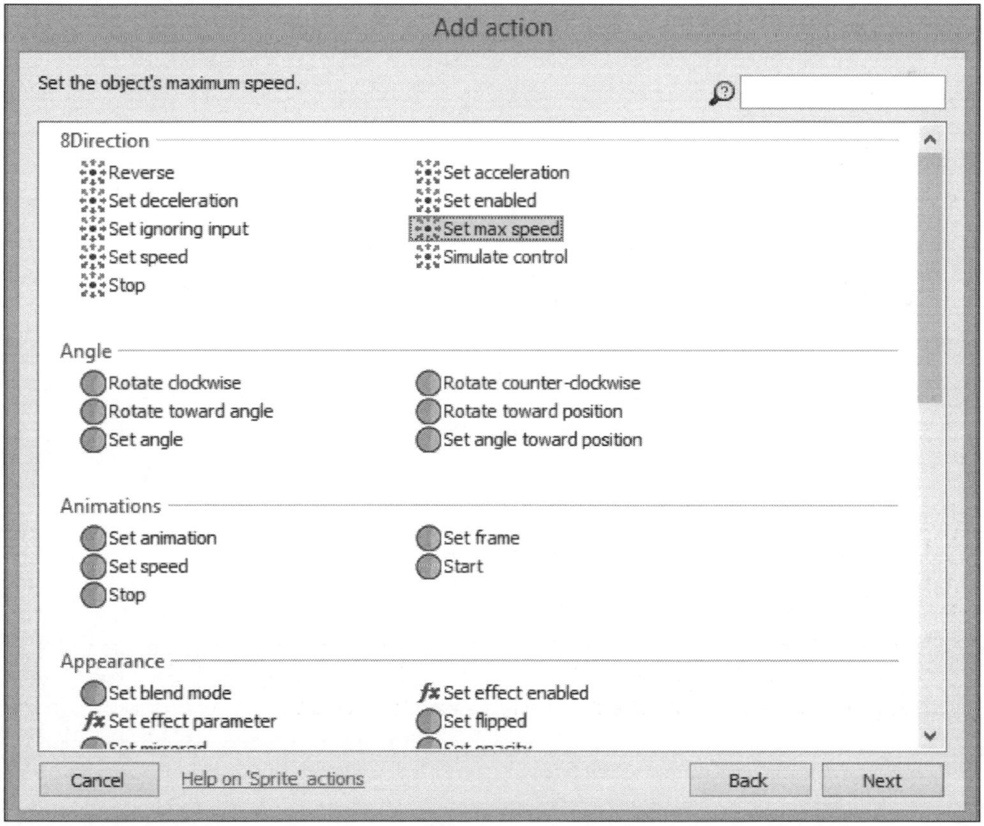

Here, you can see that by adding the **8Direction** functionality, we have added more options for actions. Select **Set max speed**. It should bring up the **Set max speed** dialog box, which is shown in the following screenshot:

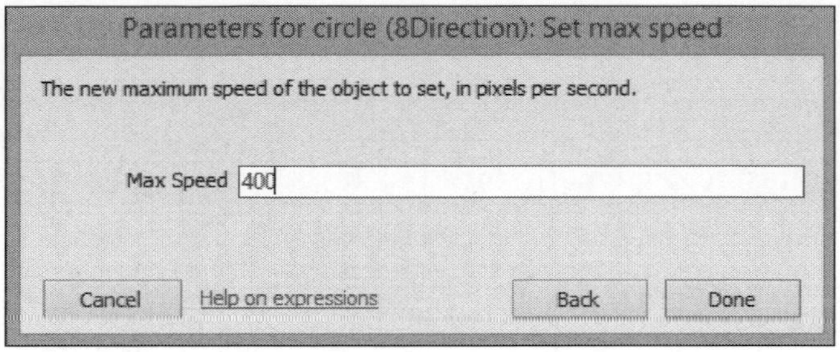

We need to set it to `400`, or whatever you want your power-up to increase the speed to. Once you are finished, click on **Done**.

Setting the duration of the speed boost

The last thing we need to do is set the duration for the increased speed. Add another action from the **Add action** window and select **System**, as shown in the following screenshot:

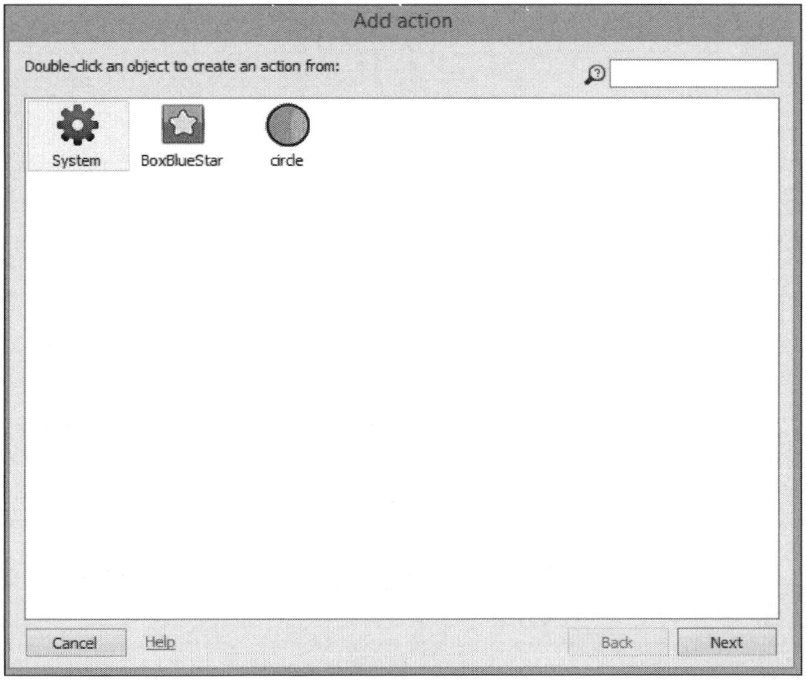

Then, we need to select the **Wait** function in order to insert a small timer. After the **Wait** command is finished, the power-up will end and the player sprite will return to a normal speed of 200. Once you select **Wait**, the **Parameters for System** dialog box will appear. Type the number of seconds you want the power-up effect to last, as shown in the following screenshot:

Restoring the player's speed to normal

After that, select the first **Set maximum speed** event and press *Ctrl* + *C* to copy. Then, select the **Wait** command and press *Ctrl* + *V* to paste. The second **Set maximum speed** command should be after the **Wait** command, as shown in the following screenshot:

Double-click the second **Set maximum speed** action and set it to 200—the original speed. Your event sheet should look like this:

Go ahead and try it out. You have just made your first game mechanics!

Summary

In this chapter, we talked about game mechanics, which are really important. Whenever you play a game, deconstruct the game into mechanics. Take note of the mechanics you like and the ones you don't like. We have learned how to add game mechanics to sprites and change their properties as well.

In the next chapter, we are going to learn how to make a game from scratch.

5

Making a Simple Shooter

Shooters are one of the best places to start when making games. Most people like to play a shooter, so they are a recognizable game archetype. The best part is that they are generally easy to make. So let's construct one!

In this chapter, we are going to learn:

- How to control the sprite with the keyboard
- How to rotate the sprite about the mouse position
- How to add bullet behavior

Starting the project

Once you have started a new project, you need to change the layout size to `640, 480`. Then, we need to add some art. The first thing we need to add is the player. Find a circular graphic and add the sprite. Make your sprite 50 by 50 pixels and change its name to `Player`.

Your layout should look like the following screenshot:

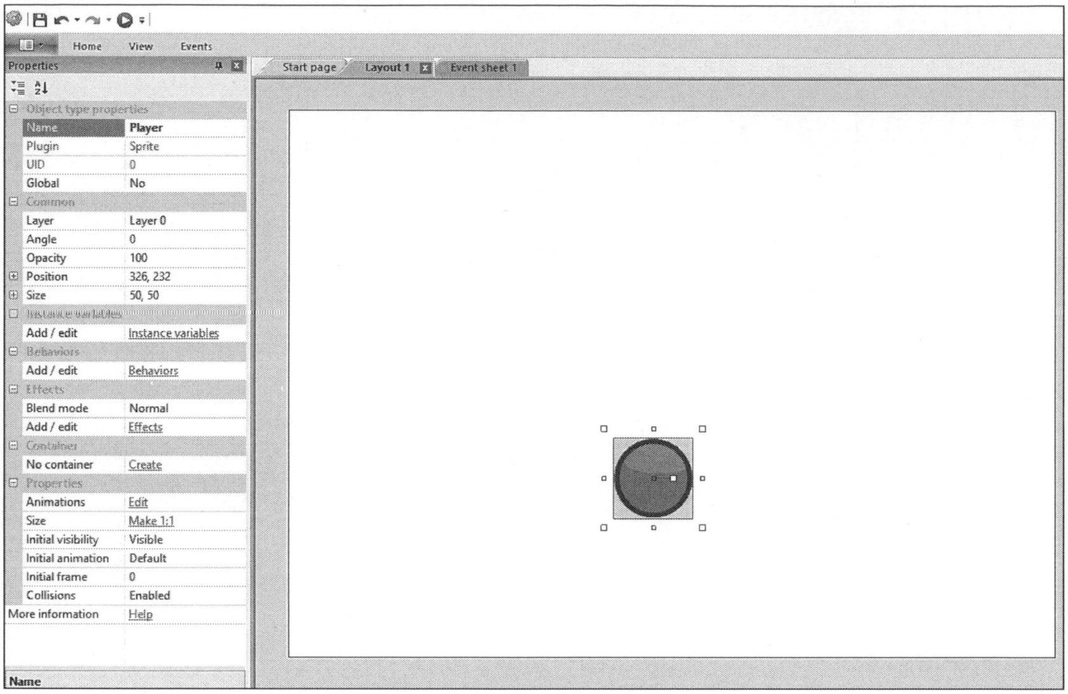

It's really important that you name the player as well as set the size, because when you make a lot of sprites, it can get confusing later on. Imagine if you had a game with 200 sprites and they were all called sprite1, sprite2, and so on; it would get confusing really fast. Whenever you set the size of an object, it is best to set the size in Photoshop or another program. When you change the size of images in game engines, the images can be distorted and as a result, they do not look good.

The next thing we need to do is create a background. In order to do this, we need to add another layer to the game. This can be done by performing the following steps:

1. Click on the **Layers** tab and then click on the plus sign (**+**).

   This will create a new layer on top of the other layer. Move **Layer 1** to the bottom; to do this, select **Layer 1** and press the down arrow.

   Layer 1 is now at the bottom and we can add our background image. While you do not need to have a background image, it is good practice to put one in because most games have them. Also, it improves the quality of the game. Add the background image. At this point, we need to change the background transparency. Currently, you have something like the following screenshot:

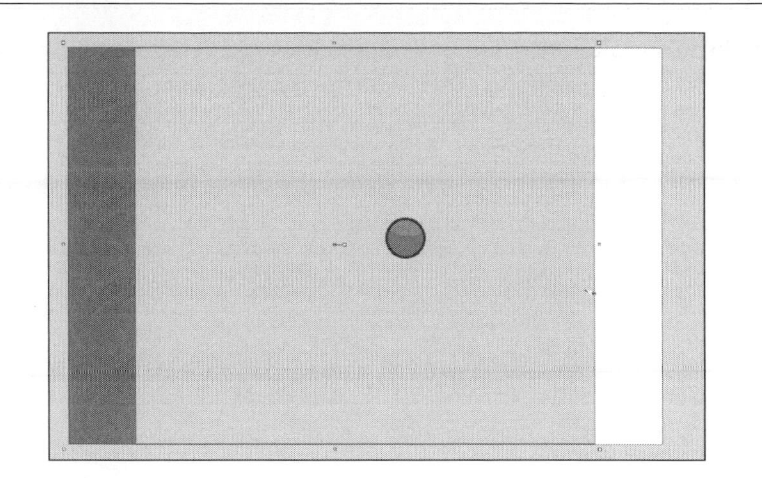

2. At the moment, the top layer isn't transparent. In order to make it transparent, select the layer and move it over to the left side of the screen where it says **Transparent**. Then, select **Yes**.

The top layer should now be transparent and you can see the background.

3. There is one more thing left to do: locking the background layer. This is done so that when we are editing the game, we do not make any accidental changes to the background. Since the background layer is static and will not be moving during the game, it is best to make it a locked layer. In the **Layers** tab, click on the lock icon at the top (as shown in the following screenshot); the background layer is now locked.

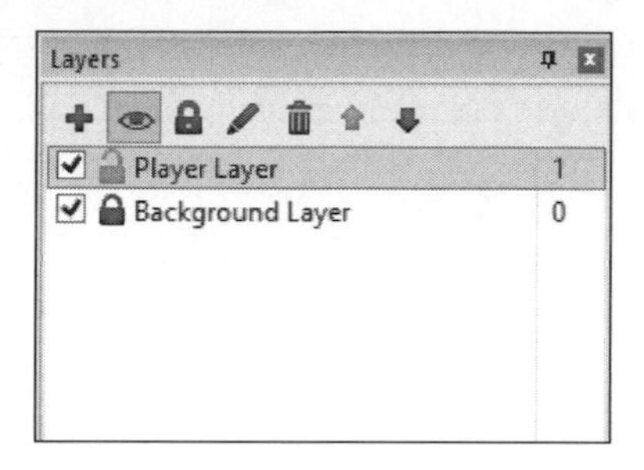

Now, we have two layers and we can start programming some of the game mechanics. We have two layers, but we will need to add more as the game goes on.

Controlling a sprite with the keyboard

Let's add some game logic to the game. Double-click on the screen in the first layout and add the keyboard and mouse objects, as shown in the following screenshot. This allows us to use the **Keyboard** and the **Mouse** in our game.

Let's set up the game logic:

1. We need to make the player move with the WASD control and rotate to the mouse location. Click on the player and add the behavior.
2. Once you see this dialog box, click on the plus sign to add a behavior.
3. Scroll down and add the **8Direction** behavior:

4. Once you have added the **8Direction** behavior, it should appear just like the preceding screenshot. Exit this window and go to the layout.

What we want is for the player to use either the arrow keys or the WASD controls to move around. It's good to have both, as players have different preferences. The following are the steps to do so:

1. First, we have to change the eight directions to four. You can have a game with the full eight directions, but four is a little easier to manage programmatically.

2. Select the box next to **8 directions** and change it to **4 directions**, as shown in the following screenshot:

Behaviors
8Direction
Max speed
200
Acceleration
600
Deceleration
500
Directions
4 directions
Set angle
360 degree (smooth)
Default contr...
Yes
Initial state
Enabled
Add / edit
Behaviors

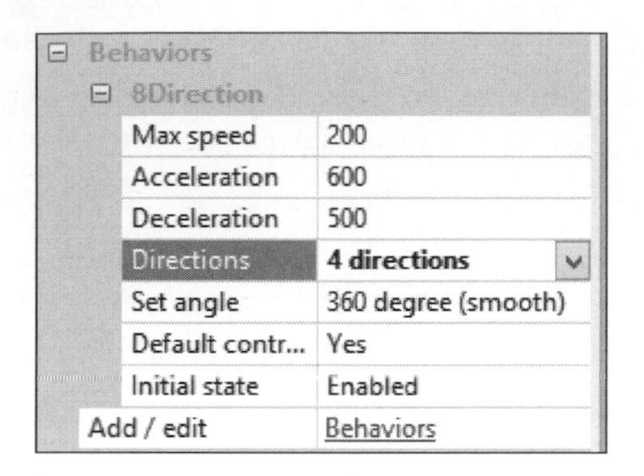

3. We also need to make sure that the angle will be determined by the mouse and not the **8Direction** behavior. From the **Set angle** dropdown list, select **No** as shown in the following screenshot:

Behaviors
8Direction
Max speed
200
Acceleration
600
Deceleration
500
Directions
4 directions
Set angle
No
Default contr...
Yes
Initial state
Enabled
Add / edit
Behaviors

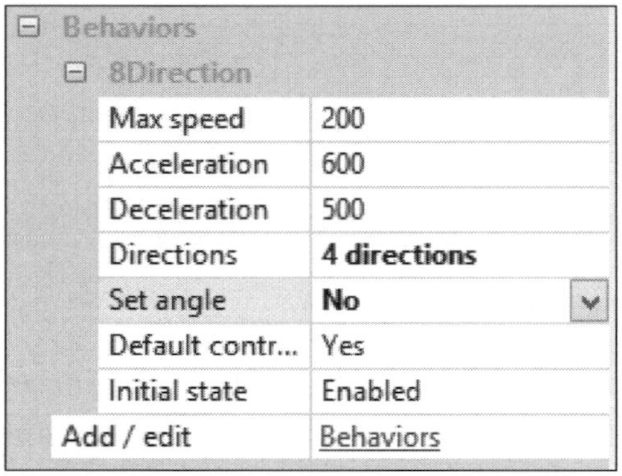

4. Before we move on, let's test the game. Press *F5* and run the game. Make sure that the controls work. Once you are satisfied, go to the event sheet and add your WASD controls.
5. Once you are in the event sheet, double-click on the background to add an event and add a **Keyboard** event.
6. Once you are in the **Keyboard** event window, select **Key is down**.
7. Once you have selected **Key is down**, select **<click to choose>** in the **Parameters for Keyboard: Key is down** window:

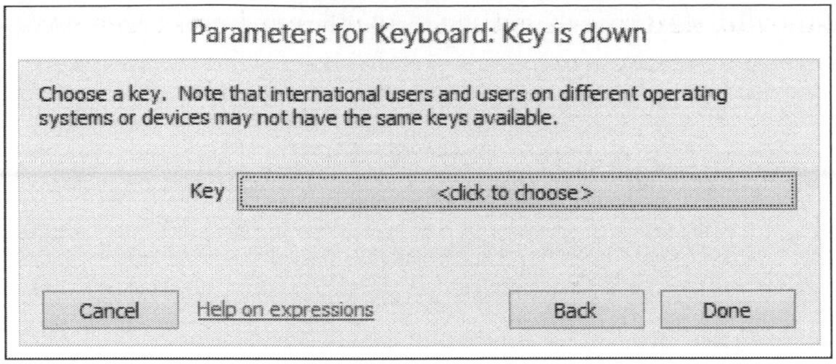

8. Once you have selected **<click to choose>**, select the key you want. In this case, it will be the *D* key:

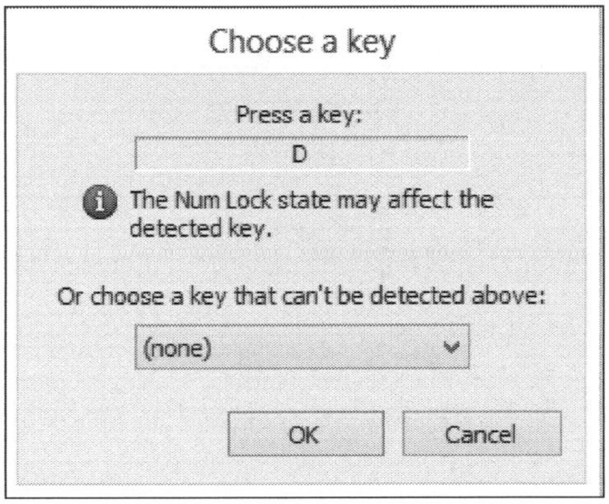

9. Once you have selected the *D* key, the event sheet should look like this:

10. Click on **Add action** and click on **Player** in the layout. Once you have clicked on **Player**, select **Simulate control** from the available options:

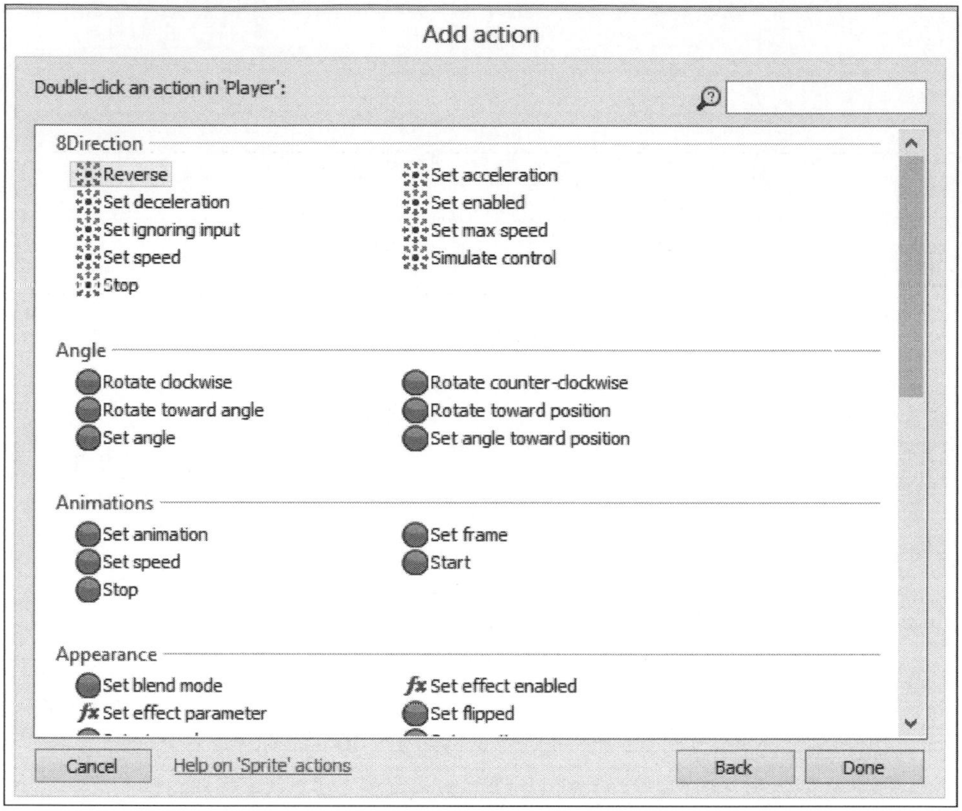

11. This will simulate the control of the **8Direction** behavior. We want to simulate the right control, so select the **Right** control as follows:

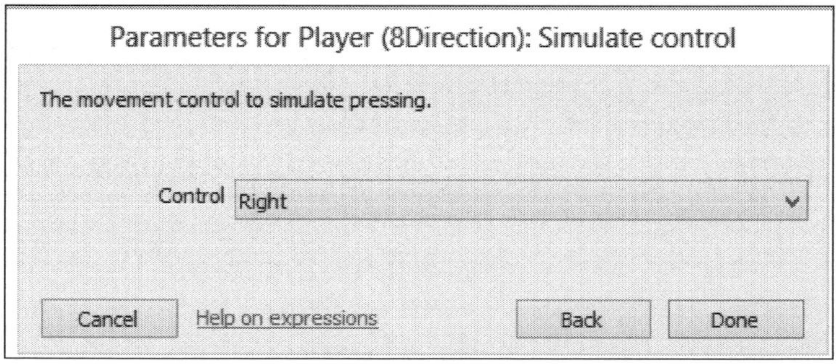

12. After you do that, the event sheet should look like this:

#	Object	Condition	Object	Action
1	Keyboard	D is down	Player	Simulate 8Direction pressing Right
				Add action

Add event

13. Copy-and-paste the keyboard layout and change the controls accordingly. In the end, the event sheet should look like this:

#	Object	Condition	Object	Action
1	Keyboard	D is down	Player	Simulate 8Direction pressing Right
				Add action
2	Keyboard	A is down	Player	Simulate 8Direction pressing Left
				Add action
3	Keyboard	W is down	Player	Simulate 8Direction pressing Up
				Add action
4	Keyboard	S is down	Player	Simulate 8Direction pressing Down
				Add action

Add event

Test and run the game. If the player moves around correctly, then we can move on. Before we do this, however, there is one more thing that needs to be addressed—restricting the player's position. The player can move off of the screen. Go to the layout and select the **Bound to layout** behavior.

Test the game again and see whether it works. It is really important to test your game; often in game development, the sooner you catch a problem, the better chance you have of fixing it.

Organizing the event sheet

Before we add the mouse controls, let's organize our event sheet. Often, if you have a cluttered development platform (in Construct 2, the event sheet), releasing your game becomes harder to achieve. It's important to point out that disorganization makes troubleshooting and fixing bugs more difficult, which may delay or prevent release. An organized development environment is more efficient. Let's add a group. Right-click on the event sheet and select **Add group** from the menu, as shown in the following screenshot:

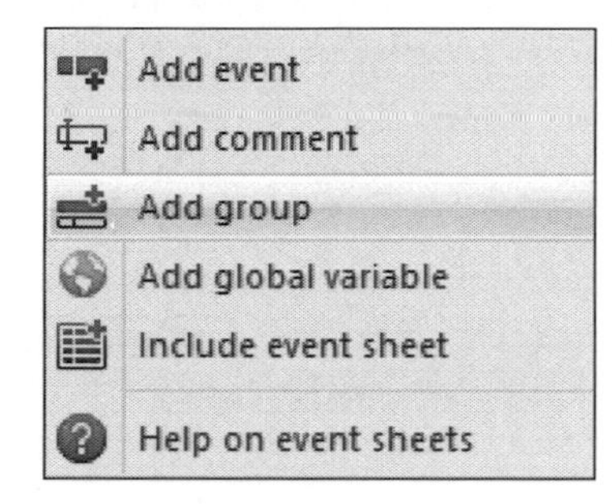
Add event
Add comment
Add group
Add global variable
Include event sheet
Help on event sheets

Name your group appropriately. Clarity is really important. You can also write an optional description. The more information you put in here, the better; when you come back to this source code in a year, you will know what is going on.

Name the group `WASD Controls` or something similar, and give it an accurate description. Then, click on **OK** and you should see something like the following screenshot:

Start page
Layout 1
Event sheet 1
Keyboard D is down
Player Simulate 8Direction pressing Right
Add action
Keyboard A is down
Player Simulate 8Direction pressing Left
Add action
Keyboard W is down
Player Simulate 8Direction pressing Up
Add action
Keyboard S is down
Player Simulate 8Direction pressing Down
Add action
WASD Controls
This sets up the WASD controls.
Add event

Now, it is time to select everything and move it into the group. Select all of the purple areas of the events, press *Shift*, and then select the bottom event. This should select all of them. You can then drag them into the group, which should look like the screenshot that follows. Note that there will be an arrow that appears at the bottom, which will tell you that the events will shift to the group.

In the following screenshot, you can see the final product of the group. You can access the contents of the group by clicking on the plus sign.

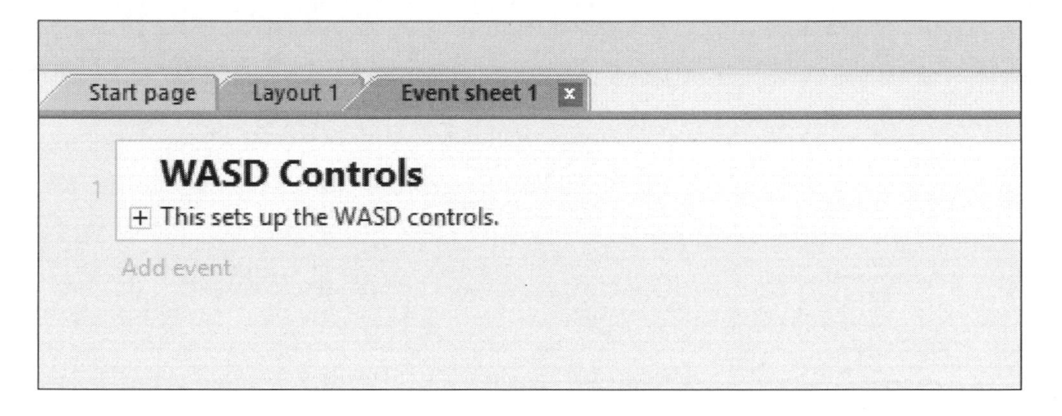

Adding mouse controls

Let's add some mouse controls. First click on **Add event** and then click on **System**. The mouse controls will allow us to use the mouse and access its properties, such as position, clicks, and movement.

Then, click on **Every tick**. The **Every tick** option will access the game loop and it will make sure that the logic for this event will always be checked.

Once you have **Every tick** selected, it should look like this:

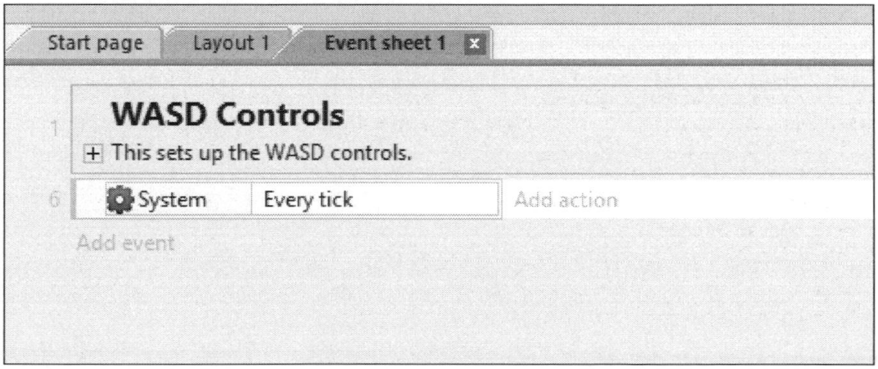

Click on **Add action** and then click on the player. Then, select **Set angle toward position** from the **Angle** list, as shown in the following screenshot:

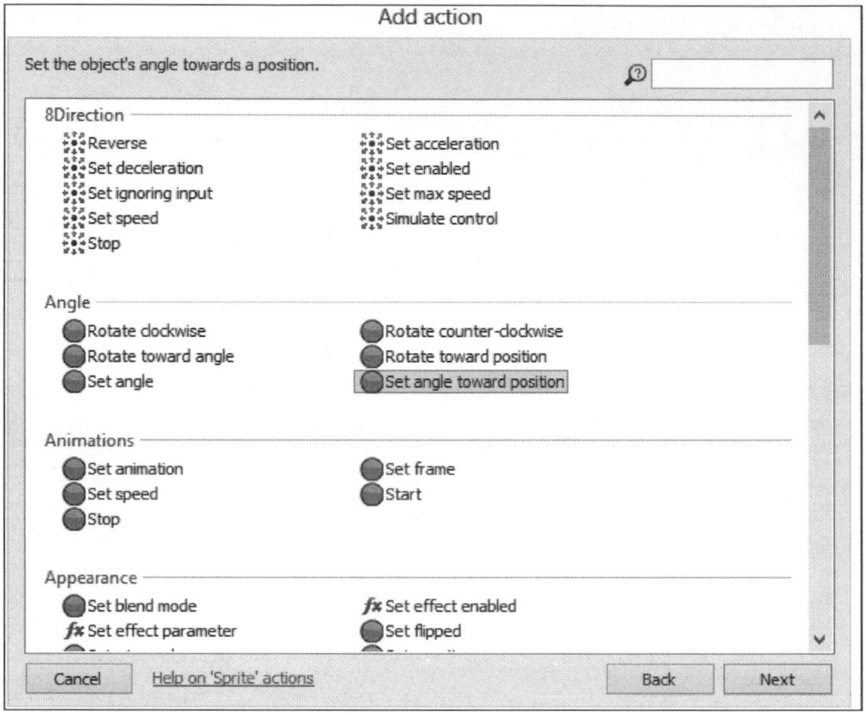

As shown in the following screenshot, type `Mouse.X` in the **X** box and type `Mouse.Y` in the **Y** box. Then, click on **Done**. This will make sure that the angle of the player will constantly be set to the mouse location. In 2D game development, we need to have two coordinates in order to find a position. These coordinates are X and Y. In order to find the position of the mouse, we need `Mouse.X` and `Mouse.Y`, which are the mouse's X and Y positions.

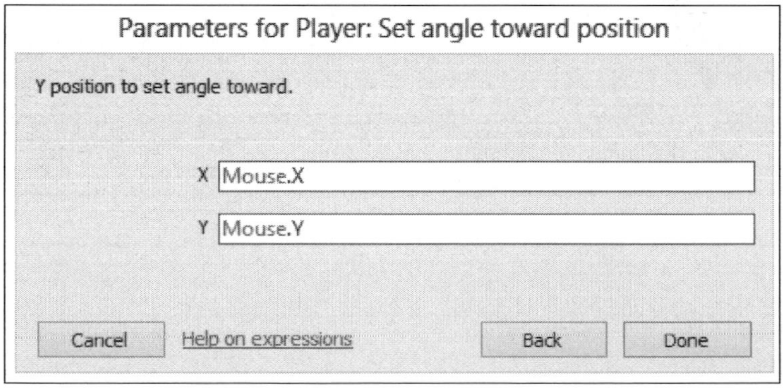

You should end up with something that looks like the following screenshot. This will now set the angle of the player to the mouse location.

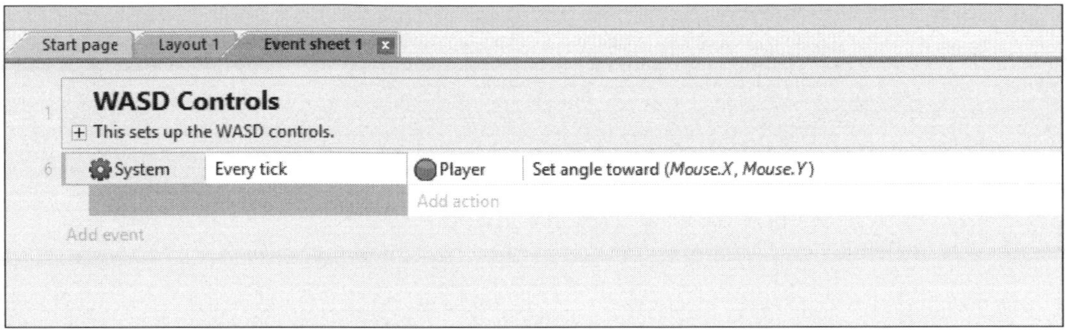

Go ahead and run the game. It should work out just fine.

Making the player shoot

Now, we need to make our player shoot. Add a sprite to the screen; we will use it as a projectile. We are going to use the same ball graphic that we used for the player. Change the name to something more appropriate, such as `Projectile`. Also, we have to set the size to `10, 10`. This is shown in the following screenshot:

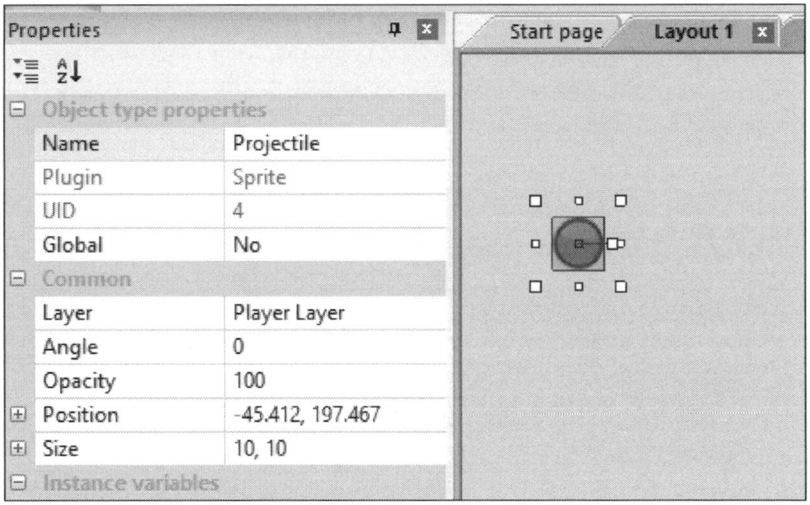

Go down in this pane and select **Behaviors**, and add a `Bullet` behavior as shown in the next screenshot. For more information, check *Chapter 2, Inputs and Controls*.

One thing that is great about Construct 2 is that the projectile speed is taken care of for you. This is great because setting up a projectile can be time consuming.

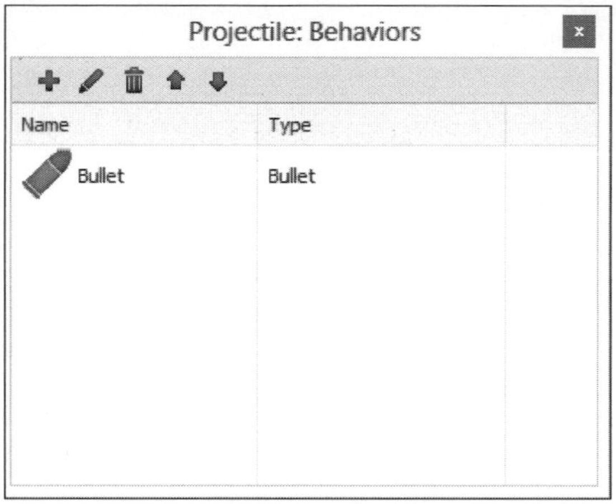

What we need to set up is for the projectile to spawn when we click the mouse. This won't be too hard. Go back to the event sheet and add a **Mouse** event. The **Mouse** event that we want to add is the **On any click** event. Since this game is really simple, we are going to use this option. If you want to link firing to a specific button, you can select **On click**.

Your project should look like the following screenshot:

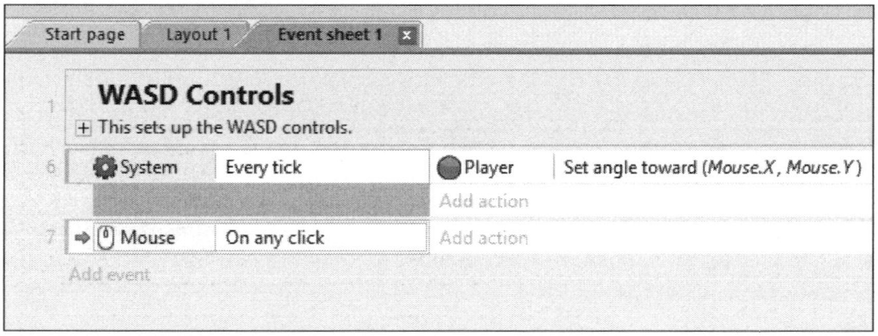

Go ahead and click on **Add action** next to **On any click**, and then select **Spawn another object**. This is shown in the following screenshot. The object we want to spawn is a projectile.

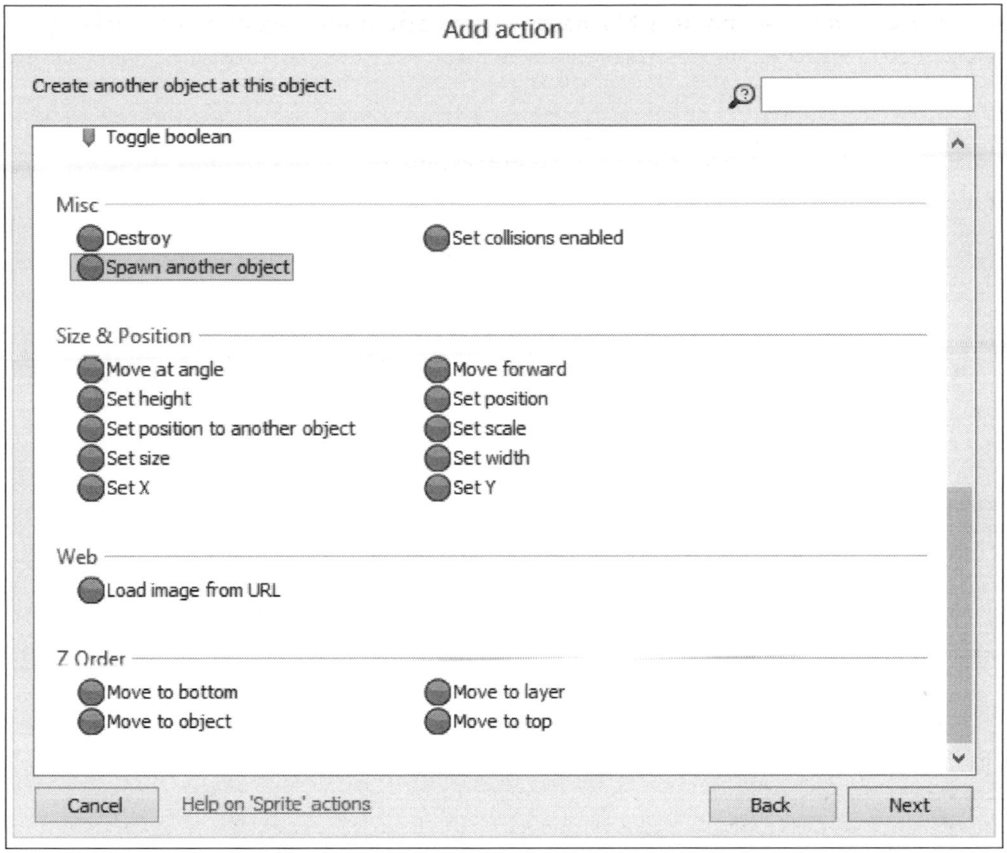

Add action

Create another object at this object.

Toggle boolean

Misc

Destroy

Set collisions enabled

Spawn another object

Size & Position

Move at angle

Move forward

Set height

Set position

Set position to another object

Set scale

Set size

Set width

Set X

Set Y

Web

Load image from URL

Z Order

Move to bottom

Move to layer

Move to object

Move to top

Cancel Help on 'Sprite' actions Back Next

Once you have clicked on the projectile, the following dialog box should appear:

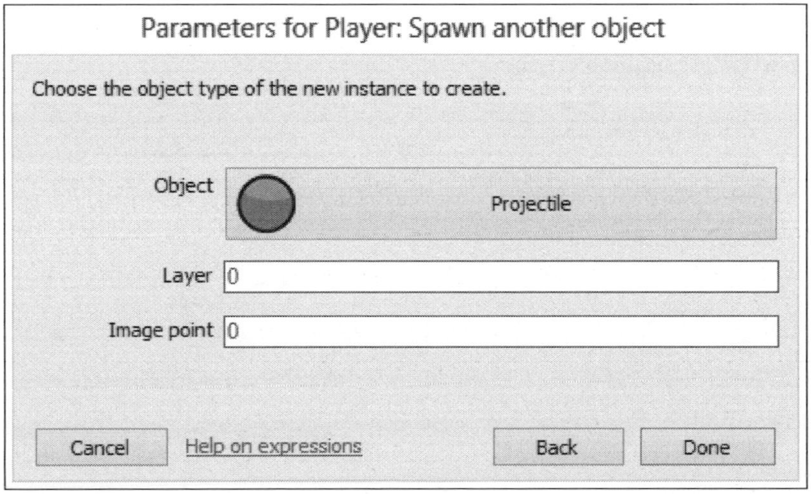

Parameters for Player: Spawn another object

Choose the object type of the new instance to create.

Object Projectile

Layer 0

Image point 0

Cancel Help on expressions Back Done

Go ahead and test your game. You should be able to move around and shoot a projectile to the mouse location.

> We have to take into account that every time you spawn a projectile, it uses a little bit of memory. Therefore, we have to destroy that projectile when we don't see it. If we do not do this, then the game can lag; this is especially a problem for mobile devices.

Click on your projectile and click on **Add behavior**. Add the **Destroy outside layout** behavior. This will destroy the projectile and free up memory when the projectile is offscreen. The **Behaviors** window should now look like the following screenshot:

Projectile: Behaviors

Name	Type
Bullet	Bullet
DestroyOutsideLa...	Destroy outside layout

You can also change the properties of the bullet under **Behaviors**, if you want to. You can change the speed, acceleration, and gravity, and you can also set whether it bounces off solids. You can set the angle and you can choose whether the projectile will be enabled or not.

One way to make your bullets appear more realistic is to add the **Gravity** option shown in the following screenshot. Gravity in games works just like gravity in the real world. For projectiles such as cannonballs, it adds a level of realism. Go ahead and try it out.

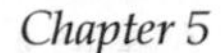

Behaviors	
Bullet	
Speed	400
Acceleration	0
Gravity	0
Bounce off s...	No
Set angle	Yes
Initial state	Enabled
DestroyOutsideL...	(no properties)
Add / edit	Behaviors

Adding the enemy

Adding enemies is a great way to add game complexity and fun. Let's add an enemy that moves towards the player. Go ahead and add an enemy to the screen. I sized the enemy `30, 30` and named the sprite `Enemy`. This is what your layout should look like:

Properties	
Layout properties	
Name	Layout 1
Event sheet	Event sheet 1
Active layer	Player Layer
Unbounded scro...	No
Layout Size	640, 480
Margins	500, 500
Effects	
Add / edit	Effects
Project Properties	View
More information	Help

Next, we need to go to our event sheet and add an **Every tick** event.

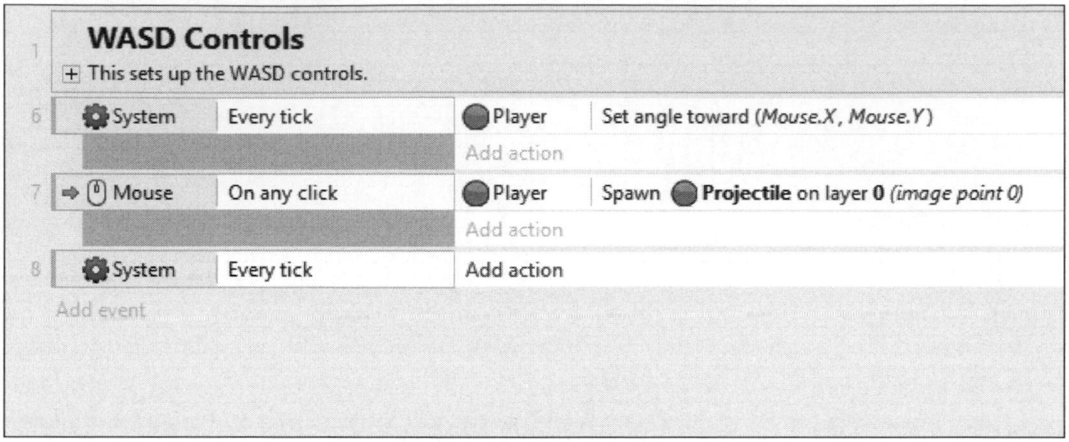

#	Object	Condition	Object	Action
1	**WASD Controls** This sets up the WASD controls.			
6	System	Every tick	Player	Set angle toward (*Mouse.X*, *Mouse.Y*)
			Add action	
7	Mouse	On any click	Player	Spawn **Projectile** on layer **0** (*image point 0*)
			Add action	
8	System	Every tick	Add action	
	Add event			

Once you have an event sheet that looks like the preceding screenshot, you can add an action for the `Enemy` sprite, such as **Rotate toward position**. Type `Player.X` in the **X** box and `Player.Y` in the **Y** box. This sets the position to the player's X and Y locations, and it is shown in the following screenshot:

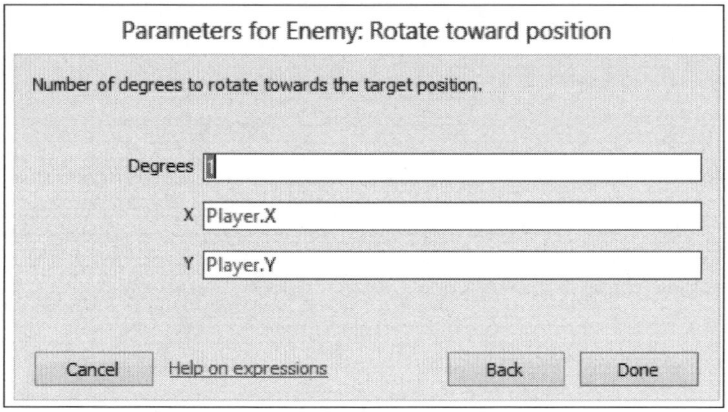

Parameters for Enemy: Rotate toward position

Number of degrees to rotate towards the target position.

Degrees 1

X Player.X

Y Player.Y

Cancel | Help on expressions | Back | Done

Once you have done that, add another action. This time, we need to move the enemy forward. Navigate to **Add action** | **Enemy** | **Move forward**, as shown in the following screenshot:

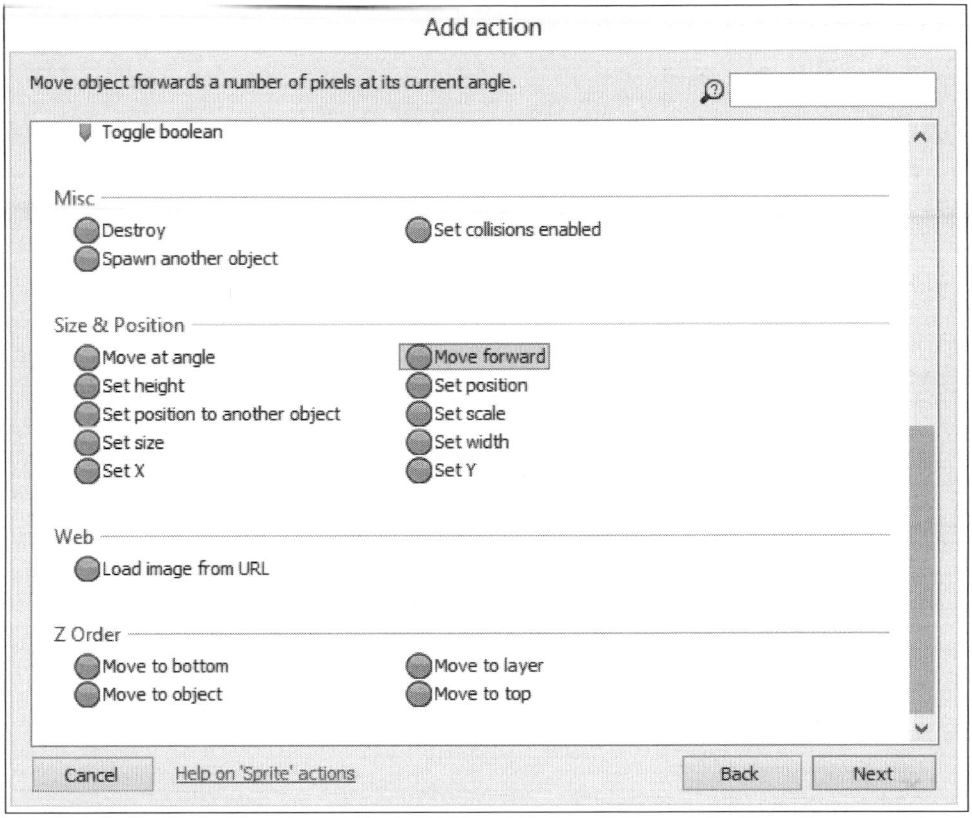

We do have to move the enemy forward a certain distance. In this case, we will set the distance to `1`. You can set the distance to another number if you wish.

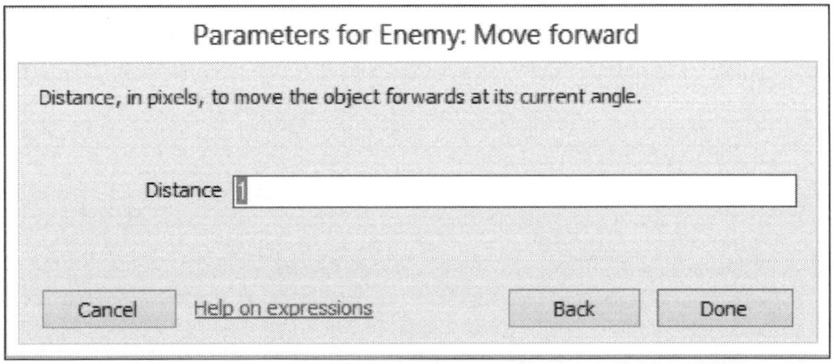

Your event sheet should look like the following screenshot. Now, the enemy constantly rotates towards the position of the player, while constantly moving the enemy forward. Run the game and try it out.

WASD Controls
This sets up the WASD controls.
System
Every tick
Player
Set angle toward (Mouse.X, Mouse.Y)
Add action
Mouse
On any click
Player
Spawn Projectile on layer 0 (image point 0)
Add action
System
Every tick
Enemy
Rotate 1 degrees toward (Player.X, Player.Y)
Enemy
Move forward 1 pixels
Add action
Add event

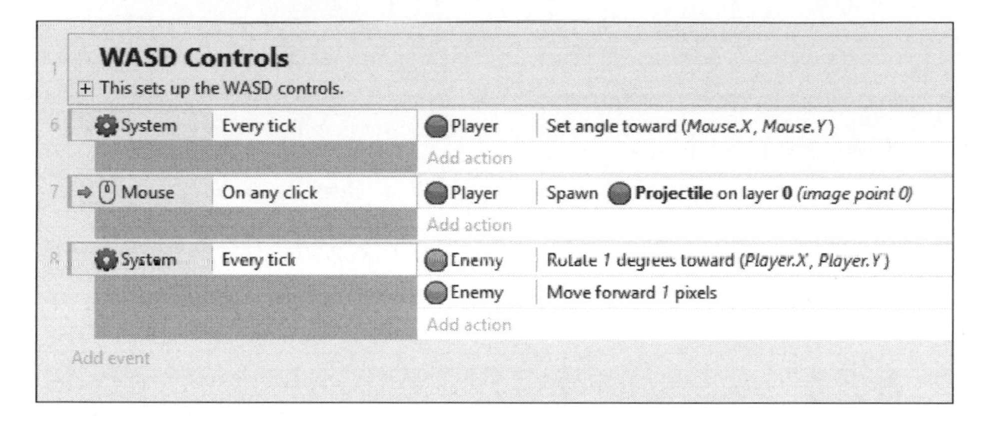

Destroying the enemy

Let's add another event. This time, we want to destroy the enemy and the projectile when the projectile hits the enemy. Navigate to **Add event** | **Projectile** | **On collision with another object**, as shown in the following screenshot:

Add event
Triggered when the object collides with another object.
Angle
Is between angles
Is clockwise from
Is within angle
Animations
Compare frame
Is playing
On any finished
On finished
On frame changed
Appearance
Compare opacity
Is flipped
Is mirrored
Is visible
Bullet
Compare distance travelled
Compare speed
Collisions
Collisions enabled
Is overlapping another object
Is overlapping at offset
On collision with another object
Cancel
Help on 'Sprite' conditions
Back
Next

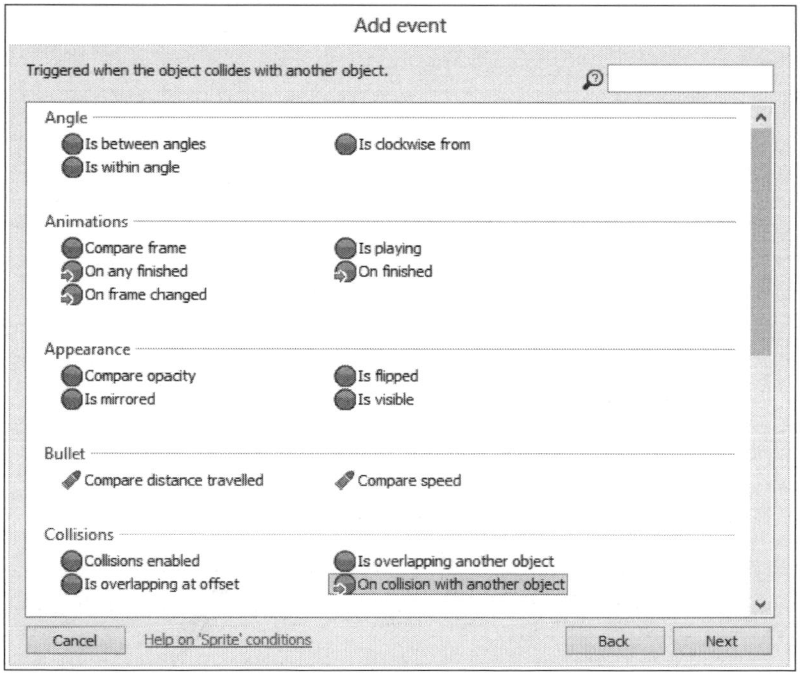

Choose **Enemy** in the dialog box that pops up, as shown in the following screenshot:

Parameters for Projectile: On collision with another object

Select the object to test for a collision with.

Object — Enemy

Cancel | Help on expressions | Back | Done

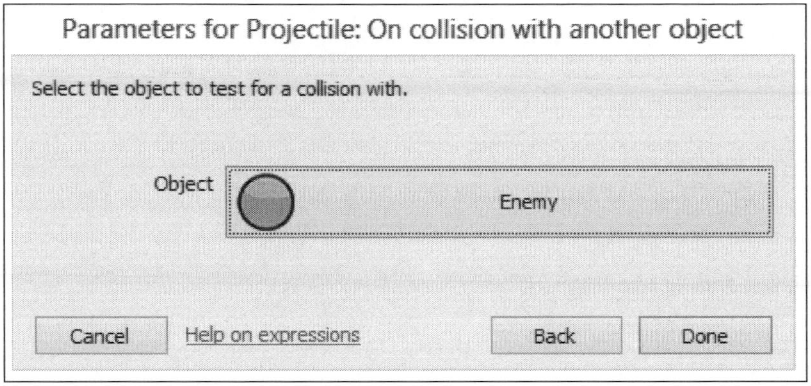

Once you have done that, add an action and choose the projectile. Scroll down until you see **Destroy**, as shown in the following screenshot. This will destroy the projectile.

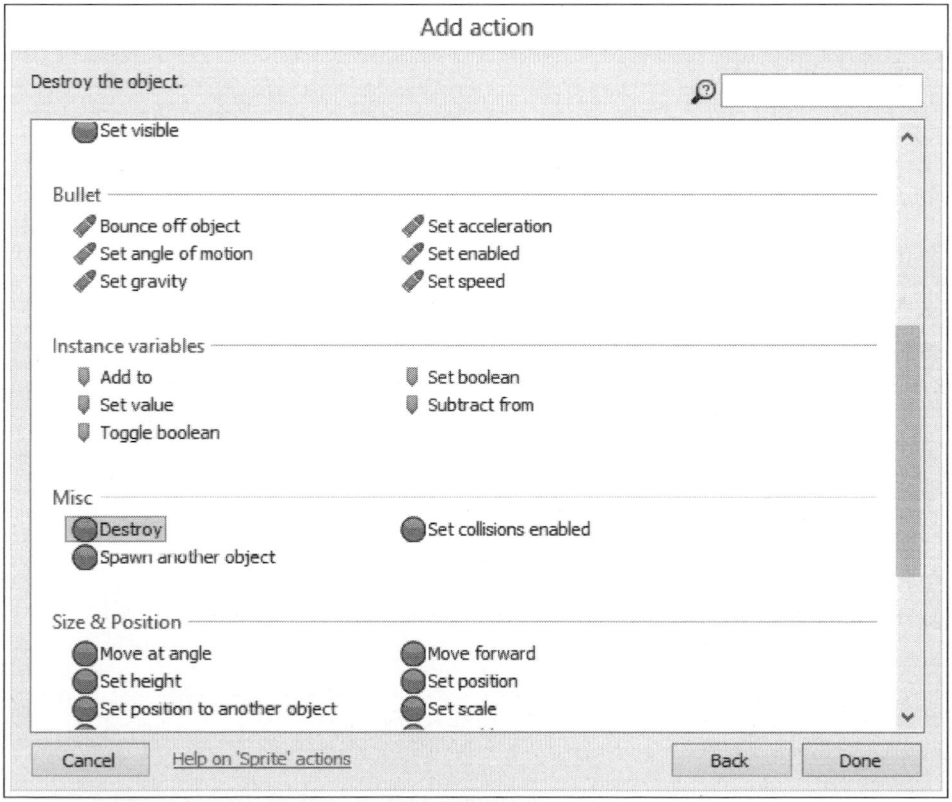

Add action

Destroy the object.

Set visible

Bullet
- Bounce off object
- Set acceleration
- Set angle of motion
- Set enabled
- Set gravity
- Set speed

Instance variables
- Add to
- Set boolean
- Set value
- Subtract from
- Toggle boolean

Misc
- Destroy
- Set collisions enabled
- Spawn another object

Size & Position
- Move at angle
- Move forward
- Set height
- Set position
- Set position to another object
- Set scale

Cancel | Help on 'Sprite' actions | Back | Done

Do the exact same thing for the enemy. You have to destroy both the enemy and the projectile. The event sheet should look like this at the end:

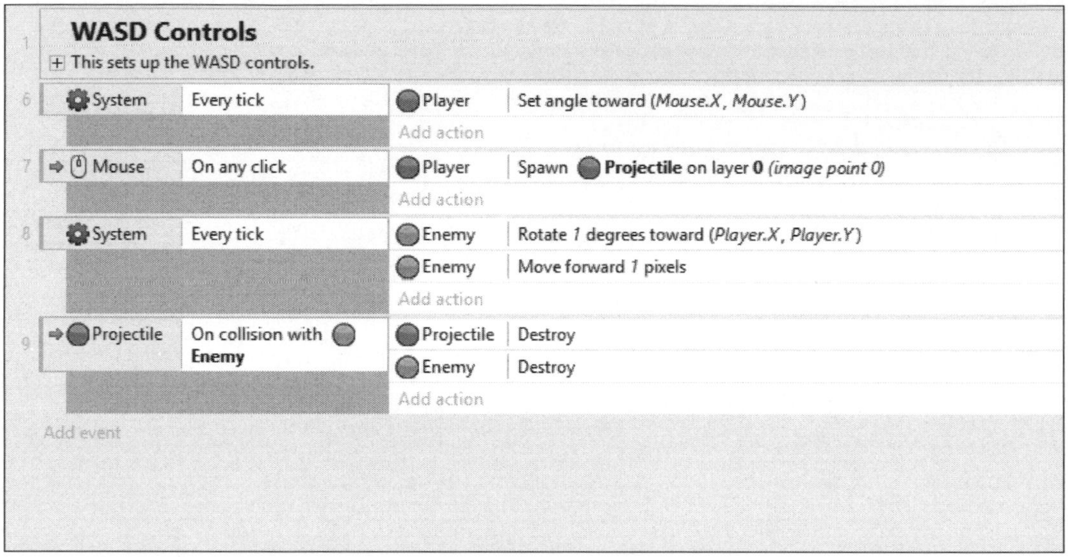

WASD Controls

+ This sets up the WASD controls.

#	Object	Condition	Object	Action
6	System	Every tick	Player	Set angle toward (*Mouse.X*, *Mouse.Y*)
			Add action	
7	Mouse	On any click	Player	Spawn **Projectile** on layer **0** *(image point 0)*
			Add action	
8	System	Every tick	Enemy	Rotate *1* degrees toward (*Player.X*, *Player.Y*)
			Enemy	Move forward *1* pixels
			Add action	
9	Projectile	On collision with **Enemy**	Projectile	Destroy
			Enemy	Destroy
			Add action	

Add event

Test out the game and see how it works. When you run the game, you should see that the enemy moves towards the player. When the projectile hits the enemy, the enemy and the projectile should be destroyed.

Adding a spawner

Now, we need to add a spawner. A spawner spawns game objects. Go ahead and add a sprite; it should look something like the following screenshot. Rename it `Spawner`.

Object type properties	
Name	Spawner
Plugin	Sprite
UID	6
Global	No
Common	
Layer	Player Layer
Angle	0
Opacity	100
Position	-142.85, 64.285
Size	250, 250
Instance variables	
Add / edit	Instance variables
Behaviors	
Add / edit	Behaviors
Effects	
Blend mode	Normal
Add / edit	Effects
Container	
No container	Create
Properties	
Animations	Edit
Size	Make 1:1
Initial visibility	Visible
Initial animation	Default
Initial frame	0
Collisions	Enabled

What we need to do is change the size of the spawner. Double-click on the spawner and select **Resize**, as shown in the following screenshot:

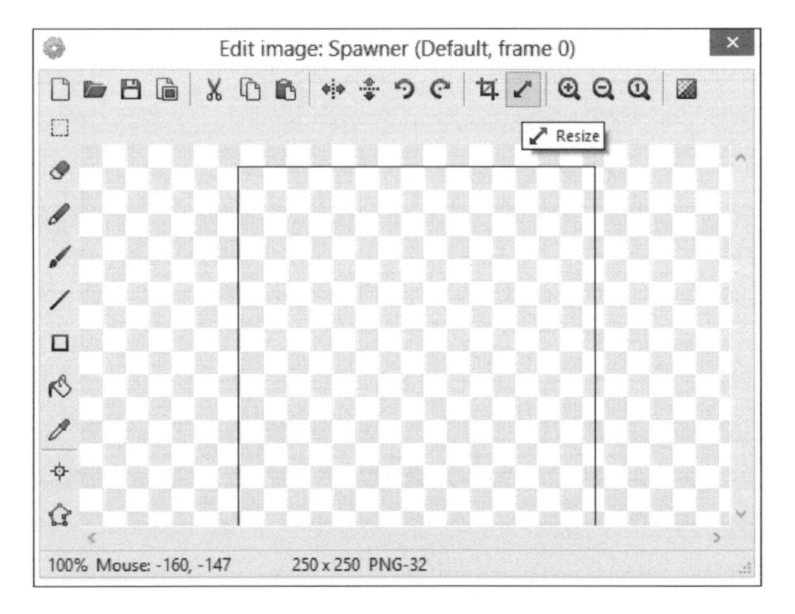

Then resize it to 50 by 50 with the help of the **Resize** option. Then, click on the paint bucket tool and fill in the color. We do this because otherwise we won't be able to see the spawner. I suggest making the spawner a bright and obvious color. We're going to make our spawner pink, as shown in the following screenshot:

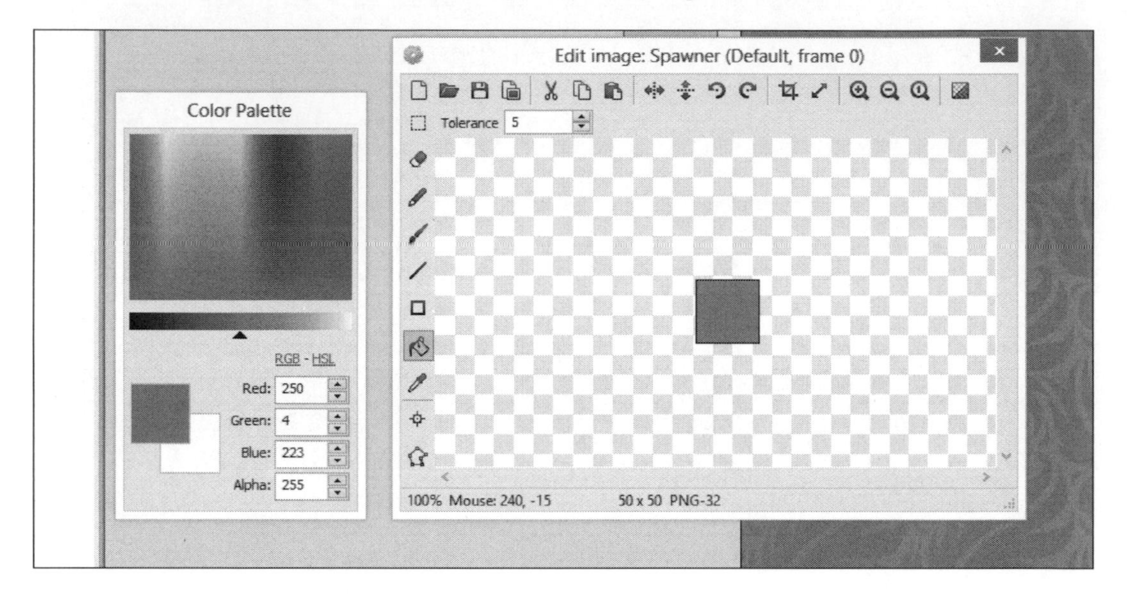

After this, click on **Close**. Now, we have to copy the spawners and put them in the playing area. You can press *Ctrl* and drag the spawner to copy quickly. If that doesn't work, you can use the copy-and-paste method. The game area should look like the following screenshot:

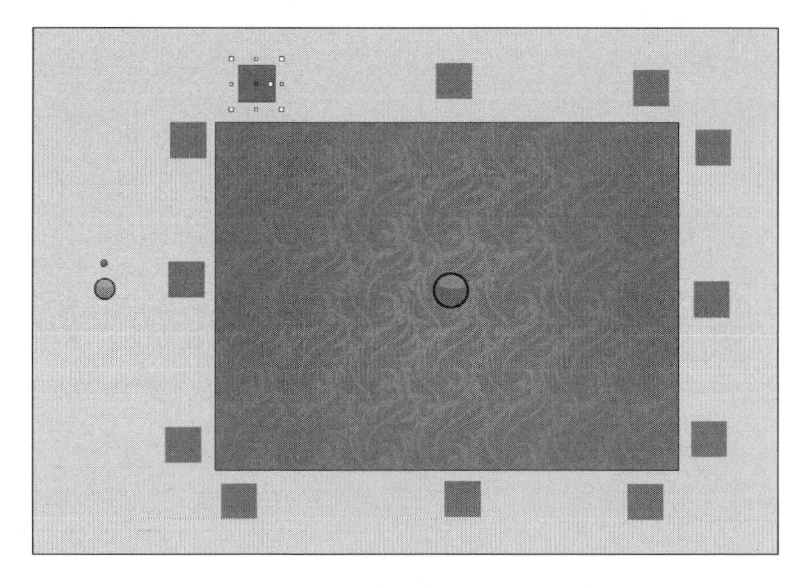

Now, we need to add functionality to the spawners. Go back to the event sheet and add an **Every X seconds** event, as shown in the following screenshot:

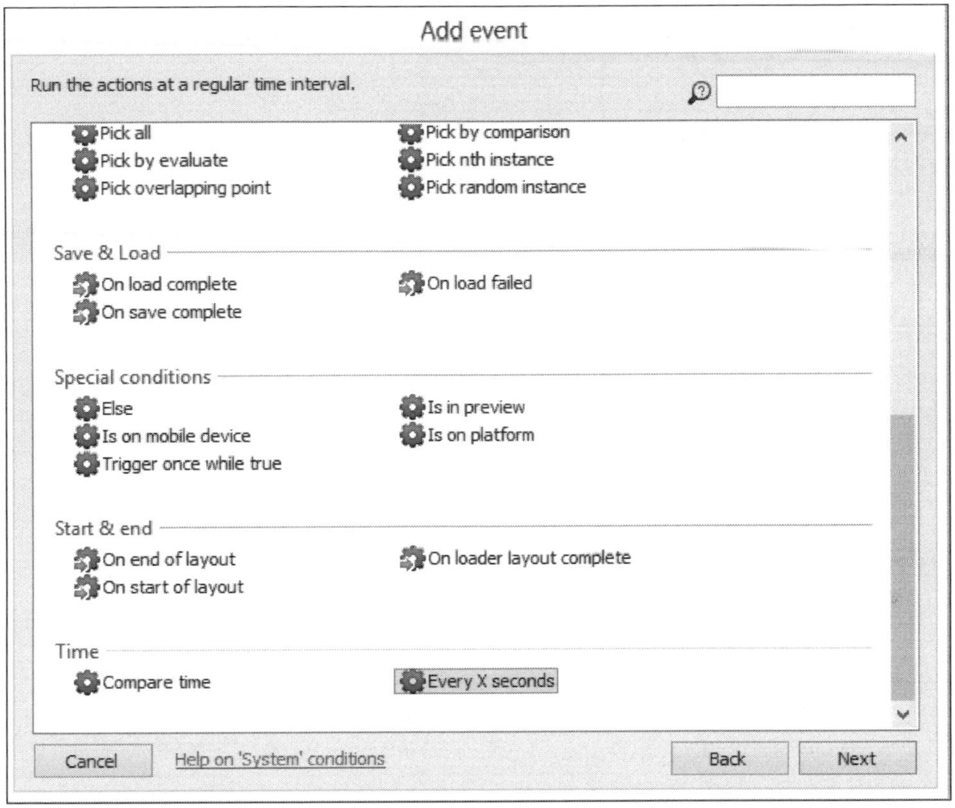

Let's add a time interval of `2.0` seconds in the **Parameters for System: Every X seconds** dialog box, as shown in the following screenshot. This will spawn an enemy at each spawner location every 2 seconds.

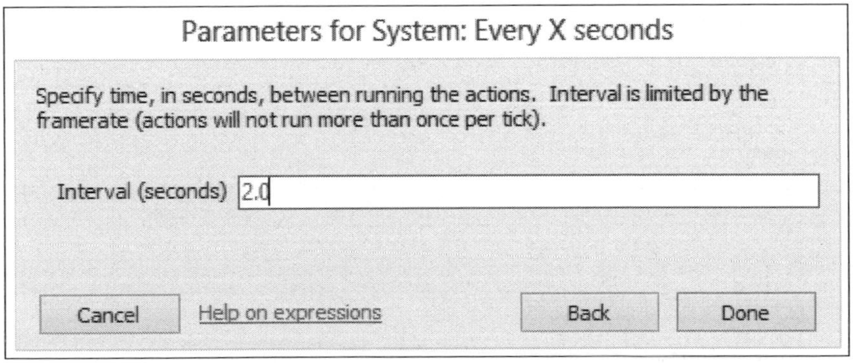

Add an action to this event by navigating to **Add action** | **Spawner** | **Spawn another object**. We want to spawn the enemy, so we select **Enemy** in the **Parameters for Spawner: Spawn another object** dialog box. This is shown in the following screenshot:

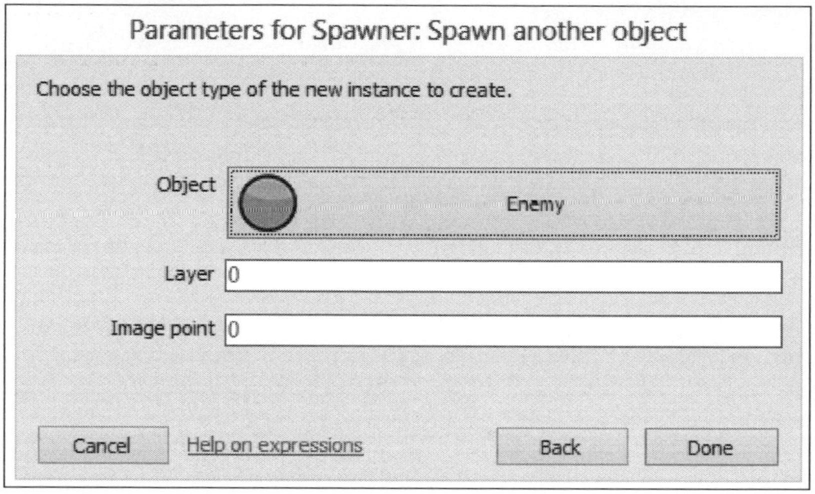

Your project should look like the following screenshot when you click on **Done**:

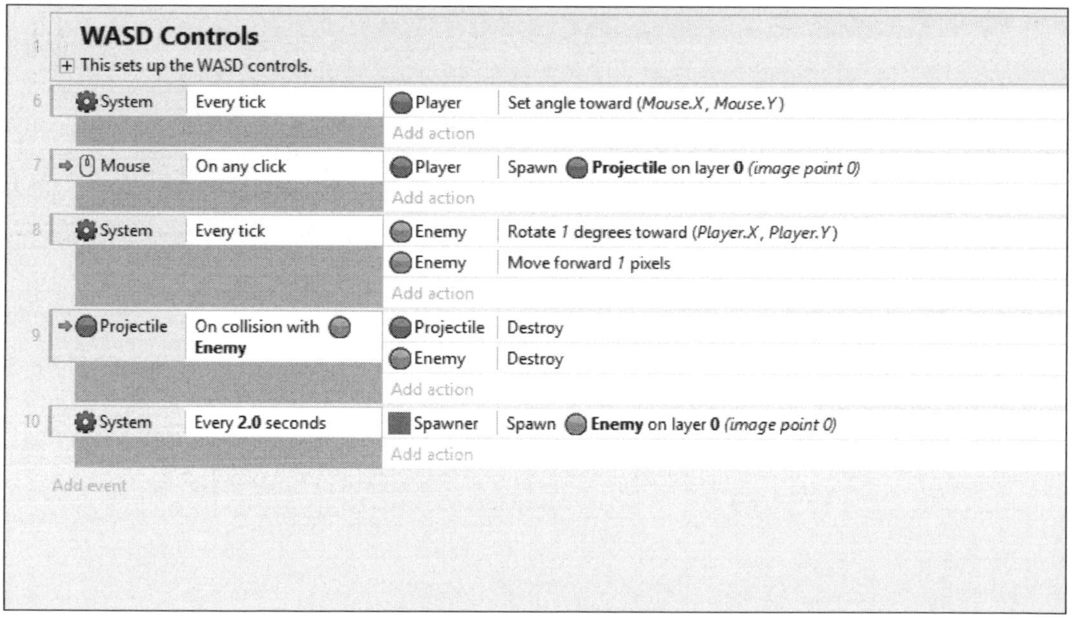

What we need to do now is add some logic for when the enemy hits the player. For this, we will restart the layout.

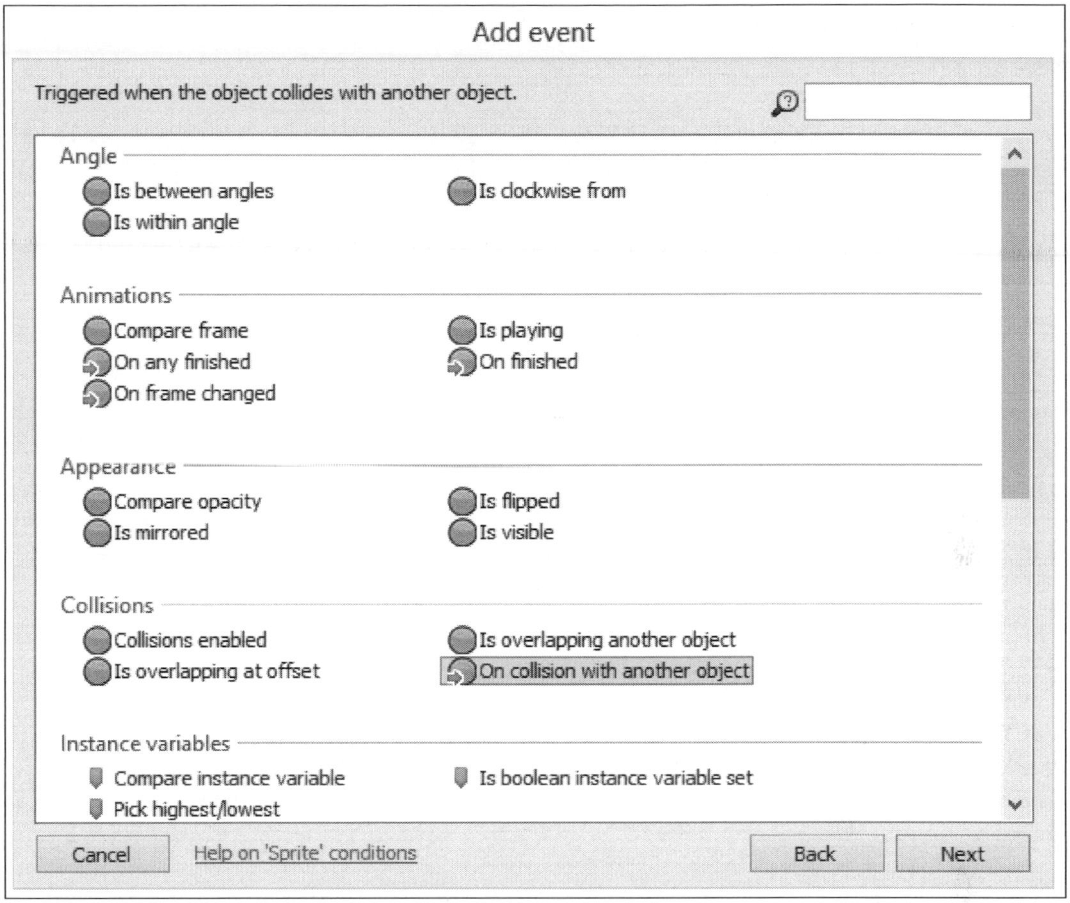

Add event

Triggered when the object collides with another object.

Angle

Is between angles
Is clockwise from
Is within angle

Animations

Compare frame
Is playing
On any finished
On finished
On frame changed

Appearance

Compare opacity
Is flipped
Is mirrored
Is visible

Collisions

Collisions enabled
Is overlapping another object
Is overlapping at offset
On collision with another object

Instance variables

Compare instance variable
Is boolean instance variable set
Pick highest/lowest

Cancel Help on 'Sprite' conditions Back Next

Then, we will add an action. Go to **System**, then select **Restart layout**. This should restart the layout.

#	Object	Condition	Object	Action
1	**WASD Controls**	This sets up the WASD controls.		
6	System	Every tick	Player	Set angle toward (*Mouse.X*, *Mouse.Y*)
			Add action	
7	Mouse	On any click	Player	Spawn **Projectile** on layer **0** *(image point 0)*
			Add action	
8	System	Every tick	Enemy	Rotate *1* degrees toward (*Player.X*, *Player.Y*)
			Enemy	Move forward *1* pixels
			Add action	
9	Projectile	On collision with **Enemy**	Projectile	Destroy
			Enemy	Destroy
			Add action	
10	System	Every **2.0** seconds	Spawner	Spawn **Enemy** on layer **0** *(image point 0)*
			Add action	
11	Enemy	On collision with **Player**	System	Restart layout
			Add action	
	Add event			

Go ahead and try out the game. There you go, you have a shooter! What you can do now is modify this code as much as you want. You have a basic shooter to play with—it's your job to add more functionality. Add more projectiles, enemies, and other cool game mechanics.

Summary

In this chapter, we learned how to make a small shooter. Shooters are one of the best games to make because most people know how to play them and they are a simple source of fun.

In the next chapter, we will learn how to make a tower defense game. Tower defense games are really easy to make and are fun to play. If you haven't played a tower defense game, Google `tower defense` and play a few.

6
Making a Tower Defense Game

Tower defense games are fun to play and (somewhat) easy to develop. Construct 2 can develop a tower defense game much more easily than if you were to code it by yourself. Before we start, if you haven't played a tower defense game before, you should go and try one to get familiar with the genre. A Google search for `tower defense game` should bring up lots of options for you to try. A tower defense game is where you set up defensive towers that protect an object from enemies. These enemies usually come in waves and when they are destroyed, the user gets some currency to buy more towers or to upgrade them. In this chapter, we will learn the following:

- How to start a new project
- How to add a turret
- How to add tower defense game logic

Starting the project

First we need to start a new project and set the **Layout Size** option to `640, 480` in the **Layout properties** panel. We do not need to have a bigger screen size for this project. Generally, for smaller web games, it's good to have this resolution as most players are used to seeing it. You can make it bigger if you want to, but this is the more standard resolution that developers use. It should look like the following screenshot:

Layout properties	
Name	Layout 1
Event sheet	Event sheet 1
Active layer	Layer 0
Unbounded scro...	No
Layout Size	640, 480
Margins	500, 500
Effects	
Add / edit	Effects
Project Properties	View
More information	Help

Once you have completed the setup, go ahead and add a background. The background should be `640, 480`. When you create art in a different program, you should make it in the same dimensions you are using in the game. You will rarely need to do a lot of resizing in the game. The following screenshot shows the background design:

Once you have set the background, change the layer. Change the current layer's name by selecting it and pressing *F2*. Change it to something such as `Background`, as shown in the following screenshot:

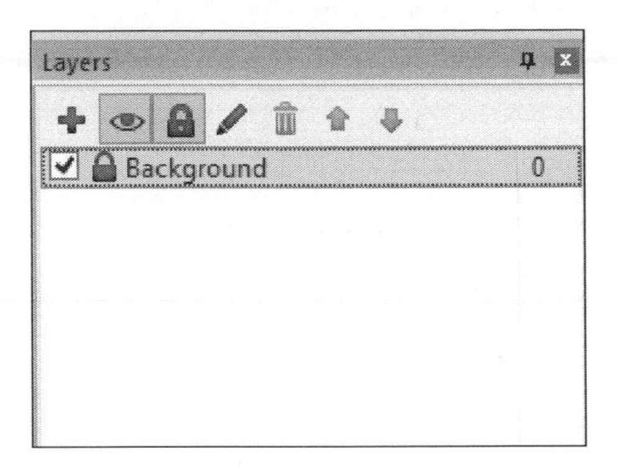

Once you have completed the previous step, lock the layer. Create a new layer to which we can add the game objects, as shown in the following screenshot:

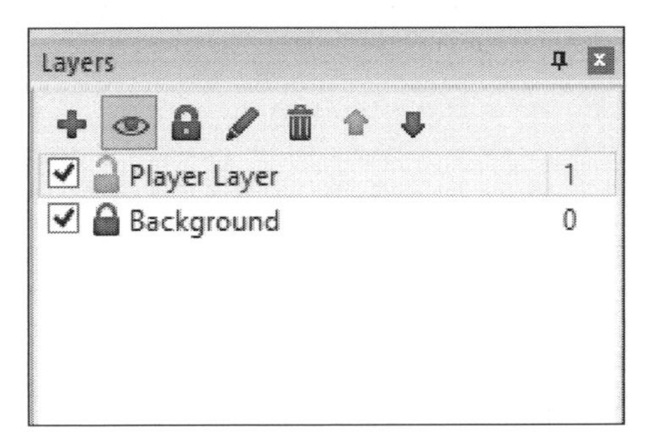

The next thing we need to do is set up **Snap to grid**. By doing so, our turrets can snap to the grid. Click on the **View** tab at the top of the screen. It is shown in the following screenshot. Once you are there, select the **Snap to grid** checkbox.

Doing so will snap any object to the grid of `32` by `32` pixels. You can change the grid size, but make sure that the grid size can be divided with the numbers of our screen resolution (which is `640` by `480`). The current grid size, `32` by `32`, does divide evenly between these two numbers.

Creating a spawn point

Let's add a sprite where we can spawn the enemies from. This is the starting point of the tower defense. In the **Insert New Object** window, double-click on **Sprite** to add a sprite, as shown in the following screenshot:

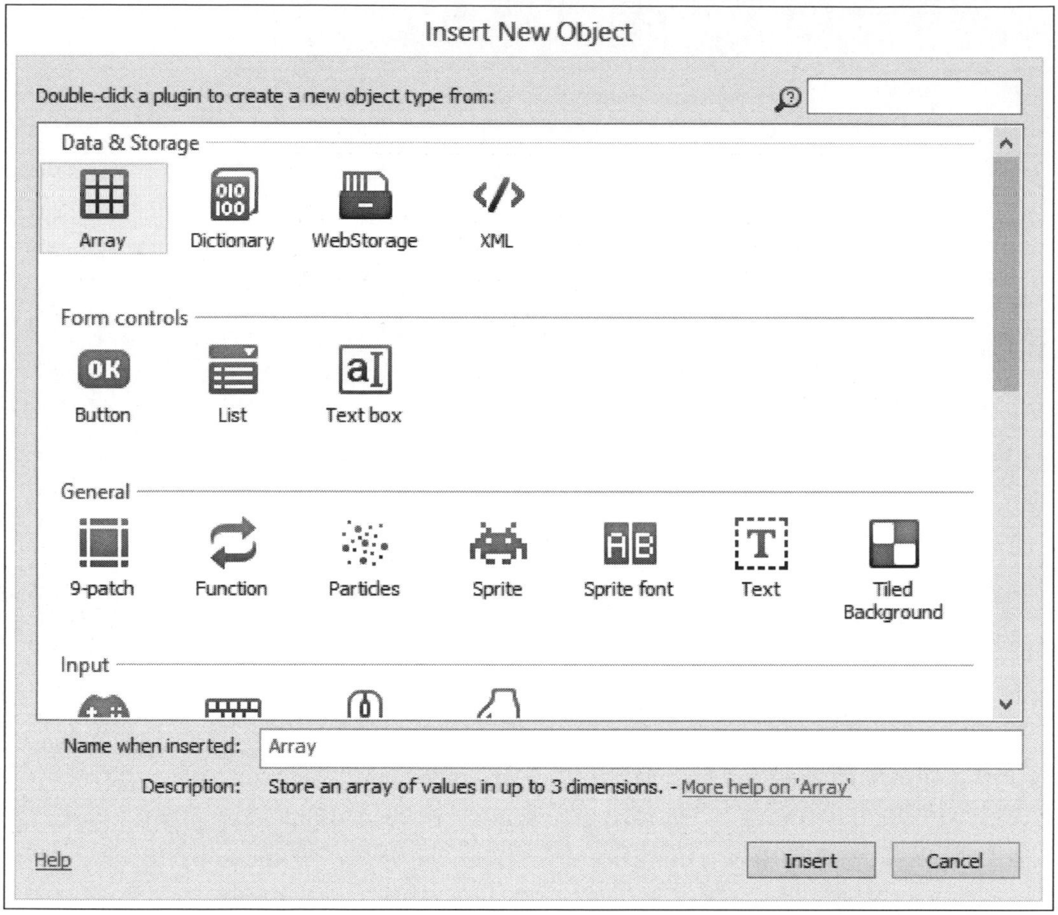

Once you have added the sprite, resize it to `32` by `32`, as shown in the following screenshot. This way, it will easily fit the grid that we have made. Click on the resize button; it looks like a double arrow and can be found at the top of the window.

Once you have resized the image, fill it with a color—for this example, we're going to use green. Make sure that this color stands out. When you are building the basics of your game, you shouldn't worry too much about the artwork. Games are more about functionality than art. This won't be the final product but it will serve us for now.

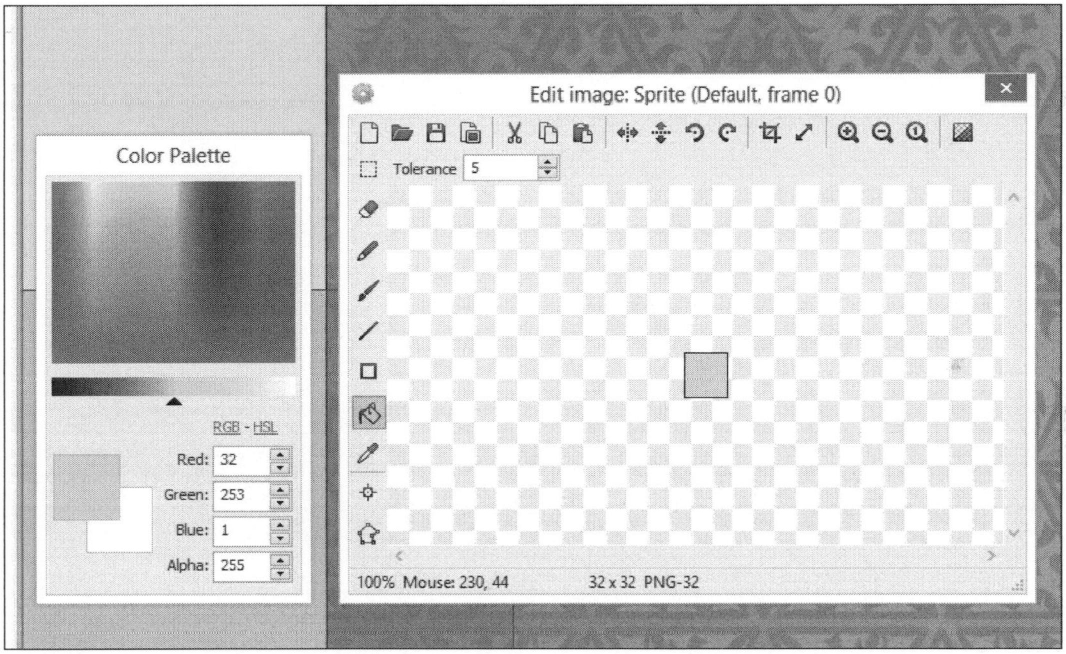

Close out of the box and move the sprite around. You should see that the square does move around in a grid pattern. This means that it jumps from location to location quite easily. The only problem is that the grid seems to be a bit off. This is because the origin is in the center of the object. We need to change the origin to the side.

Double-click on the object and click on the **Origin** tool. As you can see in the following screenshot, the origin is in the center:

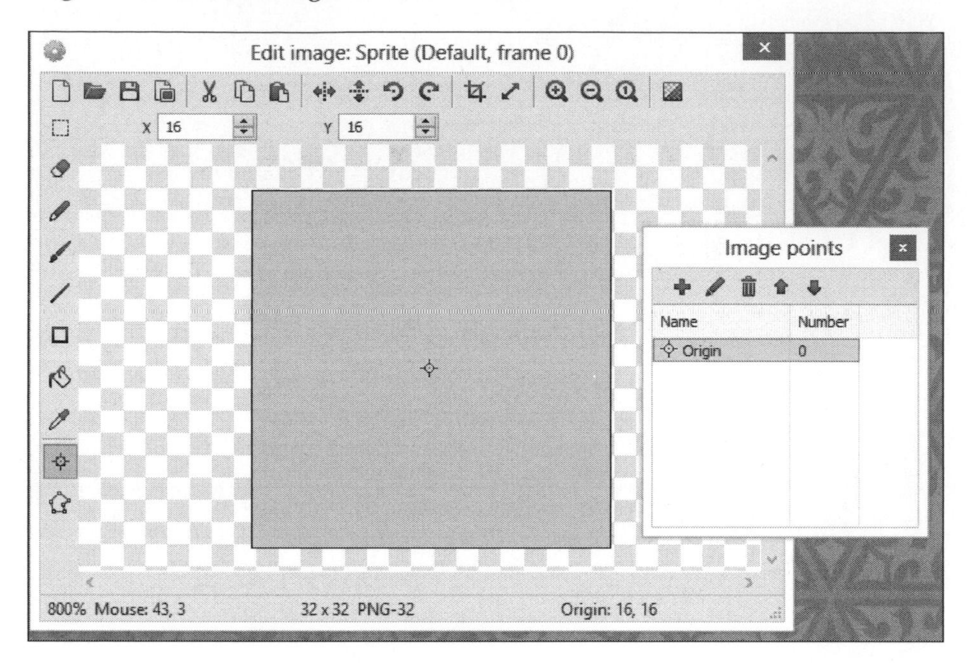

Move the origin to the side, as shown in the following screenshot:

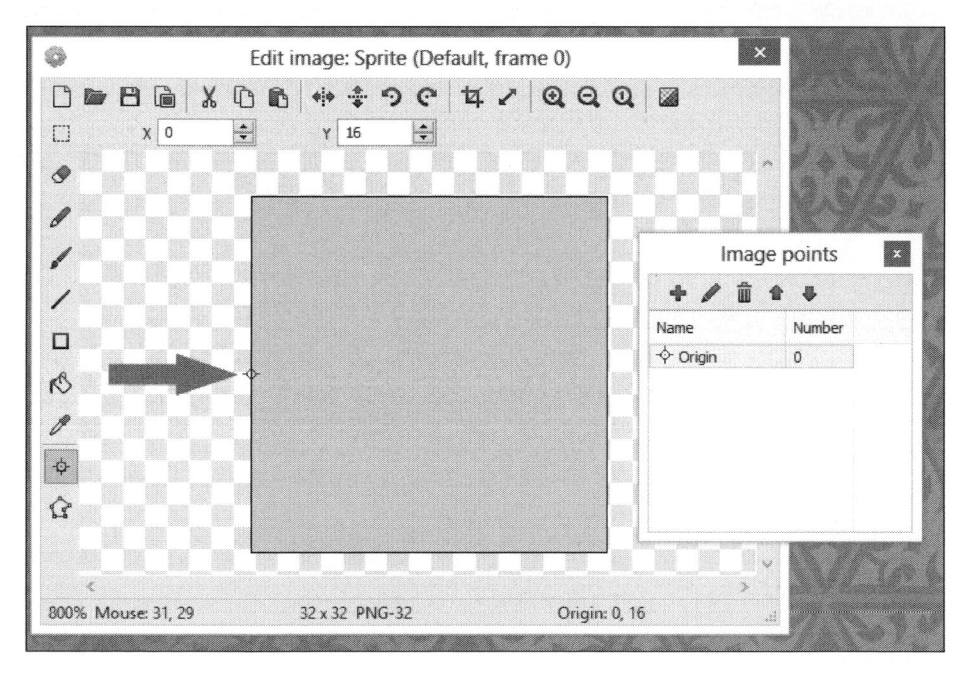

We can now have a good grid placement for our object. Your project should look something like the following screenshot:

There is one more thing we need to do: we need to change the name of the sprite to something that makes more sense. We changed the name to `Start`, as shown in the following screenshot:

Object type properties	
Name	**Start**
Plugin	Sprite
UID	1
Global	No
Common	

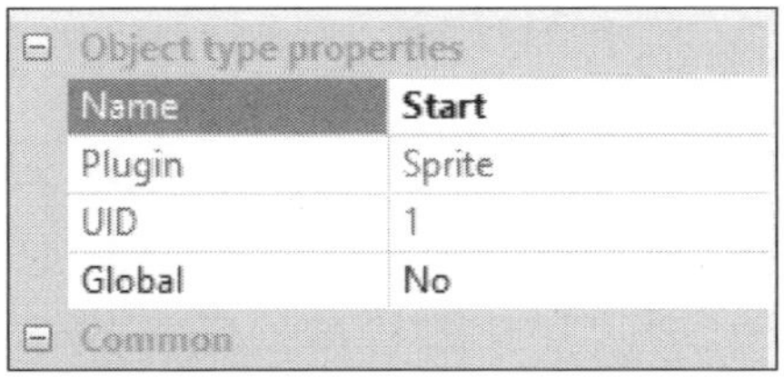

Next, we need to duplicate the sprite for the end. Right-click on the sprite and select **Clone object type**, as shown in the following screenshot. When you clone an object, you create a copy of the object to use in the game. Note that this makes an entirely new object with a new name. You cannot do this with the copy-and-paste method; when you copy-and-paste, you copy-and-paste the same object.

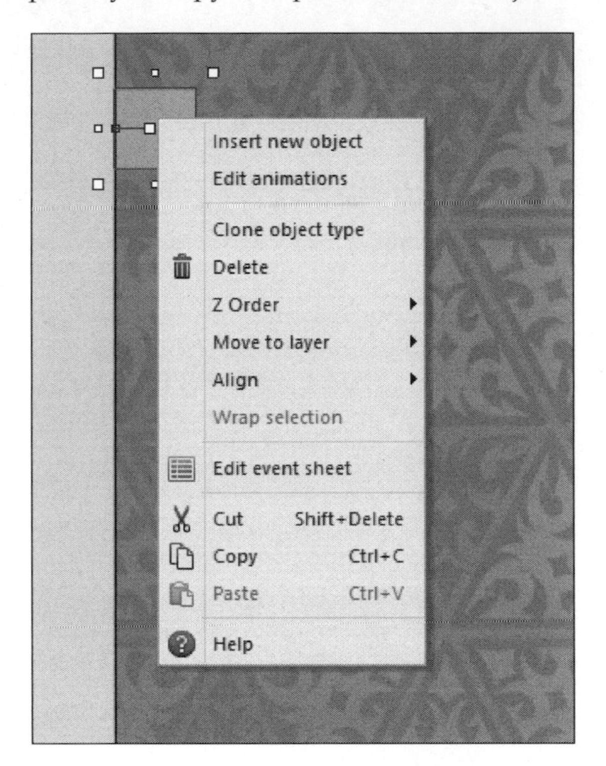

You should now have another object. Place it outside the game area, as shown in the following screenshot:

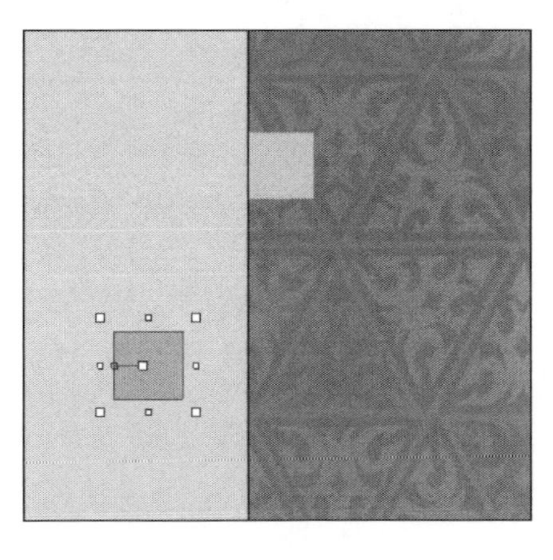

Click on this object and give it a new color. We gave it a pink color by using the paint bucket tool, as shown in the following screenshot. Now, you should see that the sprite is pink. Change the name of the game object to `End`.

Move the sprite to a place where you want your goal to be, as shown in the following screenshot:

Laying out the level

Now, it is time to place the object in the game level so that the game will be fun. Let's make another sprite with dimensions `32` by `32` and give it the color black. We will call this `PlaceTurret`. It should look something like the following screenshot. You also need to change the origin to the top-left side.

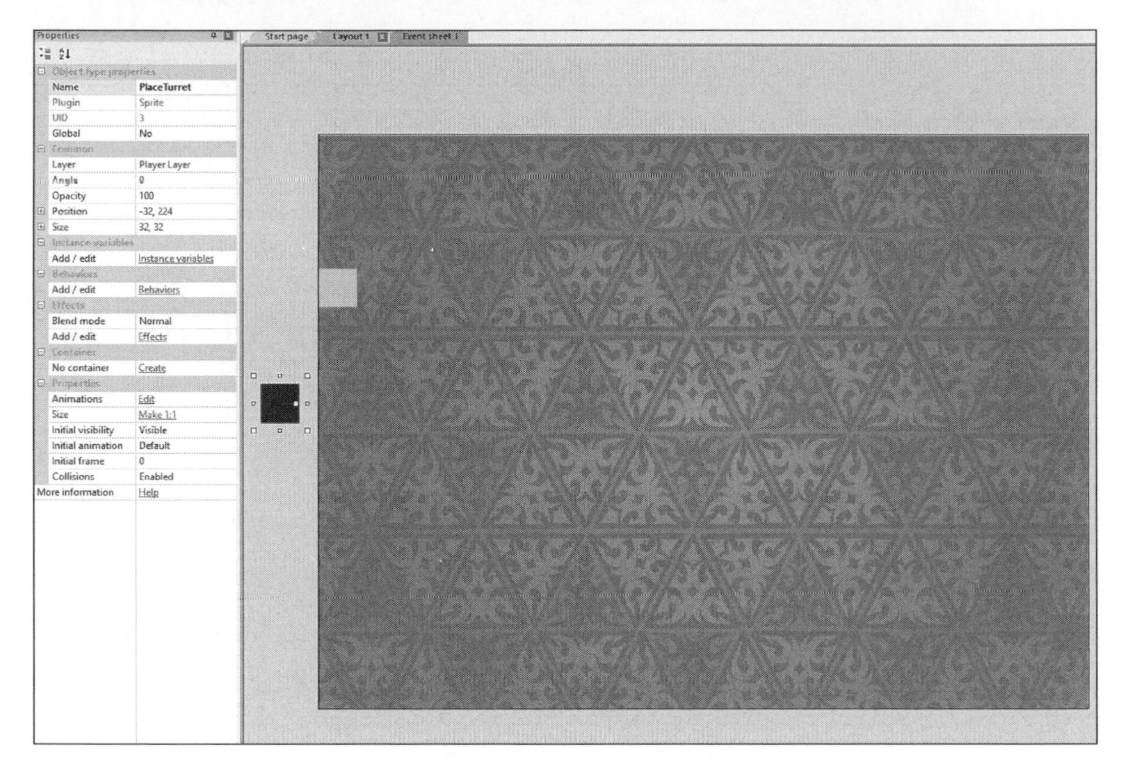

The black areas are going to be the locations where we can place turrets when we click on the screen. This will set up a path for the enemies to follow along. This is where we get into level design. I could write a dozen books on level design, but the three key things to remember are as follows:

- The levels should be playable from beginning to end
- The levels should have a win/lose condition
- The levels should provide at least one thing that is interesting for the player to see, play, or experience

You should make a few different level layouts, and then choose the best one. My level looks like the following screenshot:

Setting up the turrets

Now that we have a level, we need to add a turret. Double-click on the background, select add sprite, and then add the graphic. Make sure that the dimension of this graphic is `32` by `32`; everything that we had set up earlier needs to be on this grid. Your playing area should look like the following screenshot:

Object type properties	
Name	Turret
Plugin	Sprite
UID	14
Global	No
Common	
Layer	Player Layer
Angle	0
Opacity	100
Position	-96, 32
Size	32, 32

First, we will add some functionality using the following steps:

1. Add a **Touch** object from the **Insert New Object** window.
2. Then, go to your event sheet and add an event. This event is going to be a **Touch** event. Remember that touch events and mouse clicks are the same.

[It's better to set up the touch event for simple clicks. Now, people on mobile devices can play your game.]

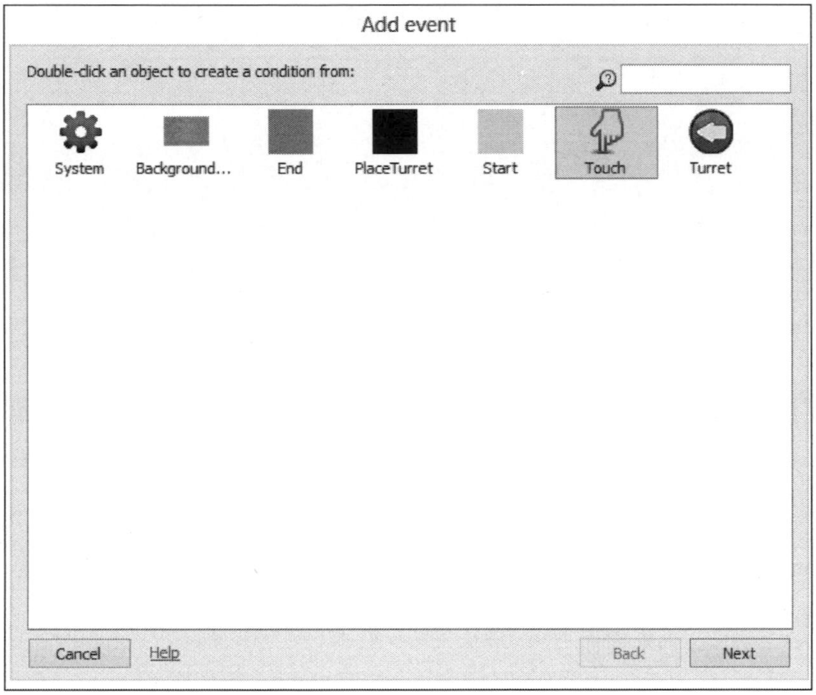

Add event

Double-click an object to create a condition from:

System Background... End PlaceTurret Start Touch Turret

Cancel Help Back Next

3. When we touch the black area, a turret is spawned. This will spawn a turret on the screen. Add an **On touched object** event, as shown in the following screenshot:

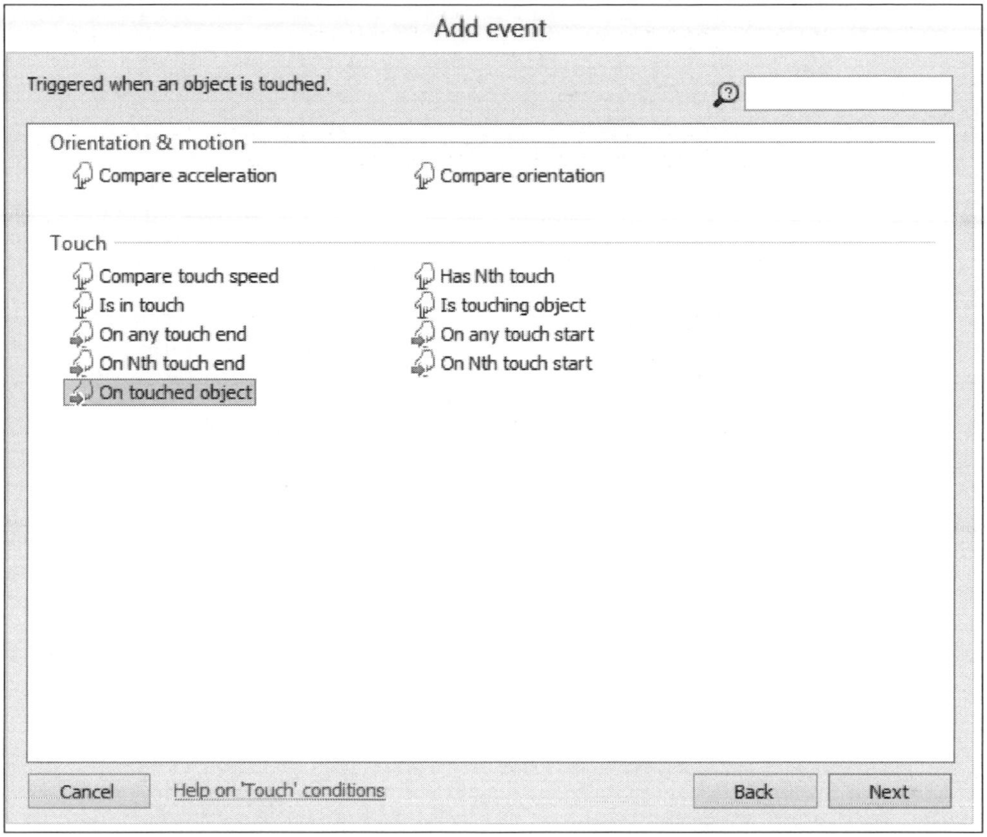

4. The object we want to be touched is the `PlaceTurret` object, as shown in the following screenshot:

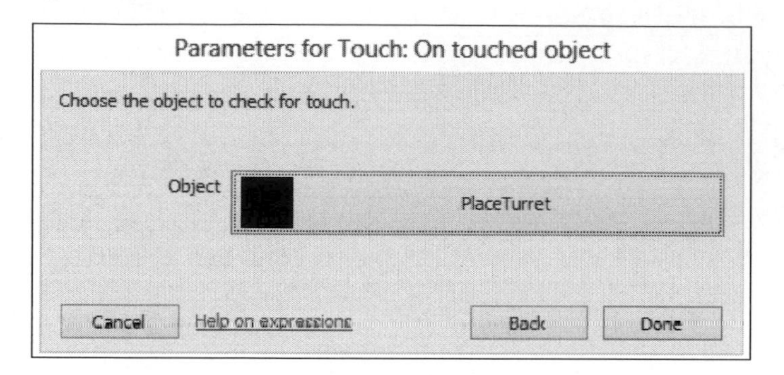

5. Click on the **Done** button and your project should look like the following screenshot:

6. Then, click on **Add action** and add a **System** action.
7. Select the **Create object** action, as shown in the following screenshot:

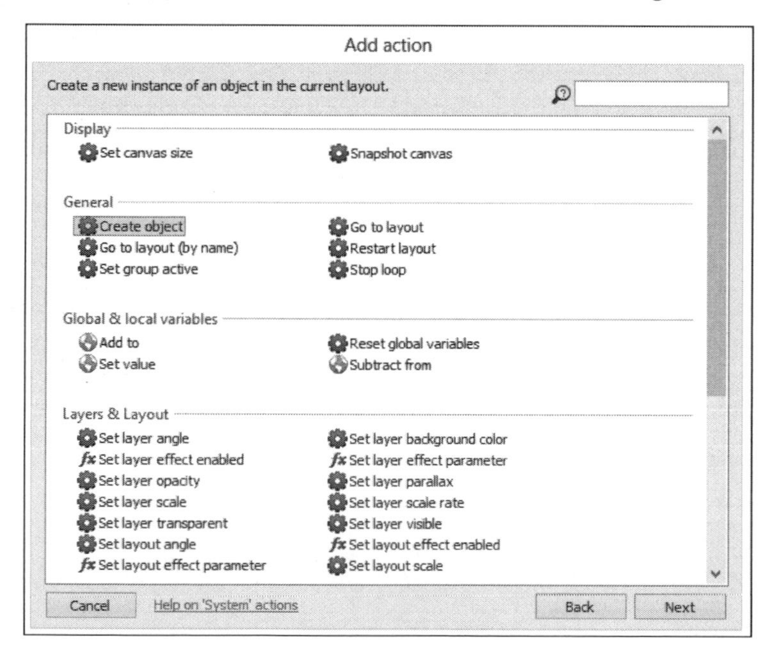

We want to create a turret object on layer 1. Remember that layer 1 is the player layer—if we spawn it on layer 0, it will be beneath the player layer and we would not be able to see the turrets. We also need to add some code. This will make sure that the turret snaps to the grid. As you can see in the following screenshot, the numbers are related to 32, which is our grid size:

Parameters for System: Create object
Name or number of the layer to create the instance on.
Object to create: Turret
Layer: 1
X: round((Touch.X - 16) / 32) * 32 + 16
Y: round((Touch.Y - 16) / 32) * 32 + 16
Cancel | Help on expressions | Back | Done

For the next part, we need to do a little bit of math. Doing so will snap the turret to the grid. The numbers represent a grid of 32 by 32. We are adding X and Y values because we need to snap to an X and Y position. You need to add the following code to your project:

```
round((Touch.X-16 /32) * 32 + 16)
round((Touch.Y-16 /32) * 32 + 16)
```

Your project should have the following elements:

Now, it's time to test our game. Press *F5* and then try it out. It should look something like the following screenshot:

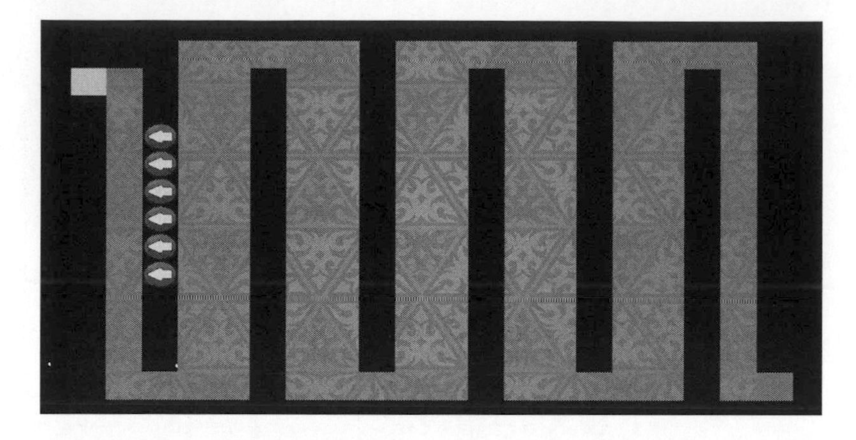

Adding enemies and projectiles

What we need to do now is put in an antagonist. Let's add a ball; in this case, we will just call it **BallGreen**. Add a projectile and make sure it isn't too big. Set the dimensions to `28` by `28` as we want it to be smaller than the walls so that it can fit and not collide. This is shown in the following screenshot:

Object type properties	
Name	BallGreen
Plugin	Sprite
UID	16
Global	No
Common	
Layer	Player Layer
Angle	0
Opacity	100
Position	-96, 96
Size	28, 28
Instance variables	
Add / edit	Instance variables
Behaviors	
Add / edit	Behaviors

Let's also put in a projectile. Add a purple ball, rename it `Projectile`, and set the **Size** property to `10, 10`, as shown in the following screenshot:

Object type properties	
Name	Projectile
Plugin	Sprite
UID	17
Global	No
Common	
Layer	Player Layer
Angle	0
Opacity	100
Position	-96, 0
Size	10, 10
Instance variables	
Add / edit	Instance variables

Put the green ball on the screen so that we can now test some of the functions. Your project should look like the following screenshot:

Rotating the turret

Now we need to make the turret rotate to the green ball. Go to the event sheet, click on **Add event**, select **System**, and then select the **Every tick** event.

Once you have these changes in your event sheet, you can add an action to the turret. Go to the **Add action** sheet and add the **Rotate toward position** action.

In the **Parameters for Turret** window, set the **Degrees** textbox to `10`. This is the speed with which the turret will rotate. You generally want a high rotation speed so that the turret can rotate on time. Remember that the turret does indeed rotate towards the object. It is best to have this speed as fast as possible because if it is too slow, then the turret will not be able to *aim* and hit the target. In the **X** textbox, type `BallGreen.X` and type `BallGreen.Y` in the **Y** textbox, as shown in the following screenshot. This rotates the X and Y position of the green ball.

Parameters for Turret: Rotate toward position

Number of degrees to rotate towards the target position.

Degrees 10

X BallGreen.X

Y BallGreen.Y

Cancel Help on expressions Back Done

Your project should now look like the following screenshot:

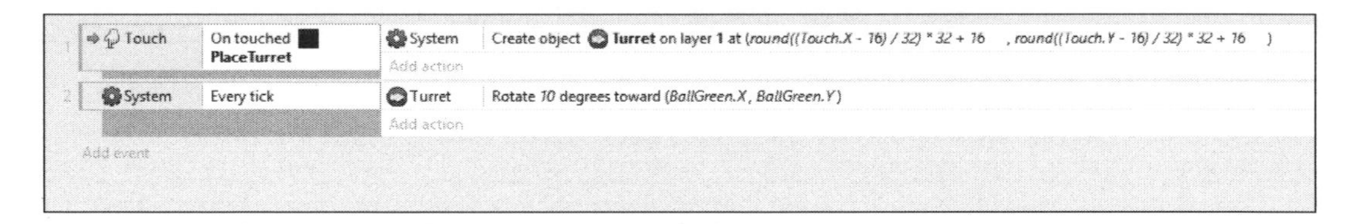

Go ahead and test the game. Add a turret and see whether it rotates towards the green ball.

Firing the turret

Now that the turret rotates, we can go ahead and add a projectile. Go and add another event. This time, it will be set to **Every X seconds**.

After you have added this event, add an action. This time, it will be for the turret. Select **Spawn another object**.

The object that we want to spawn is **Projectile**, as shown in the following screenshot. We want to spawn it on layer 1, where we have spawned all the rest of our game objects (except the background) so far.

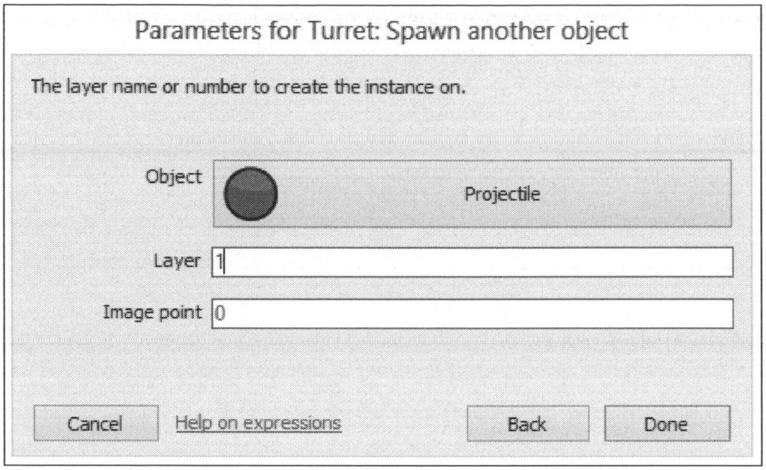

Go ahead and run your game; it should work out pretty well. You will notice that the turret offscreen keeps firing. One thing that we need to do is add a **Destroy outside layout** behavior. We cannot just delete the offscreen sprite, as we need to have a reference for when we want to add more sprites. Sometimes, if you delete all of the instances of a sprite, the game will crash. So, add the behavior for the turret, as shown in the following screenshot:

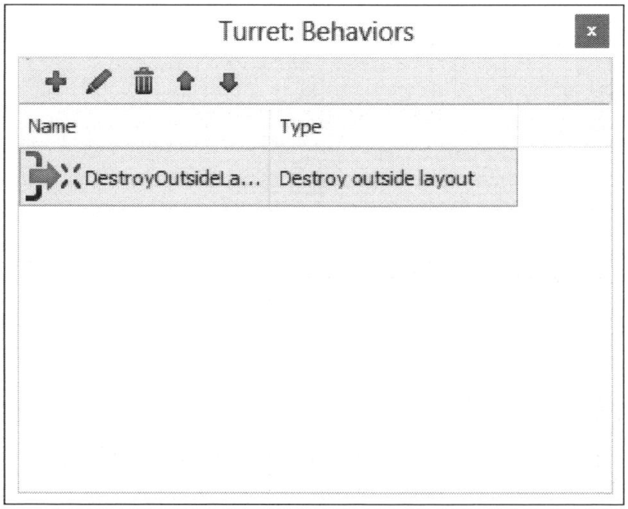

Go back to your event sheet and add an event. This event will check whether the projectile hits the green ball. Select **Add event** and select the projectile. Then, select **On collision with another object**.

We want the projectile to collide with the green ball, so select **BallGreen** as the object, as shown in the following screenshot:

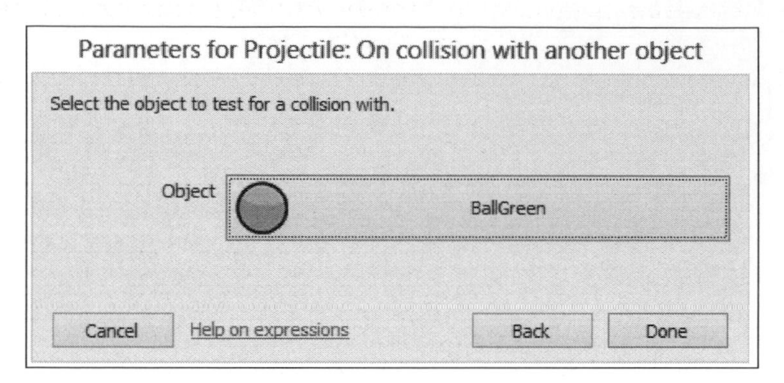
Parameters for Projectile: On collision with another object
Select the object to test for a collision with.
Object
BallGreen
Cancel
Help on expressions
Back
Done

After all of this, your event sheet should look like the following screenshot:

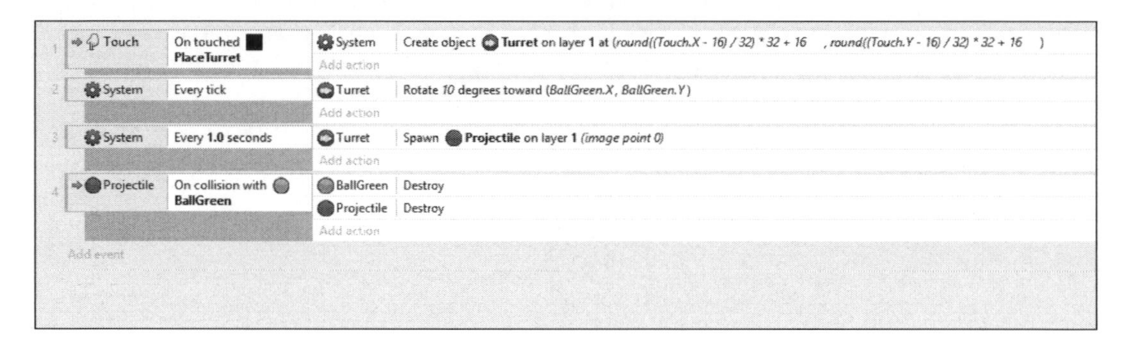
Touch
On touched PlaceTurret
System
Create object Turret on layer 1 at (round((Touch.X - 16) / 32) * 32 + 16 , round((Touch.Y - 16) / 32) * 32 + 16)
Add action
System
Every tick
Turret
Rotate 10 degrees toward (BallGreen.X, BallGreen.Y)
Add action
System
Every 1.0 seconds
Turret
Spawn Projectile on layer 1 (image point 0)
Add action
Projectile
On collision with BallGreen
BallGreen
Destroy
Projectile
Destroy
Add action
Add event

One thing that you will notice is that the turrets keep on firing. We want them to fire only when the wave of green balls is advancing. This is actually pretty easy to fix. Go to your event sheet and right-click on it, and then select **Add global variable** from the contextual menu as shown in the following screenshot:

Add event
Add comment
Add group
Add global variable
Include event sheet
Help on event sheets

The **New global variable** window will appear; enter something appropriate for your global variable name (see the following screenshot). For the purpose of this example, we will call the variable `isWave`. At the time of writing, there are no global Boolean variables. So, we are going to add a number variable. In this case, `0` will be false and `1` will be true; so when the `isWave` is set to `1`, the wave of green balls will spawn.

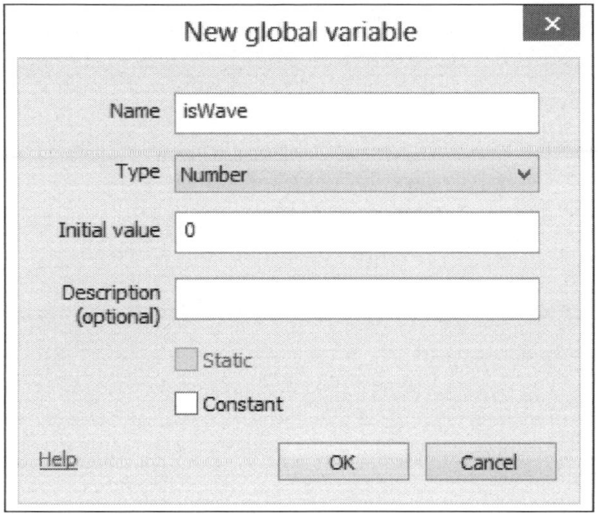

After these settings, your event sheet should look like the following screenshot:

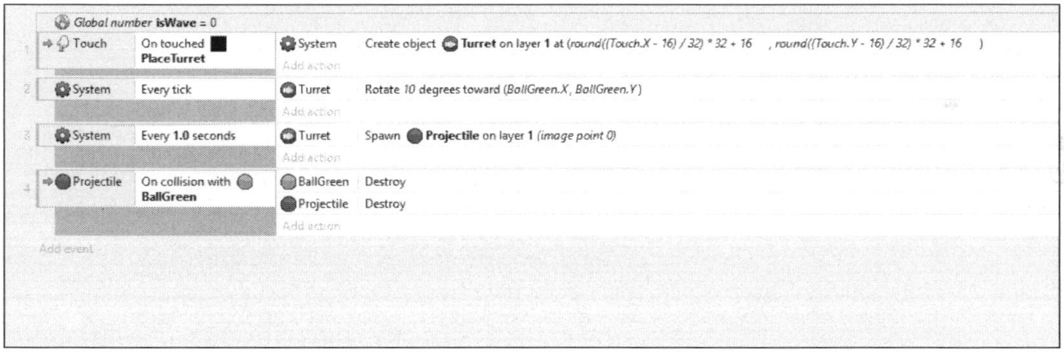

Add a **System** event that will be **Compare variable**, as shown in the following screenshot. In game design, you compare variables and act accordingly. What we are going to do is compare the variable **isWave** to see whether it is `0` or `1`, that is, true or false.

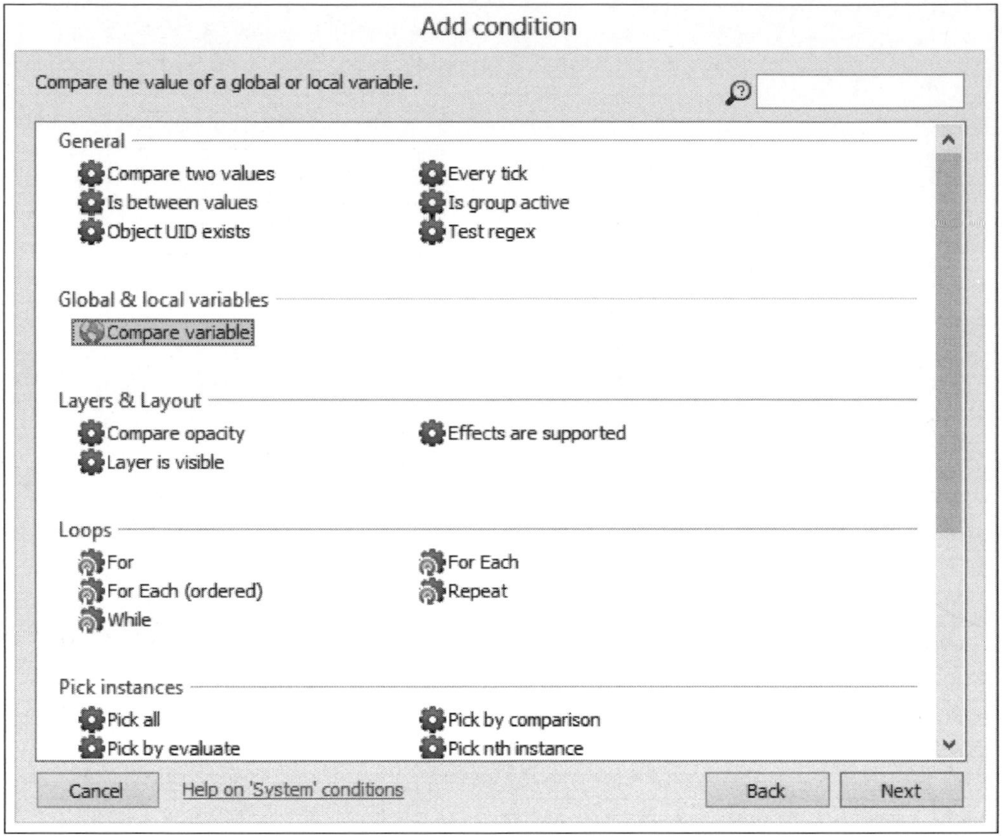

Add condition

Compare the value of a global or local variable.

General
Compare two values
Is between values
Object UID exists
Every tick
Is group active
Test regex

Global & local variables
Compare variable

Layers & Layout
Compare opacity
Layer is visible
Effects are supported

Loops
For
For Each (ordered)
While
For Each
Repeat

Pick instances
Pick all
Pick by evaluate
Pick by comparison
Pick nth instance

Cancel | Help on 'System' conditions | Back | Next

Make sure that we are comparing to check whether the variable is equal to `1`, as shown in the following screenshot. This means that when the default is `0`, we do not want the turret to fire. When we set the variable to `1`, the turrets should fire.

Parameters for System: Compare variable

Value to compare to the variable.

Variable: isWave

Comparison: = Equal to

Value: 1

Cancel | Help on expressions | Back | Done

After this, we need to make sure that there is some sort of button for the user to use. What you need to do is add an orange sprite and call it `WaveButton`. Place it somewhere that makes sense to the player, such as in the top-left corner, as shown in the following screenshot:

Now, we need to go back to our event sheet and add another event. Double-click on the event sheet and add a **Touch** event. We are going to add an **On touched object** event, as shown in the following screenshot:

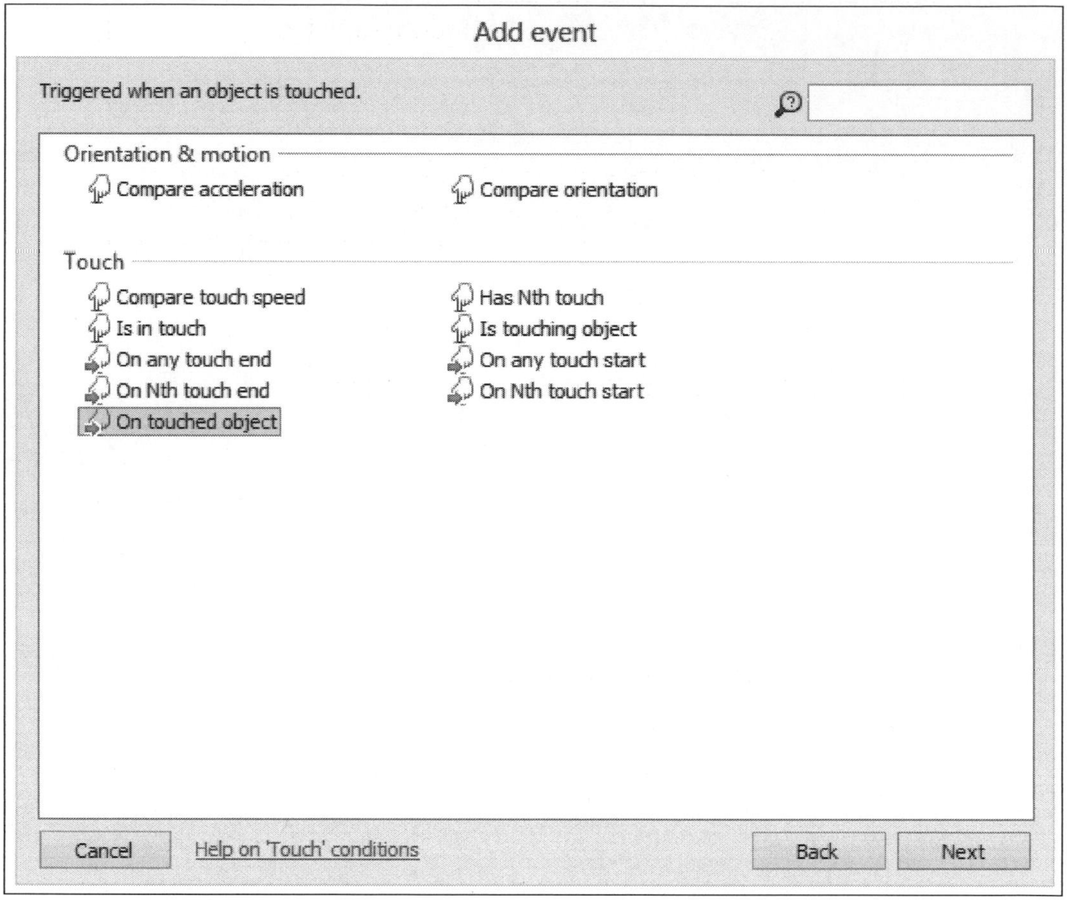

Add event

Triggered when an object is touched.

Orientation & motion

Compare acceleration
Compare orientation

Touch

Compare touch speed
Has Nth touch
Is in touch
Is touching object
On any touch end
On any touch start
On Nth touch end
On Nth touch start
On touched object

Cancel
Help on 'Touch' conditions
Back
Next

We want to check whether the event is touching the wave button. We can do so by selecting the **WaveButton** option in the **Parameters for Touch: On touched object** dialog box, as shown in the following screenshot:

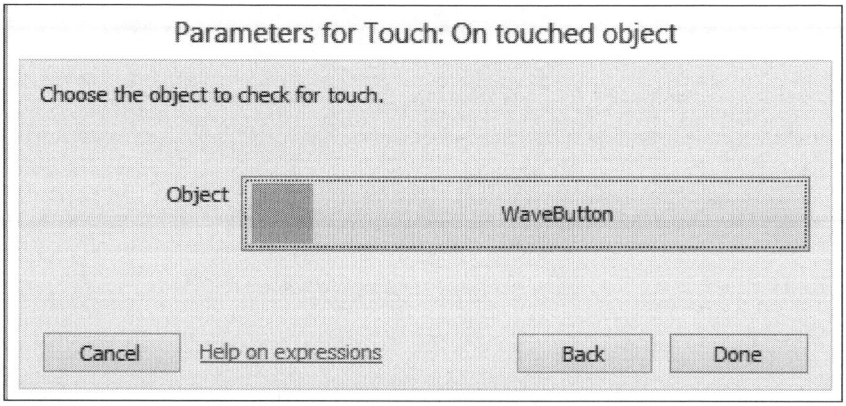

Now, add an action. This action is going to be **System, set variable,** and we are going to set **isWave** to `1`. It should look like the following screenshot:

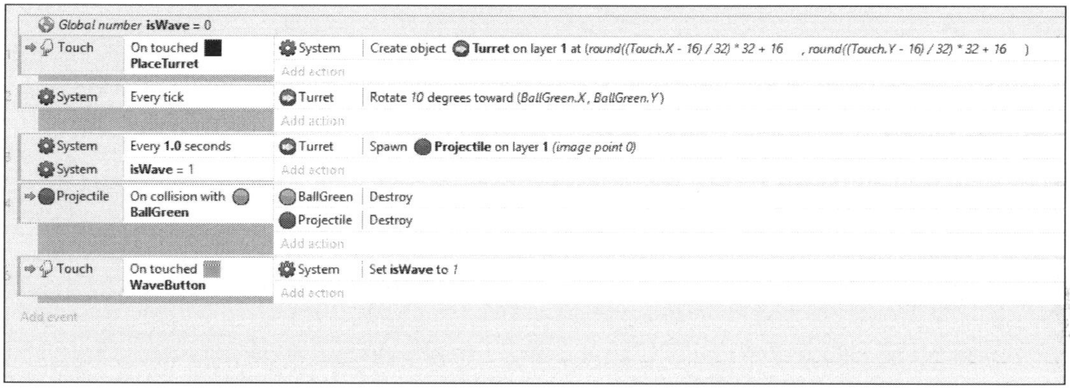

Go ahead and try out the game. You should see that when you press the **WaveButton**, the turrets start shooting!

Setting up the path for the enemy

Next, we need to add the spawning green balls that are our enemy sprites, and in order to do that we need to add the **Pathfinding** behavior. **Pathfinding** sets a path from one area to another. We are going to use the **Pathfinding** functionality of Construct 2 to make the balls move from the start to the finish line. Add a **Pathfinding** behavior to the green ball, as shown in the following screenshot:

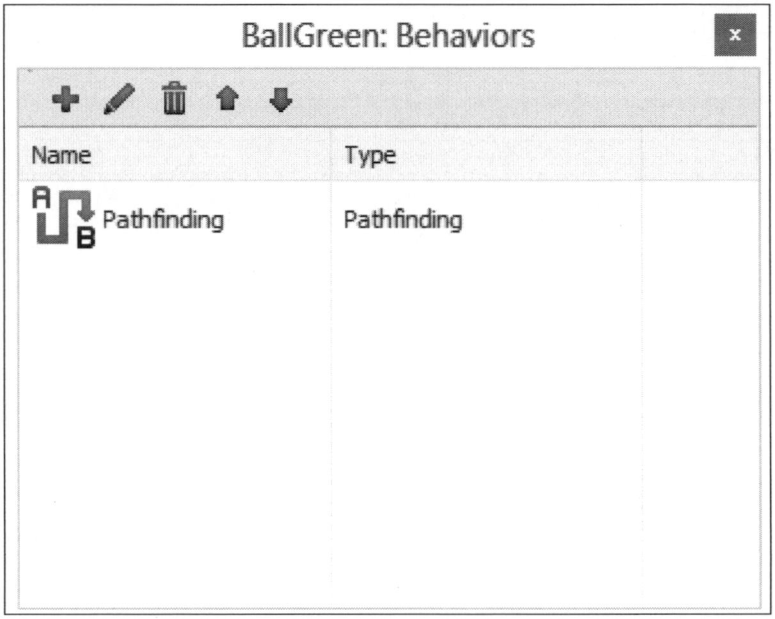

BallGreen: Behaviors

Name	Type
Pathfinding	Pathfinding

Once you have done this, go back to the event sheet and add an **On start of layout** event, as shown in the following screenshot:

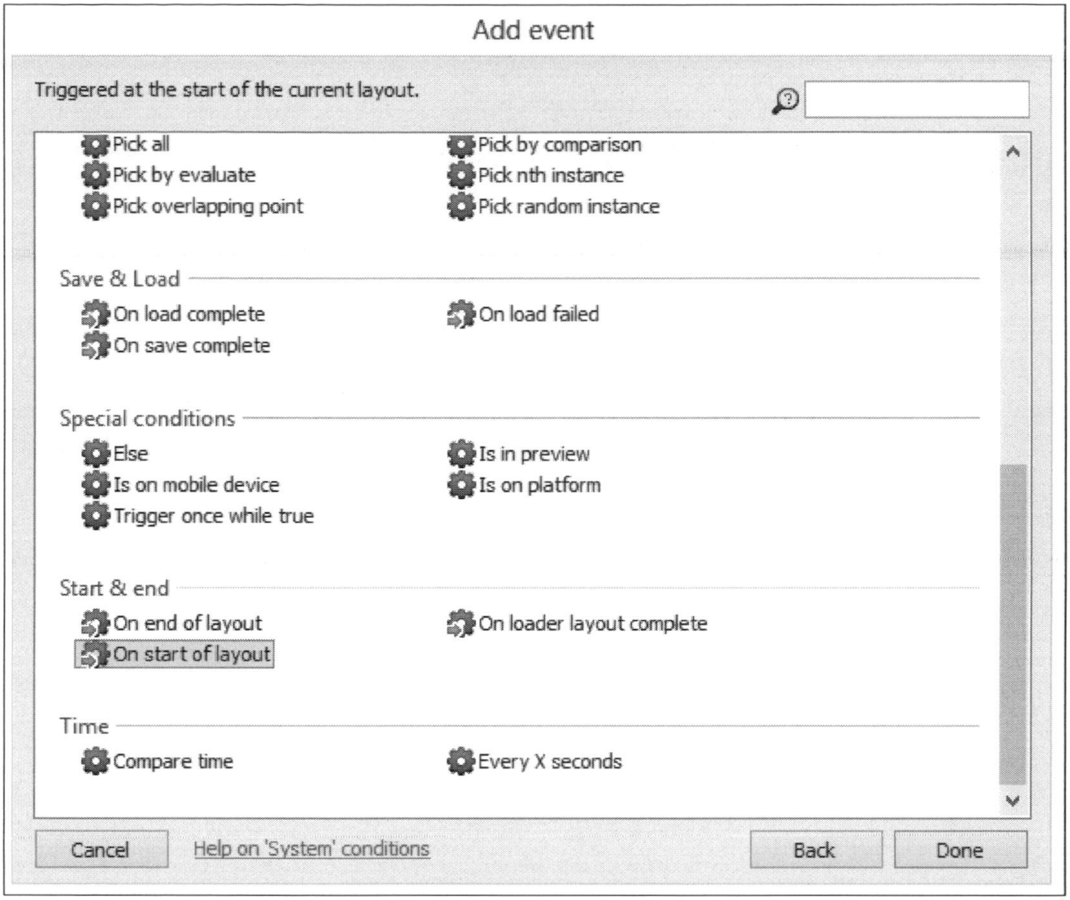

Add event

Triggered at the start of the current layout.

Pick all
Pick by comparison
Pick by evaluate
Pick nth instance
Pick overlapping point
Pick random instance

Save & Load
On load complete
On load failed
On save complete

Special conditions
Else
Is in preview
Is on mobile device
Is on platform
Trigger once while true

Start & end
On end of layout
On loader layout complete
On start of layout

Time
Compare time
Every X seconds

Cancel
Help on 'System' conditions
Back
Done

After that, add an action. Select the **BallGreen** object and select **Find path** as the action, as shown in the following screenshot. In order to set the path, you have to first set it. You can set the path to positions of objects, inputs such as touch and mouse, and specific locations.

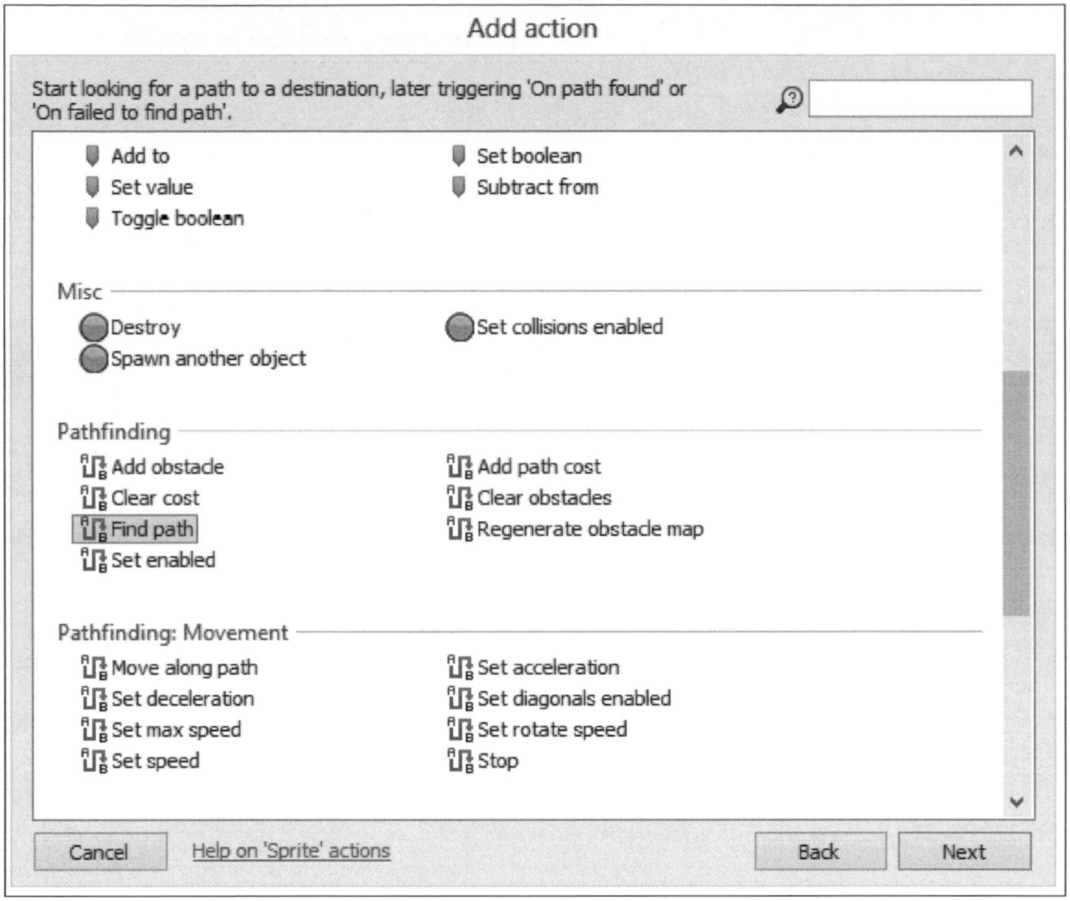

We have to specify where we want the path to go. Since we want the green balls to go all the way to the end of the path, we can type in `End.X` and `End.Y`, as shown in the following screenshot. The end of the course is the pink block we had set up earlier. So in this case, **Pathfinding** is finding a position of an object.

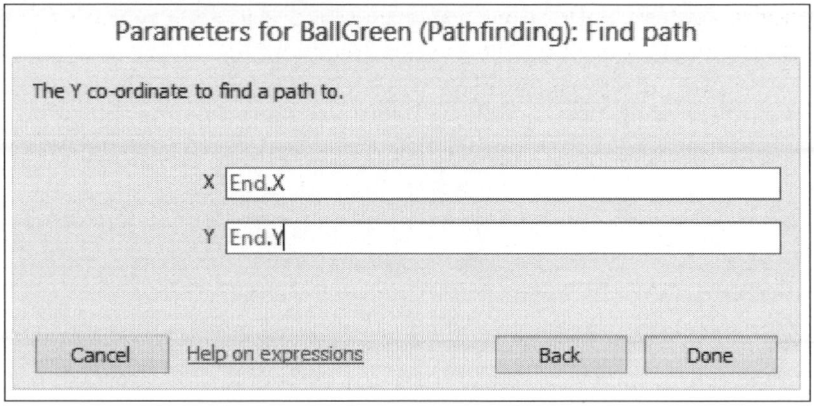

Parameters for BallGreen (Pathfinding): Find path

The Y co-ordinate to find a path to.

X End.X

Y End.Y

Cancel Help on expressions Back Done

Once you have the **Find path** action set up, you should add another event. Select **BallGreen** and then select **On path found**, as shown in the following screenshot. Once a path is found, we can perform an action.

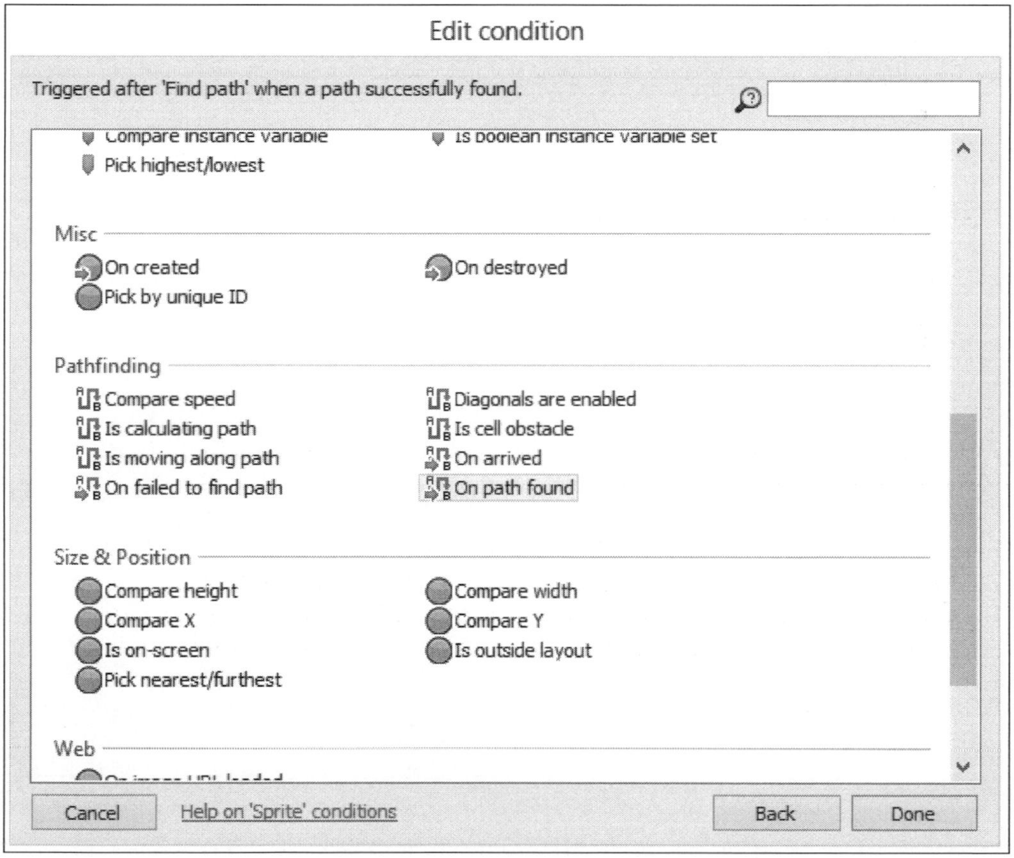

Edit condition

Triggered after 'Find path' when a path successfully found.

Compare instance variable Is boolean instance variable set
Pick highest/lowest

Misc
On created On destroyed
Pick by unique ID

Pathfinding
Compare speed Diagonals are enabled
Is calculating path Is cell obstacle
Is moving along path On arrived
On failed to find path On path found

Size & Position
Compare height Compare width
Compare X Compare Y
Is on-screen Is outside layout
Pick nearest/furthest

Web

Cancel Help on 'Sprite' conditions Back Done

Add an action and select **BallGreen**, and then select **Move along path** as shown in the following screenshot. This will move the green ball along the path that it found.

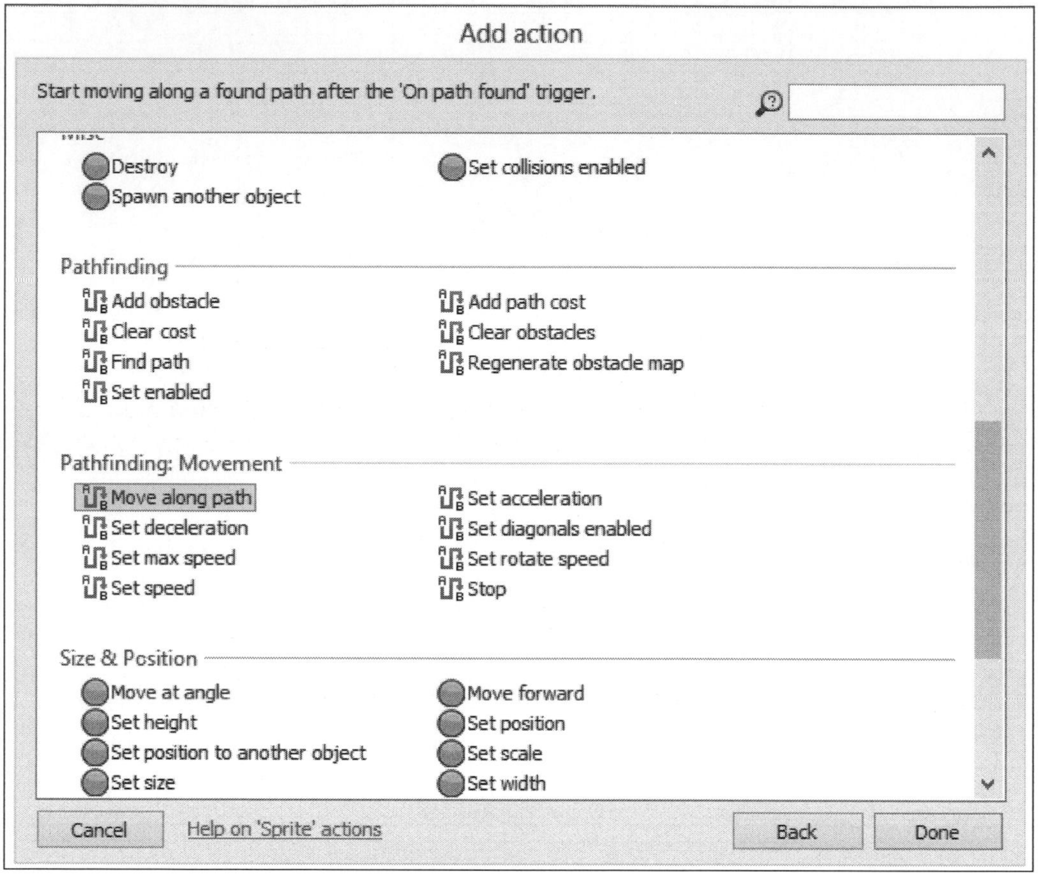

Go ahead and try out the game. You will probably notice that the ball ignores the walls. In order to fix this, we have to do two things. First, click on the **PlaceTurret** graphic and add a **Solid** behavior, as shown in the following screenshot:

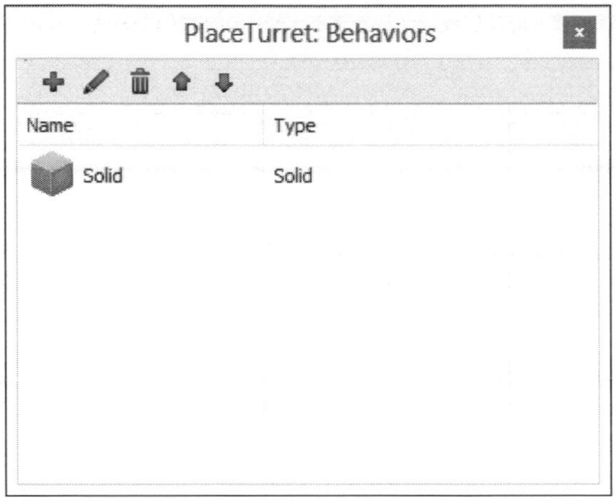

Then, we have to add another event. We have to add another action to the **On start of layout** event. Add a green ball, and then add an **Add obstacle** action. This will add an **Obstacle** for **Pathfinding**.

We want to put the **PlaceTurret** object as **Obstacle**, as shown in the following screenshot:

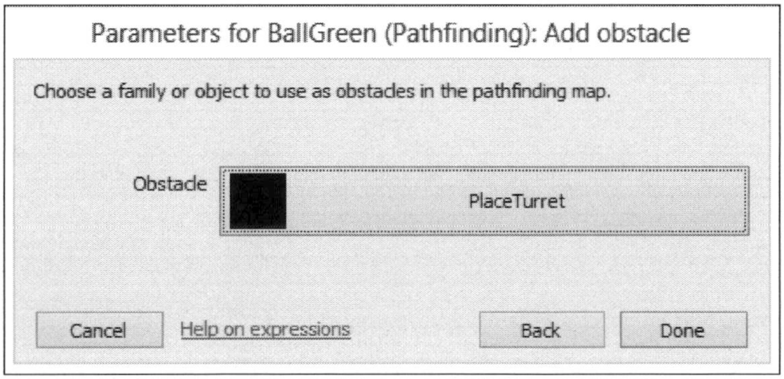

Your event sheet should look like the following screenshot:

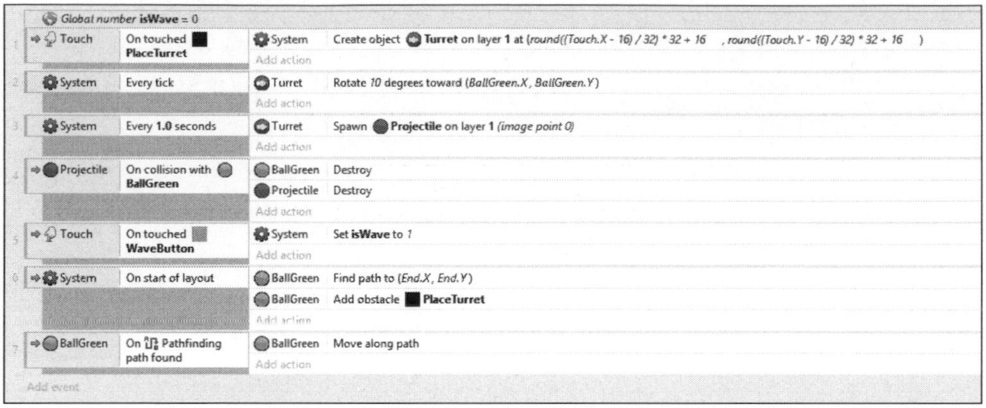

Run the game and you will see that the ball might not move the way you want it to. I have changed the settings of the ball. The following are my settings:

```
Cell size:10
Cell border: 5
Obstacles: Solid
Max speed:200
Acceleration: 9999
Deceleration: 9999
Rotate speed: 135
Rotate object: Yes
Diagonals: Enabled
Initial state: Enabled
```

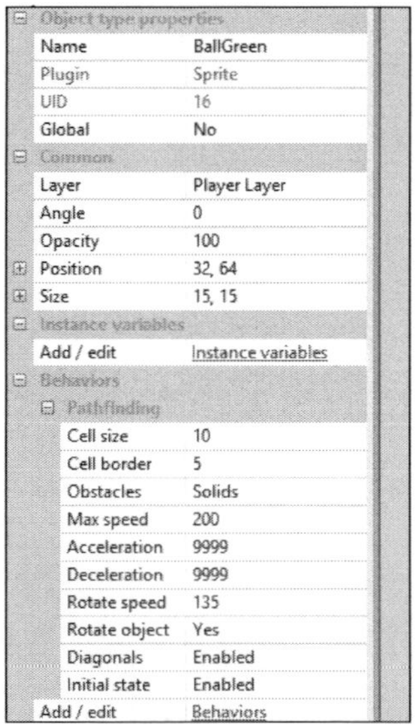

Setting up an enemy wave

We need to set up the amount of green balls that get spawned. When we push the **WaveButton**, a new wave should start. Let's go ahead and add a global variable by right-clicking on the event sheet and adding a global variable. Let's call it `waveCount` and set its **Initial value** to `3`, as shown in the following screenshot:

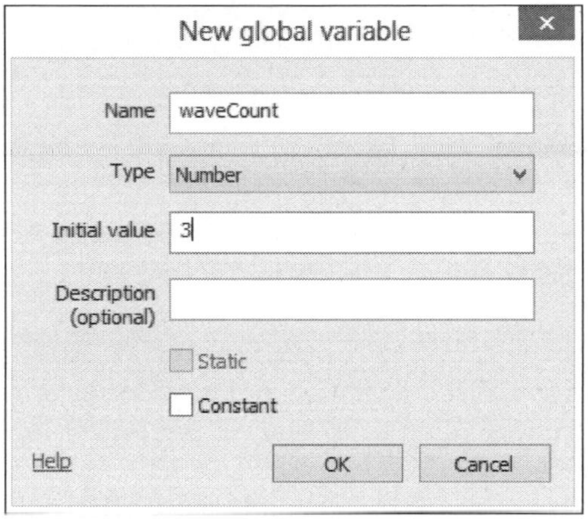

New global variable

Name	waveCount
Type	Number
Initial value	3
Description (optional)	
	Static
	Constant

Help OK Cancel

Create another variable called `ballCount`. Set its **Initial value** to `0`. The wave count is going to count how many total green balls are going to be spawned in a wave, and the ball count will count how many balls are on screen. We need both of these variables in order to make it work. Generally, you want to try and use the least amount of variables as possible—but often the least amount can still be a lot of variables. Even in some small games I've seen, the variable count exceeds 200.

Once you have created this global variable, let's use it. Add an event to the green ball and select the **On created** event, as shown in the following screenshot:

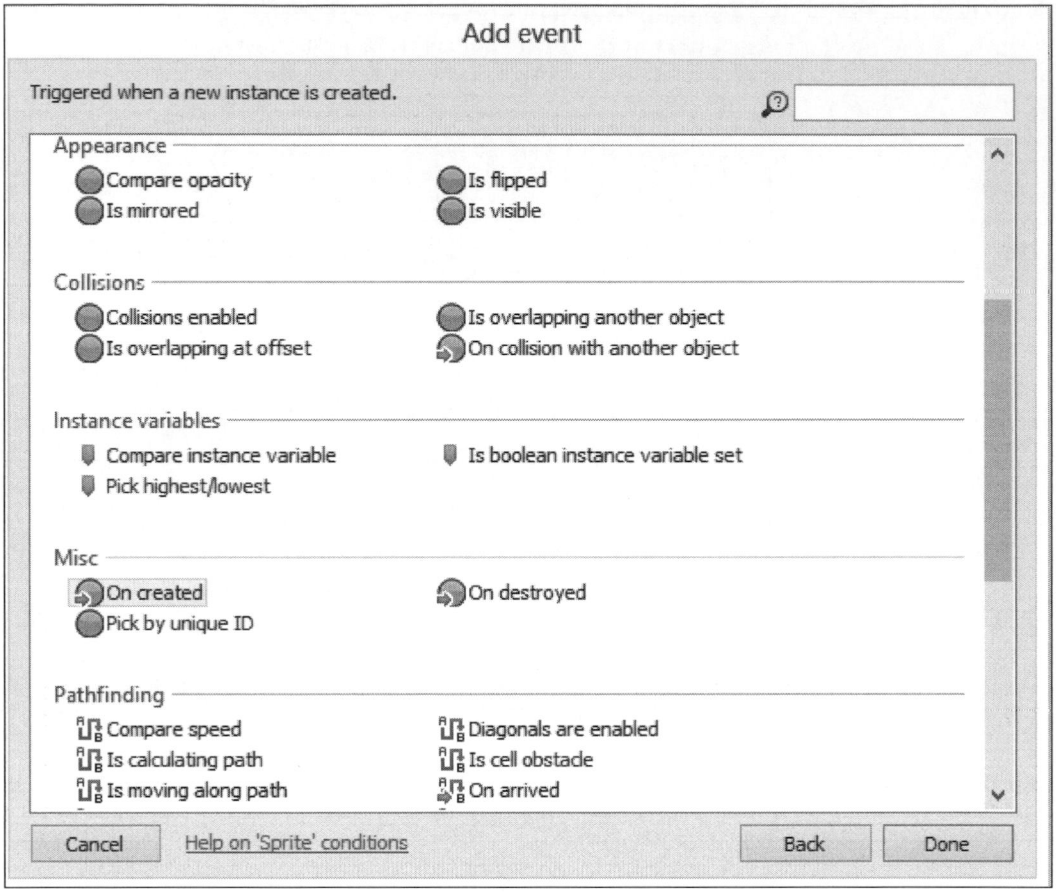

Once you have these settings in your event sheet, click on **Add action** to add another action. In this case, we are going to add `1` to the ball count. Navigate to **System | Add to** and change the settings, as shown in the following screenshot:

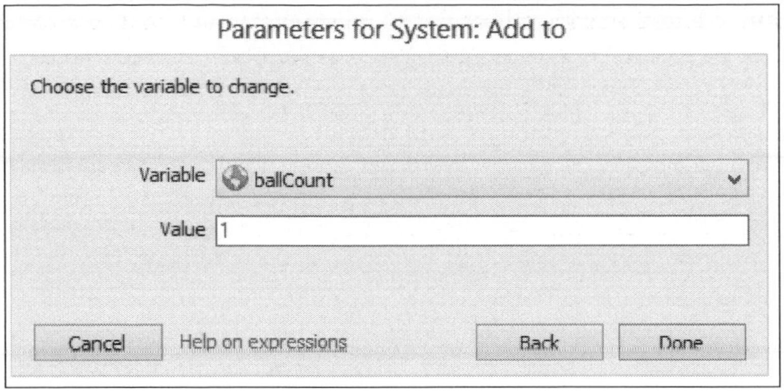

Parameters for System: Add to

Choose the variable to change.

Variable: ballCount

Value: 1

Cancel | Help on expressions | Back | Done

We need to do this in order to count how many balls are on the screen. As soon as the object is created, we add one to the ball count. Let's add another event. This event will be a **Compare variable** event, as shown in the following screenshot:

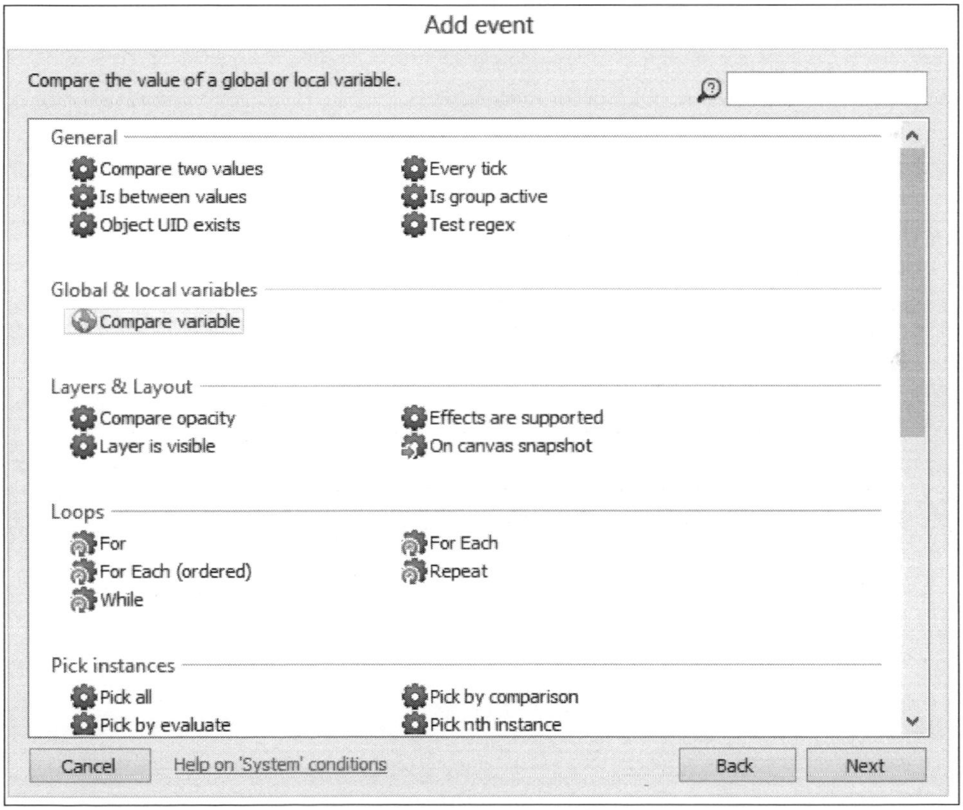

Add event

Compare the value of a global or local variable.

General

Compare two values
Every tick
Is between values
Is group active
Object UID exists
Test regex

Global & local variables

Compare variable

Layers & Layout

Compare opacity
Effects are supported
Layer is visible
On canvas snapshot

Loops

For
For Each
For Each (ordered)
Repeat
While

Pick instances

Pick all
Pick by comparison
Pick by evaluate
Pick nth instance

Cancel | Help on 'System' conditions | Back | Next

We can use this **Compare variable** event to compare variables. We can compare numbers or other variables. We are going to compare the global variable **isWave** to `1`, as shown in the following screenshot. This means that when the wave is occurring, such as when the game has started, the game starts and the enemies spawn.

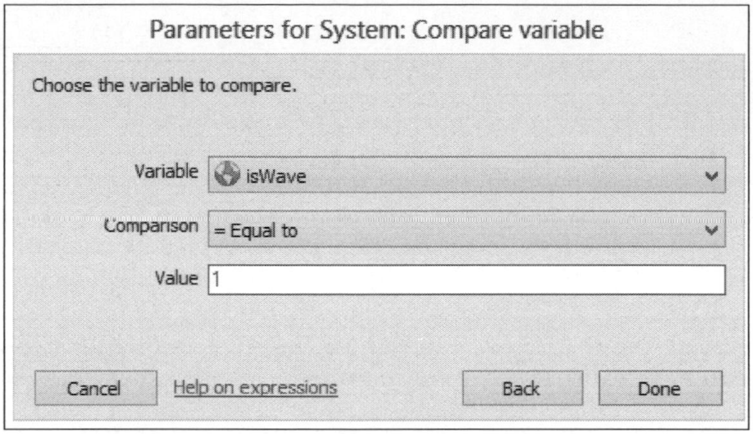

Click on **isWave =1** and press *C*. This will add another condition. This means in order for the following actions to take place, both of these conditions have to be true. Select **System** and **Compare variable**. This time, we will compare **ballCount** to being less than or equal to **waveCount**. In the **Value** field, select **waveCount** as shown in the following screenshot:

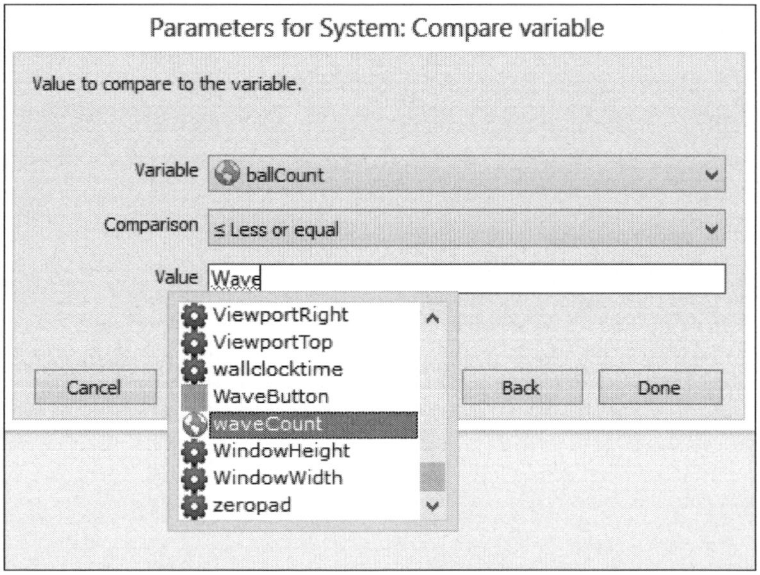

Select **isWave** again and press C. This will add another condition. In this case, we are going to add an **Every X seconds** condition, as shown in the following screenshot:

Add condition

Run the actions at a regular time interval.

Pick all
Pick by comparison
Pick by evaluate
Pick nth instance
Pick overlapping point
Pick random instance

Save & Load
On load complete
On load failed
On save complete

Special conditions
Else
Is in preview
Is on mobile device
Is on platform
Trigger once while true

Start & end
On end of layout
On loader layout complete
On start of layout

Time
Compare time
Every X seconds

Cancel
Help on 'System' conditions
Back
Next

Your event sheet should look like the following screenshot:

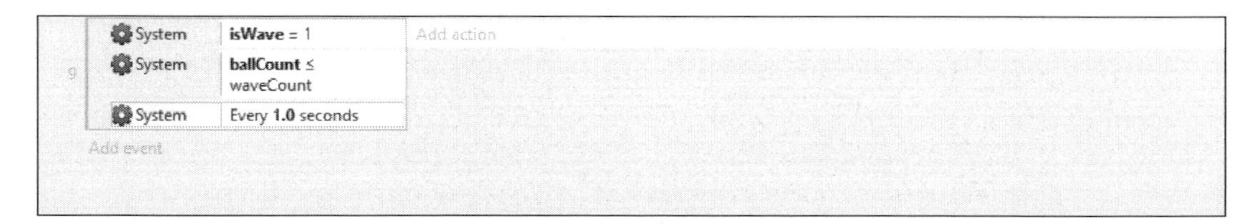

Now, we have to add another action. This action is going to be for the start block. Select **Spawn another object** from the available options in the **Add action** window, as shown in the following screenshot:

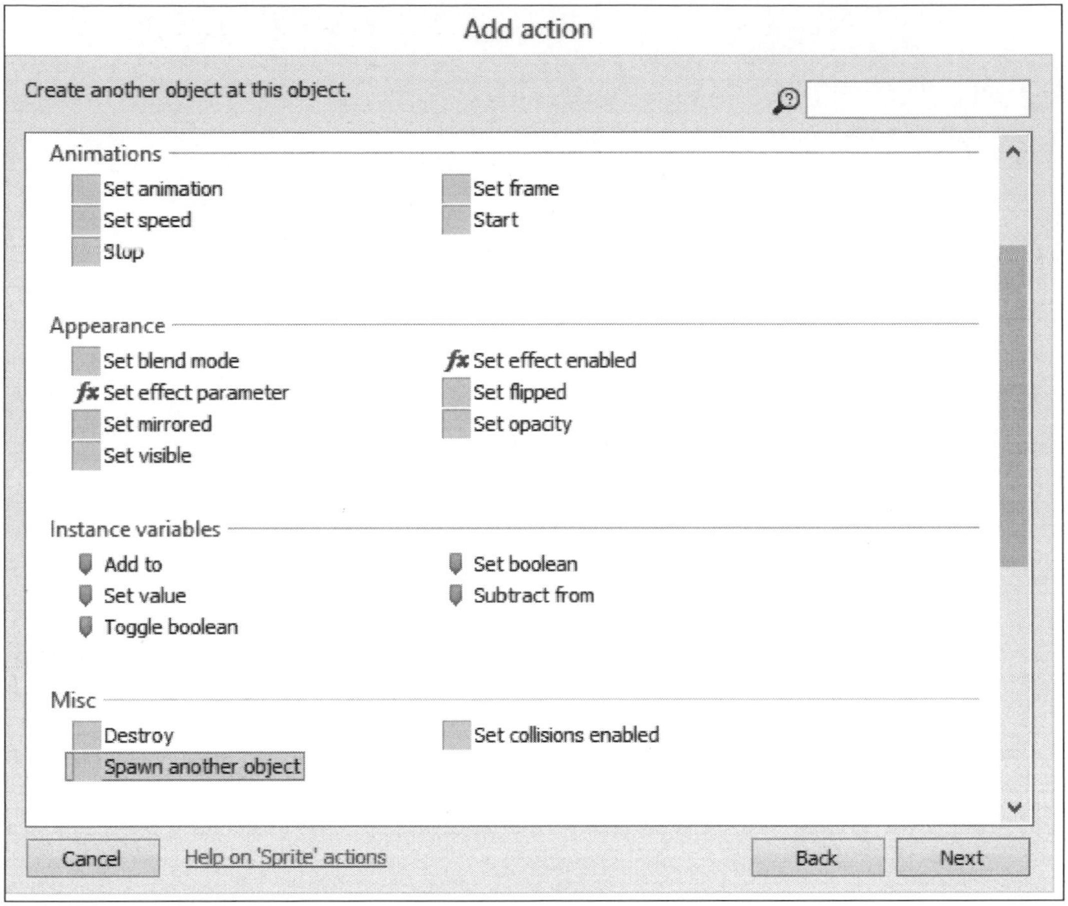

We are going to spawn the **BallGreen** object. We are also going to set the **Layer** value to `1` with **Image point** set to `1`, as shown in the following screenshot. We need to have the object spawn on the top layer. We haven't discussed image points yet, but we need to set one up.

Parameters for Start: Spawn another object

Use 0 for the object's origin, or the name or number of an image point to spawn the object from.

Object BallGreen

Layer 1

Image point 1

Cancel Help on expressions Back Done

Once you have this in your event sheet, go back to your layout and double-click on the **Start** box. We then need to add another image point. The image has a default image point called **Origin**. Any other image point after **Origin** is called **Imagepoint**. Click on the **Image points** dialog box and click on the plus icon, as shown in the following screenshot:

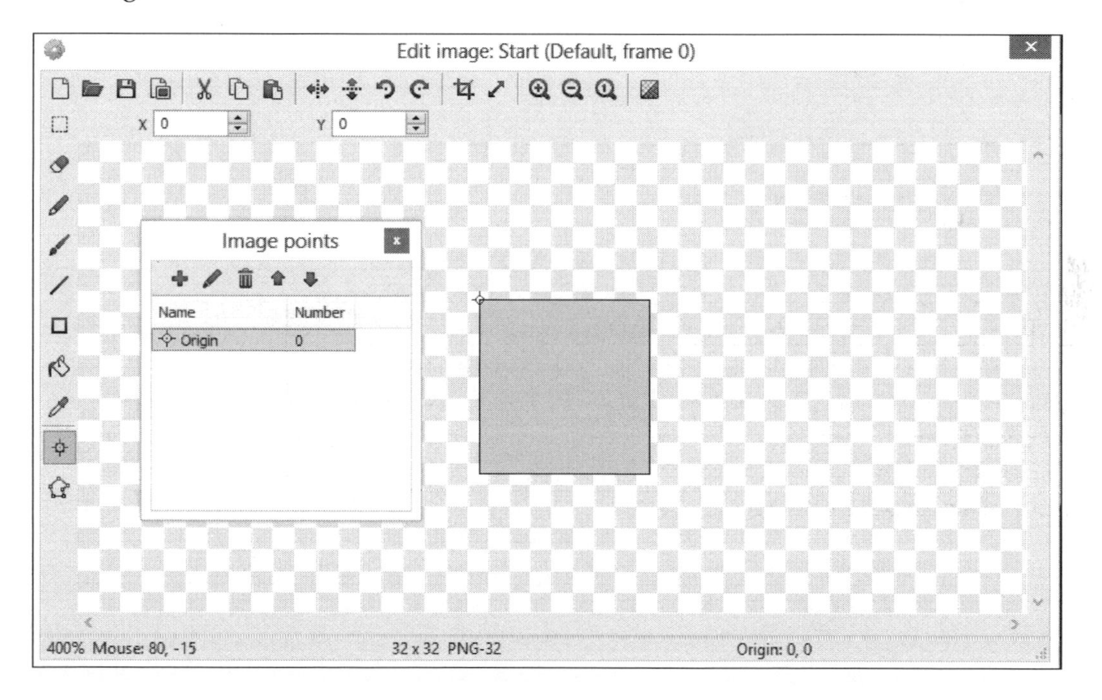

Doing so should automatically add an image point. Note that **Imagepoint** has a different icon than **Origin**. The image point is not the origin; it is simply a place where we can point to on the sprite. Place the image point outside where you want the green ball to spawn. This is really handy because this would be much harder to do in other environments. Your image box should look something like the following screenshot:

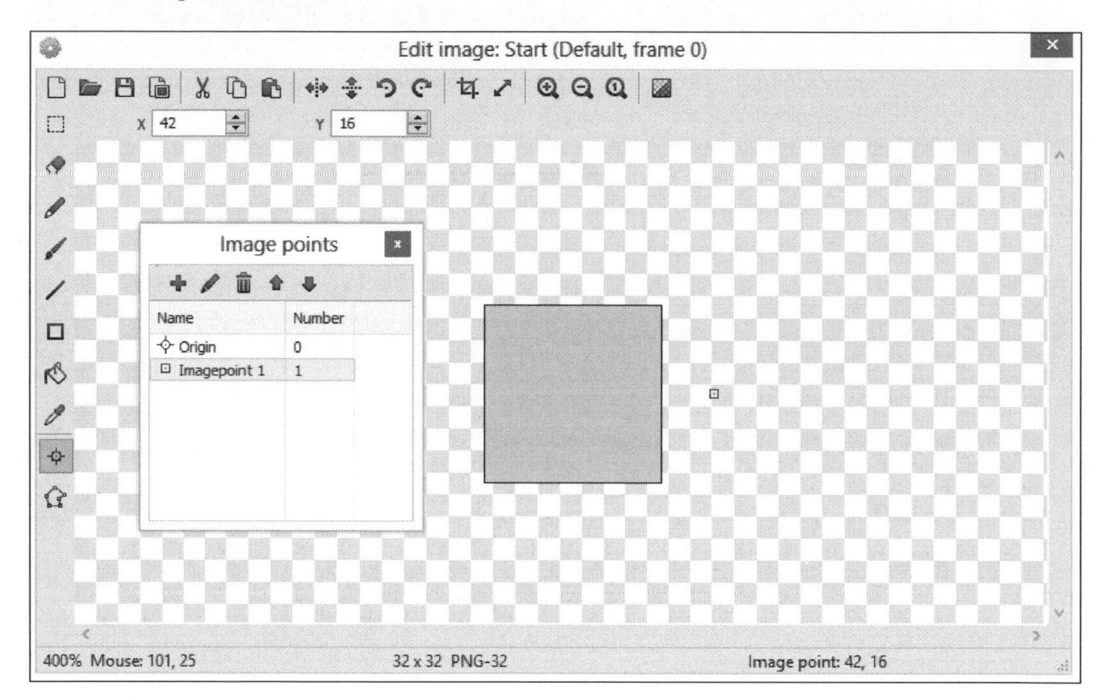

Now, we are almost ready. Let's go back to our event sheet and find **BallGreen** and find **Find path to** action. Select it and press *Ctrl* + *C* to copy the action. Find the **BallGreen** object's **On created** event and paste the action. In this case, the order does not matter. Generally, the order of actions does matter; if you are making a game and you find that your game doesn't work properly, go through the action logic and see whether it makes sense. The following screenshots show what it looks like before and after:

6	System	On start of layout	BallGreen	Find path to (*End.X*, *End.Y*)
			BallGreen	Add obstacle **PlaceTurret**
			Add action	

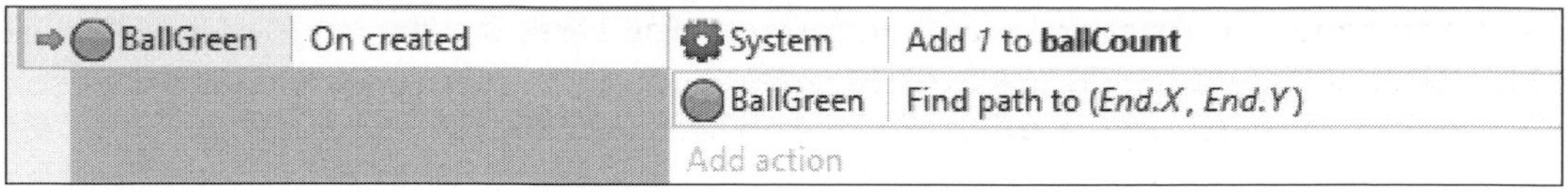

BallGreen	On created	System	Add *1* to **ballCount**
		BallGreen	Find path to (*End.X*, *End.Y*)
			Add action

We are almost finished. What we need to do next is add two **Compare variable** events. Let's compare whether **isWave** is to equal to **1** and **ballCount** is equal to **0**. The next thing we have to do is add an action. This action will set the value of **isWave** to **0**. The way this works is that once all of the balls have been spawned, we need to turn off the spawner. We do this by setting **isWave** back to **0**.

Your event sheet should look like the following screenshot:

10	System	**isWave** = 1	System	Set **isWave** to *0*
	System	**ballCount** = 0		Add action
	Add event			

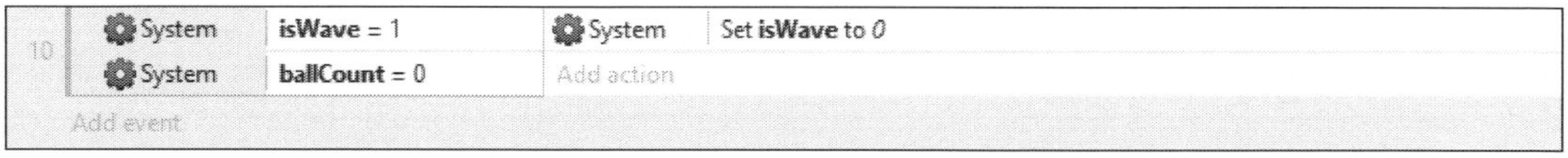

Next, let's go to the **Projectile on collision with green ball** event and add an action. Add a **System** action and choose **Subtract from**, as shown in the following screenshot:

Add action

Subtract from the value of a global or local variable.

Display
Set canvas size
Snapshot canvas

General
Create object
Go to layout
Go to layout (by name)
Restart layout
Set group active
Stop loop

Global & local variables
Add to
Reset global variables
Set value
Subtract from

Layers & Layout
Set layer angle
Set layer background color
Set layer effect enabled
Set layer effect parameter
Set layer opacity
Set layer parallax
Set layer scale
Set layer scale rate
Set layer transparent
Set layer visible
Set layout angle
Set layout effect enabled
Set layout effect parameter
Set layout scale

Cancel
Help on 'System' actions
Back
Next

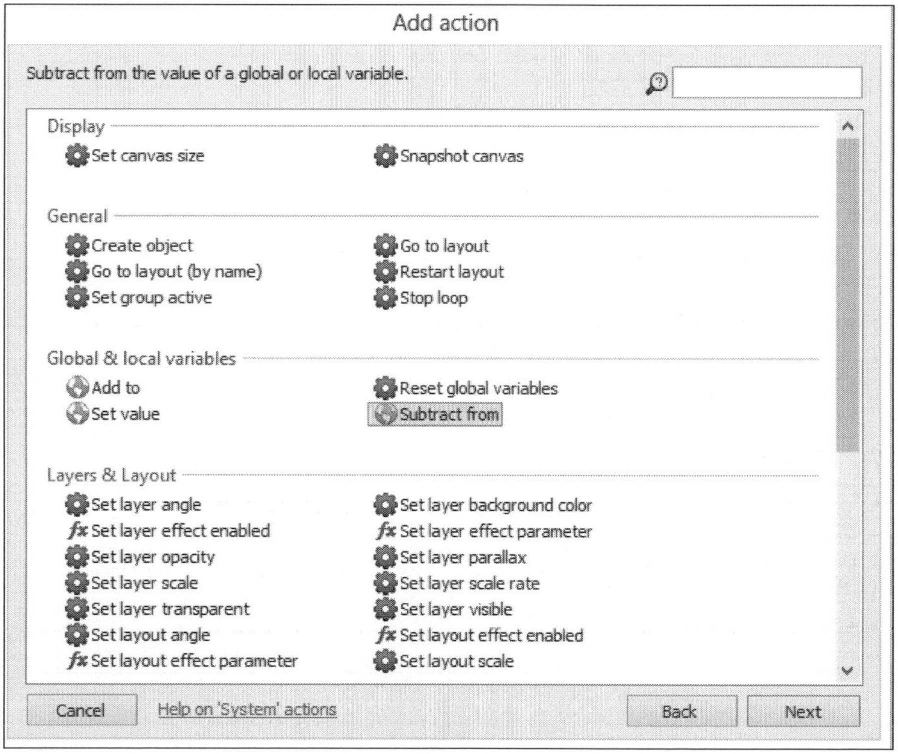

We are going to subtract from ball count. We are going to set the value of the variable to `1`, as shown in the following screenshot. When the projectile destroys the ball, this will subtract the number of balls we have on the screen.

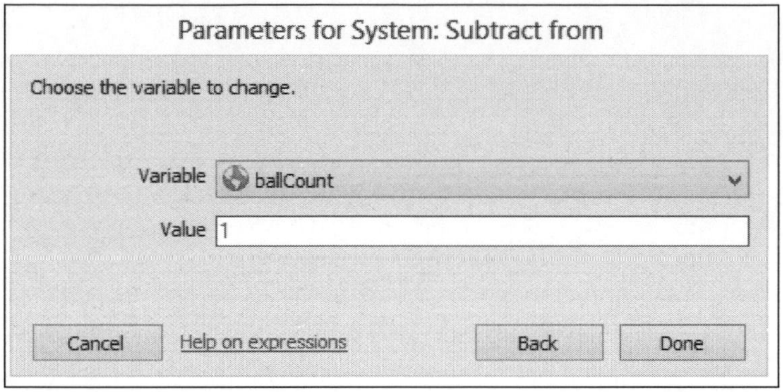

Summary

In this chapter, we learned how to make a tower defense game. Tower defense games are one of the best games to make because most people know how to play them and they are a simple source of fun. In the next chapter, we will learn how to make a physics puzzle game. Physics puzzle games are also easy to make and are quite a bit of fun.

7

Making a Puzzle Physics Game

Puzzle physics games are fun to play and relatively easy to make. In Construct 2, these games are actually really easy to make. In this chapter, we are going to make a puzzle physics game similar to Angry Birds or Crush the Castle.

In this chapter, we will cover the following topics:

- How to make a puzzle physics game
- How to add physics to game objects
- Adding HUD elements that reflect the game

Starting the project

First, we need to start with a new project. Open up a new project and set the layout size to `1500, 480`. In this game, we are going to move the "camera" around. This means that we will move the field of view to a game object.

Setting the background layer

Once you have opened a new project, set up the background layer. In this case, we have a ground and a sky. You should make sure that the background is on its own layer and make sure that there is a game object layer as well. This is what your project should look like:

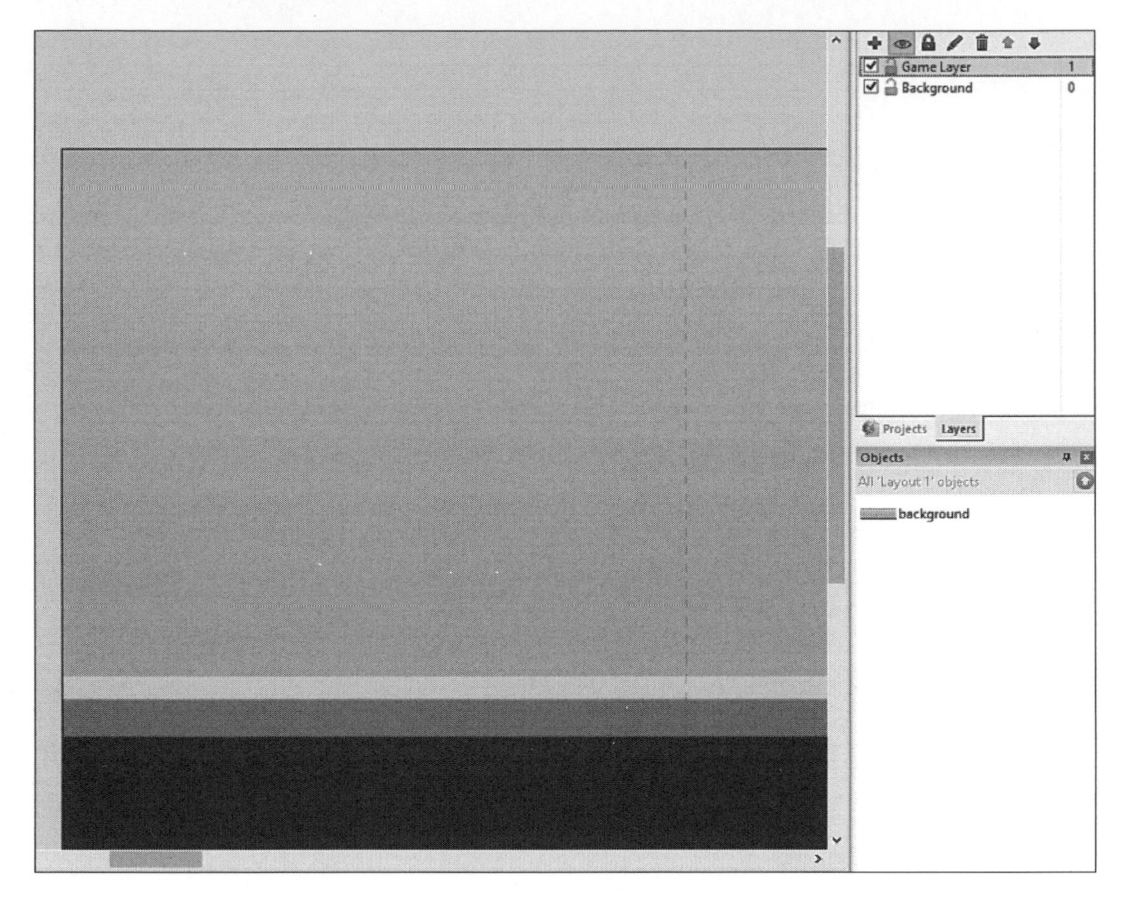

Adding the cannon

Once you have these layers, add a cannon (seen in the screenshot that follows). Name it something, such as `cannon`, so that we do not get confused—it is important to name your game objects appropriately.

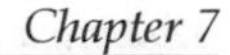

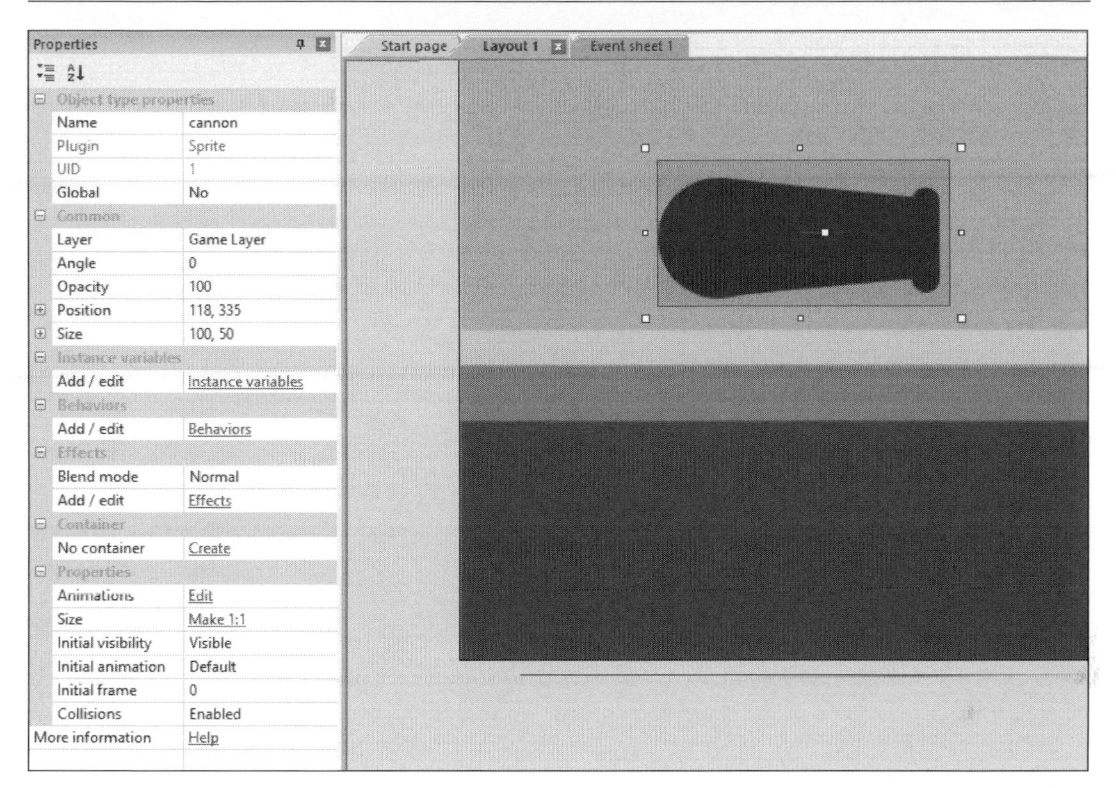

Before we continue, make sure that the cannon is on the game object layer and the background is on the background layer. Lock the background layer (by clicking on the lock icon) so that we do not accidentally modify it:

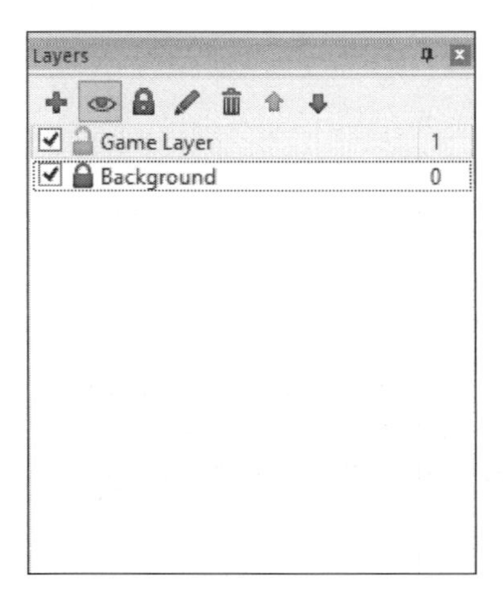

Adding sprites

We then need to add some blocks. These will serve as objects to interact with in the game. As shown in the following screenshot, we added a block and named it something that makes sense. We named it `block`.

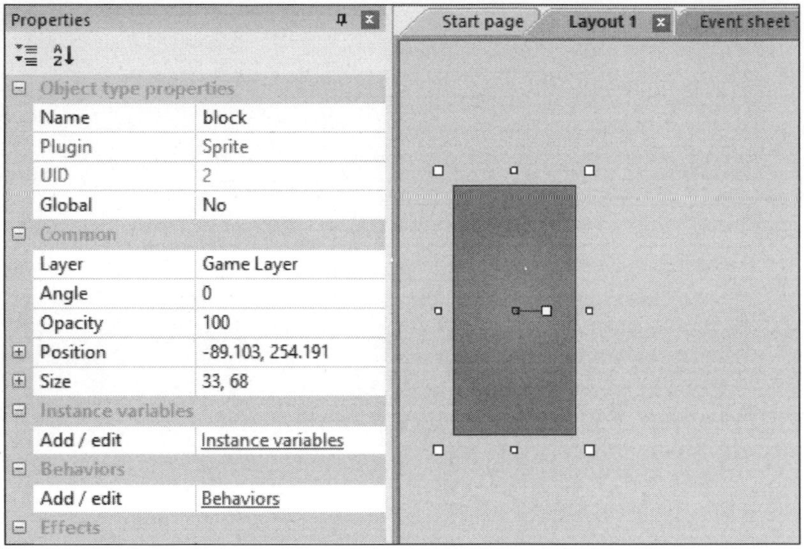

Once you have added a block, add a cannonball. We used a circular object and named it `cannonBall`, and it is shown in the following screenshot:

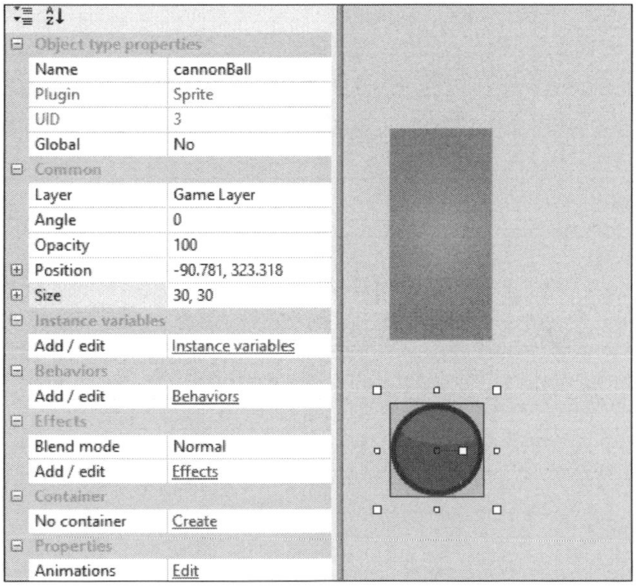

Finally, we need to have some kind of goal. In this case, we added a circle with a star on it and named it `goalBall`, as shown in the following screenshot:

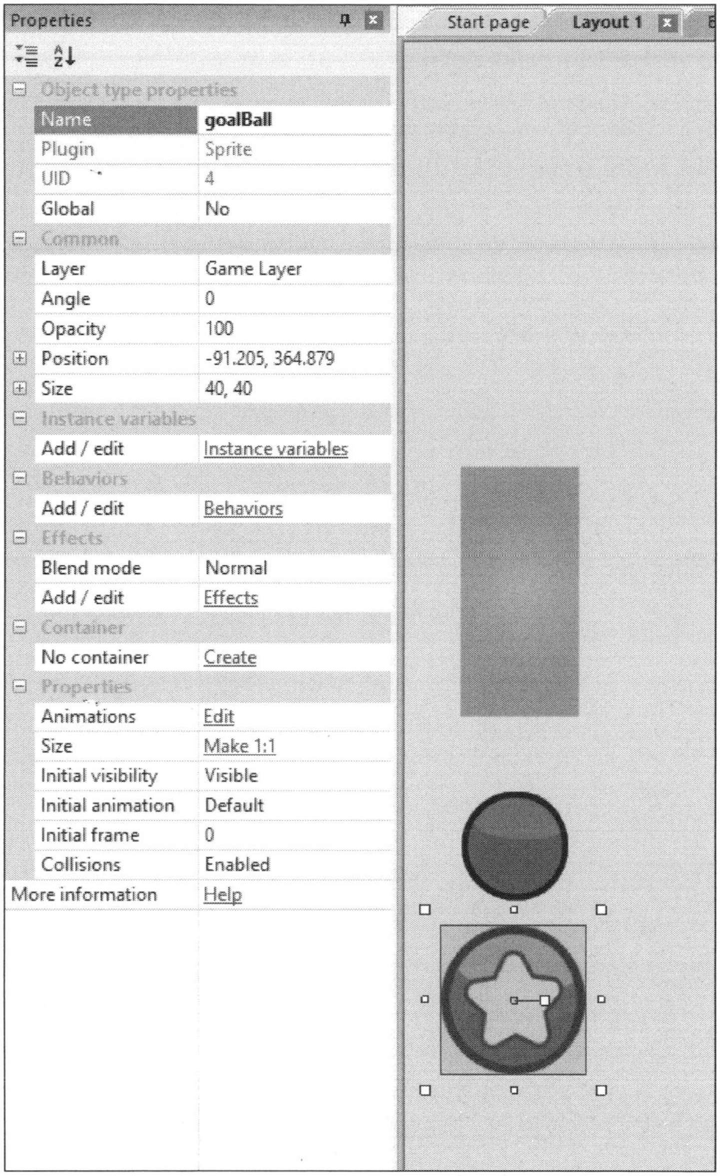

Properties

Start page | Layout 1

Object type properties	
Name	goalBall
Plugin	Sprite
UID	4
Global	No
Common	
Layer	Game Layer
Angle	0
Opacity	100
Position	-91.205, 364.879
Size	40, 40
Instance variables	
Add / edit	Instance variables
Behaviors	
Add / edit	Behaviors
Effects	
Blend mode	Normal
Add / edit	Effects
Container	
No container	Create
Properties	
Animations	Edit
Size	Make 1:1
Initial visibility	Visible
Initial animation	Default
Initial frame	0
Collisions	Enabled
More information	Help

Adding functionalities

Now that we have most of our sprites in the game, let's go and add some functionality. Double-click on the layout and add the **Mouse** functionality, as shown in the following screenshot:

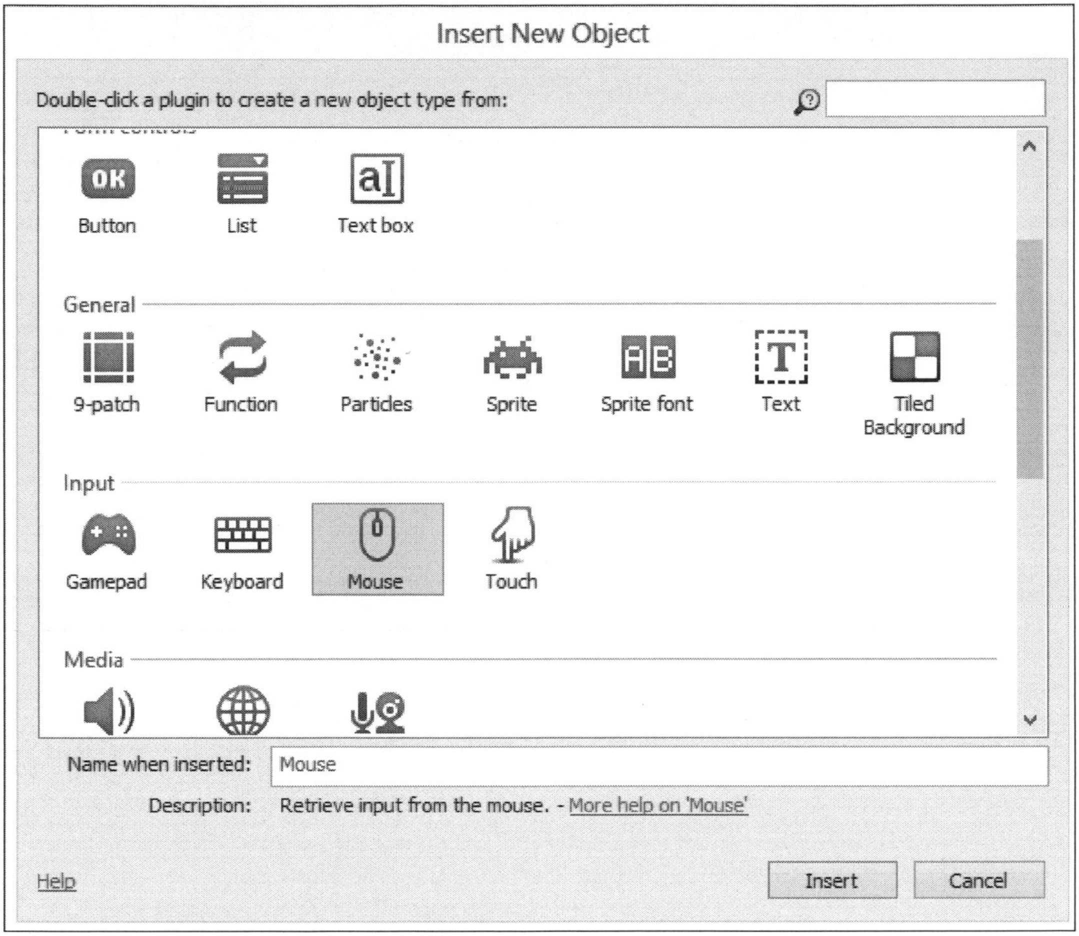

Rotating the cannon

Now, we are ready to make our game. Let's go to the event sheet and add an **Every Tick** event by navigating to **System** | **Every Tick**. Once you have added that, add an action. In this case, it's going to be for the cannon sprite and the action should be **Rotate toward position**. Check the following screenshot:

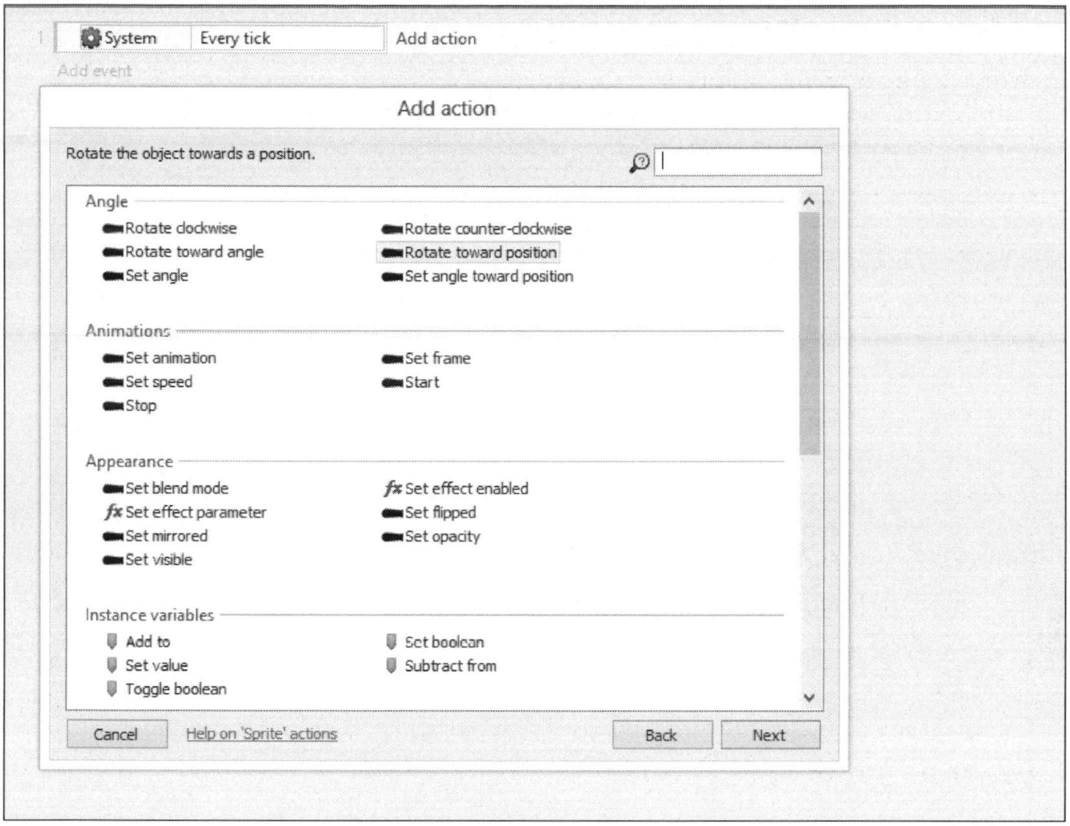

We are going to rotate the cannon with the mouse. Luckily, this is really easy to do in Construct 2.

Let's move the cannon by 10 degrees (this is the speed at which the cannon rotates). In the **X** box, type `mouse.x` and type `mouse.y` in the **Y** box. This will rotate the cannon to the position of `Mouse.X` and `Mouse.Y`, or simply the mouse position. This is shown in the following screenshot:

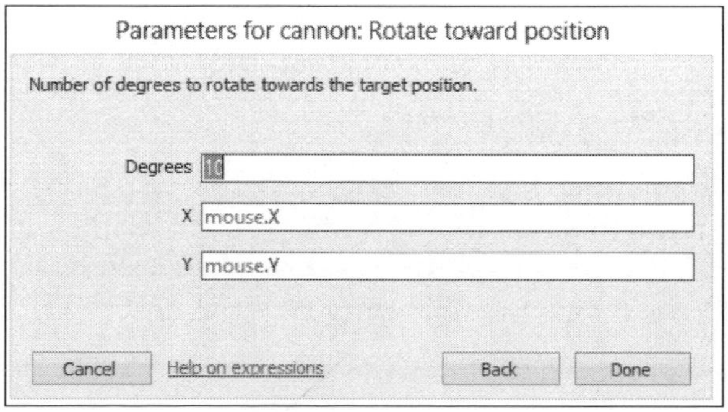

Run the game and test it out. It is good to test early and often. Make sure you save often as well. You will notice that the cannon does not rotate the way we want it to—the reason is that the cannon rotates around **Origin**. Let's double-click on the cannon and move **Origin** closer to the back of the cannon. Run the game again to test it.

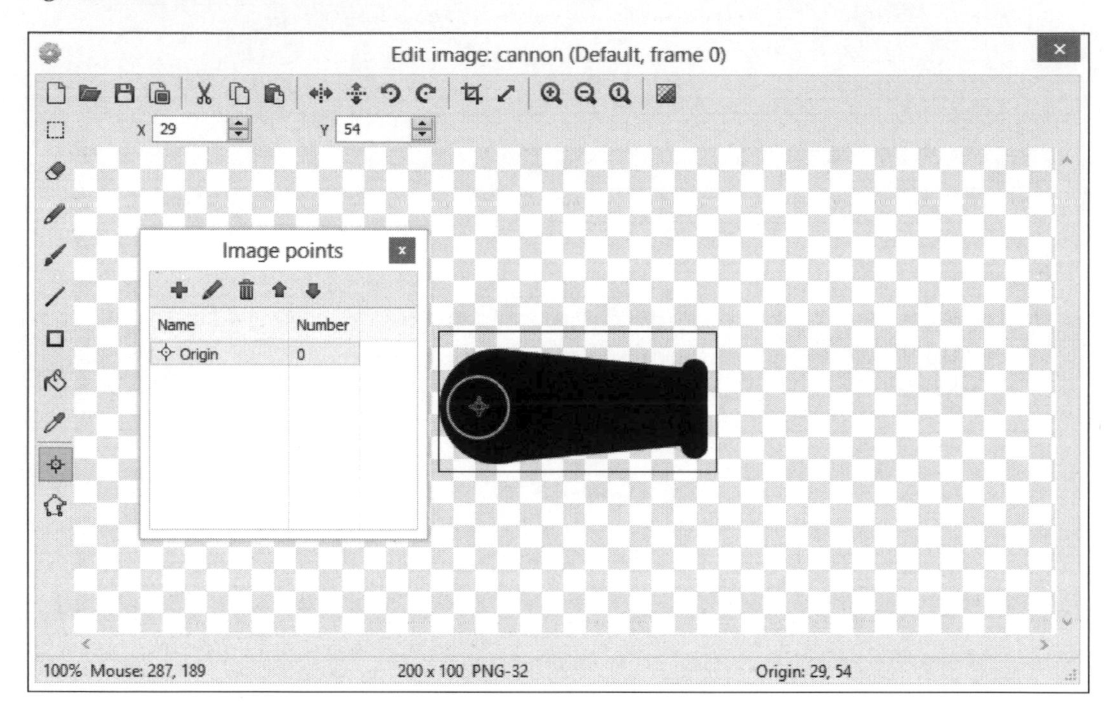

You will notice that the cannon rotates freely, while what we want to do is clamp it so that it only rotates in a certain area. Go back to the event sheet and select the **Every Tick** event. Press the *C* key to add another condition and add a **Compare two values** condition, as shown in the following screenshot:

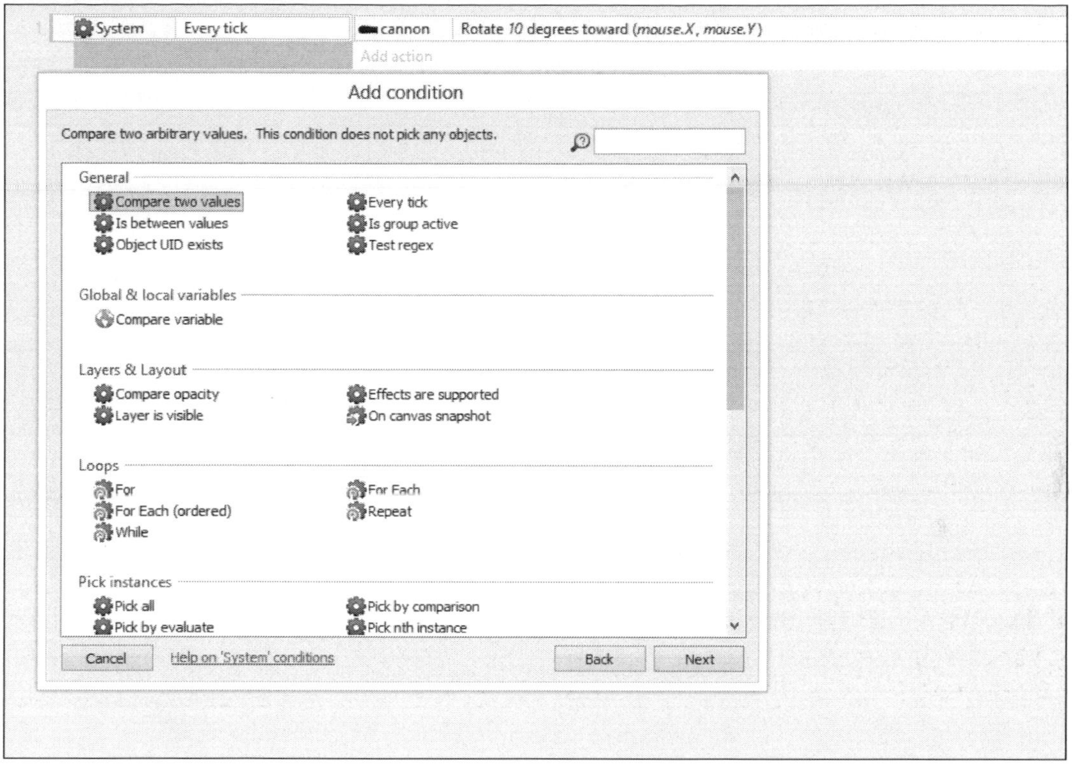

To ensure that the cannon only rotates in a set area, we have to make the range of the mouse greater than the position of the cannon. To do this, make the position greater than the X position of the cannon and less than the Y position of the cannon. Set the `mouse.X` value to be of **≥ Greater or equal** in the **Comparison** field, as shown in the following screenshot:

Parameters for System: Compare two values

Enter the first value to compare. This condition does not pick any objects - it is a simple value comparison.

First value: mouse.X

Comparison: ≥ Greater or equal

Second value: 118

Cancel | Help on expressions | Back | Done

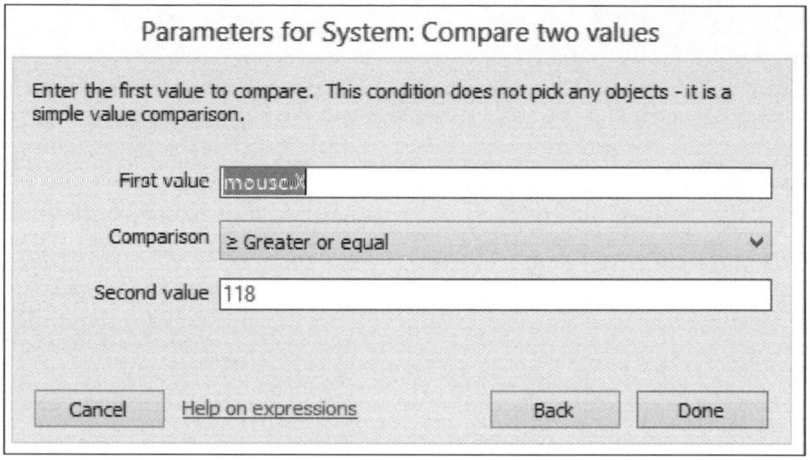

Once you have compared the X position, repeat the exact same steps for the Y position; however, make sure that the `mouse.Y` is **≤ Less than or equal** in the **Comparison** field instead of **≥ Greater than or equal**. The event sheet should now look like the following screenshot:

	Condition		Action
System	Every tick	cannon	Rotate *10* degrees toward (*mouse.X*, *mouse.Y*)
System	mouse.X ≥ 118	Add action	
System	mouse.Y ≤ 335		

Add event

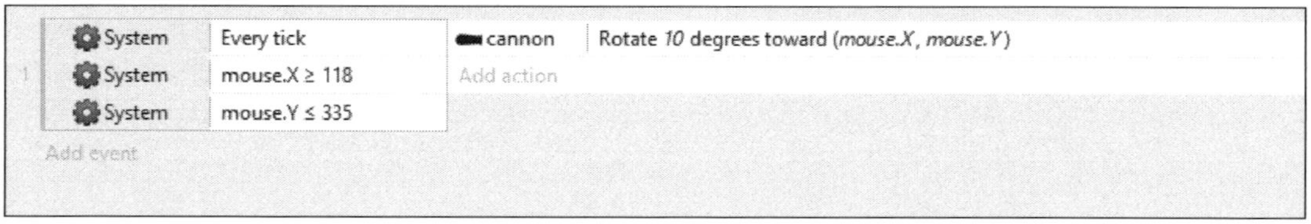

Creating a cannonball

We need to create a cannonball to fire at the other game objects. Hence, we will create and add in a projectile—a cannonball—for the cannon to fire. Add a **On any click** event by navigating to **Mouse** | **On any click**.

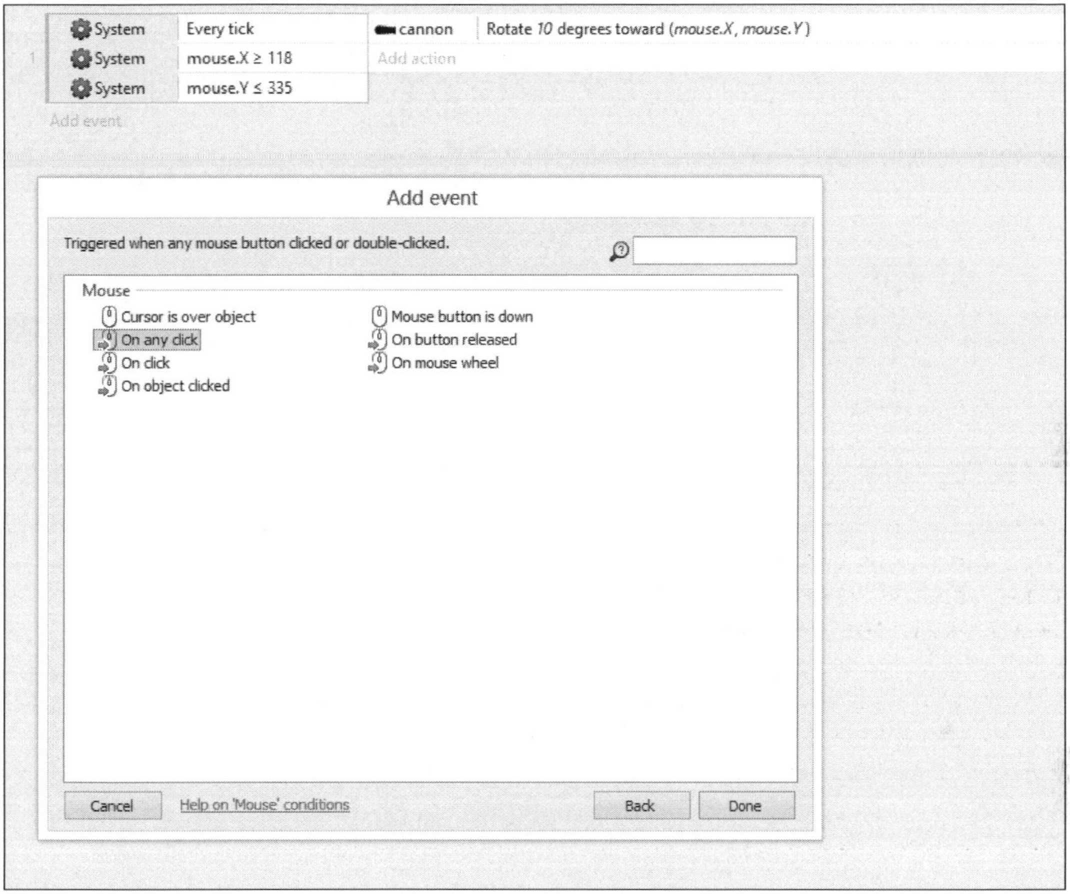

Then, add a **Spawn another object** action on the cannon, as shown in the following screenshot. We are going to spawn the cannonball when we click the mouse button.

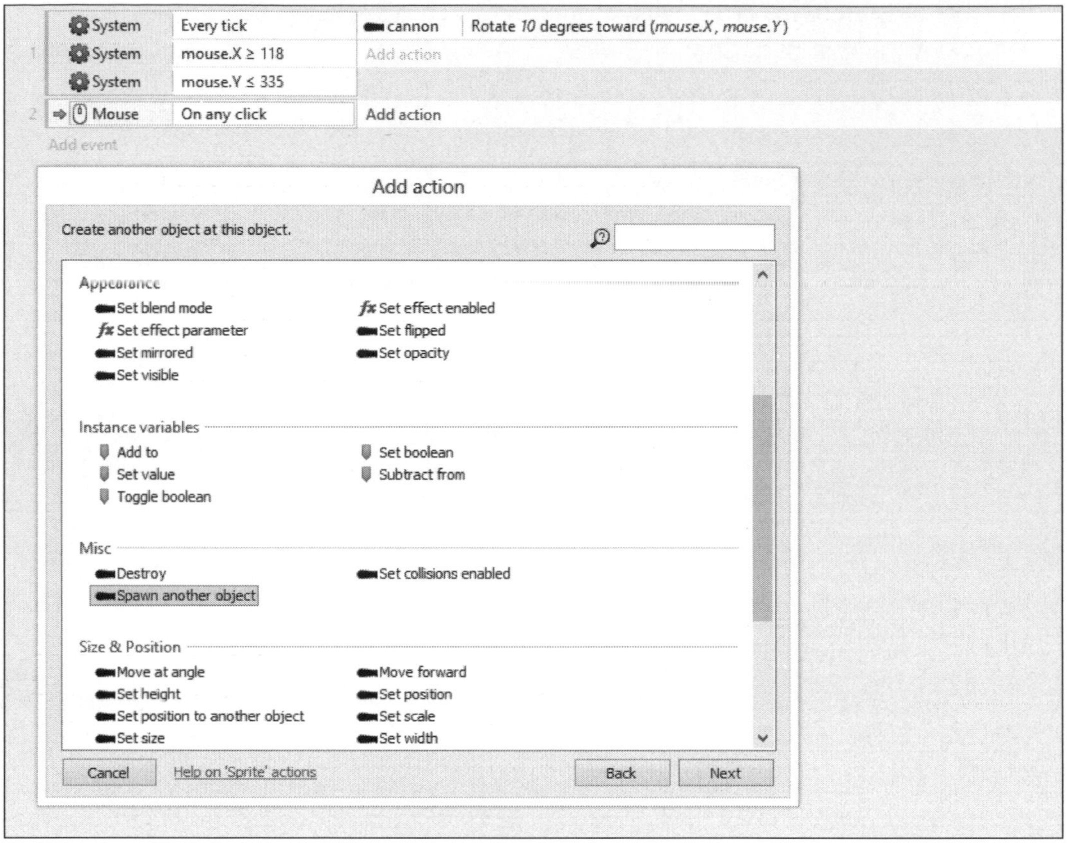

The object is, of course, going to be the cannonball.

> This is where naming your game objects clearly really makes a difference—particularly if you have more than 200 game objects.

Spawning the cannonball

In order to make the cannonball actually "fire", we need to spawn the cannonball first. Set the `cannonBall` object to spawn on **Layer** with the value `1` at **Image point** with the value `1`. This is shown in the following screenshot:

Parameters for cannon: Spawn another object

Use 0 for the object's origin, or the name or number of an image point to spawn the object from.

Object: cannonBall

Layer: 1

Image point: 1

Cancel | Help on expressions | Back | Done

Creating the spawning image point

But wait! We still have to set up an **Image point** 1! Double-click on the cannon and add an image point by pressing the plus (**+**) sign. Put the image point next to the front of the cannon, as shown in the following screenshot. The image point is where the cannonball will spawn from.

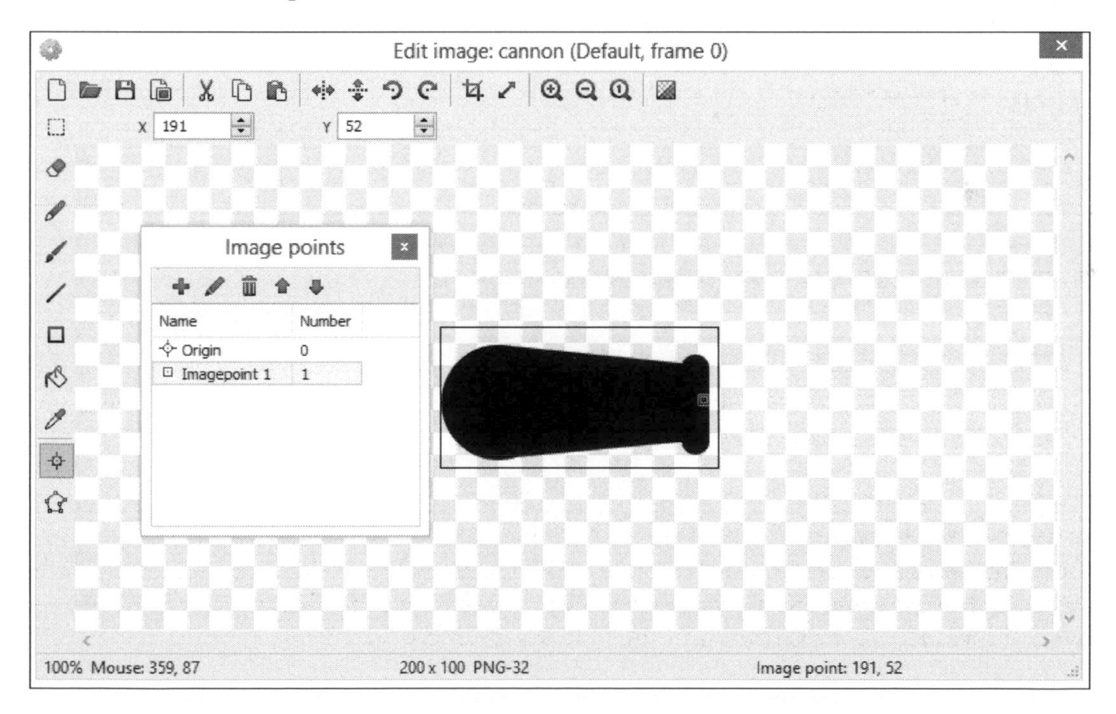

Adding physics

Run the game again and you will see that the cannonball does not act like a cannonball. We need to add some physics to it! Click on the cannonball and add the **Physics** behavior as shown in the following screenshot:

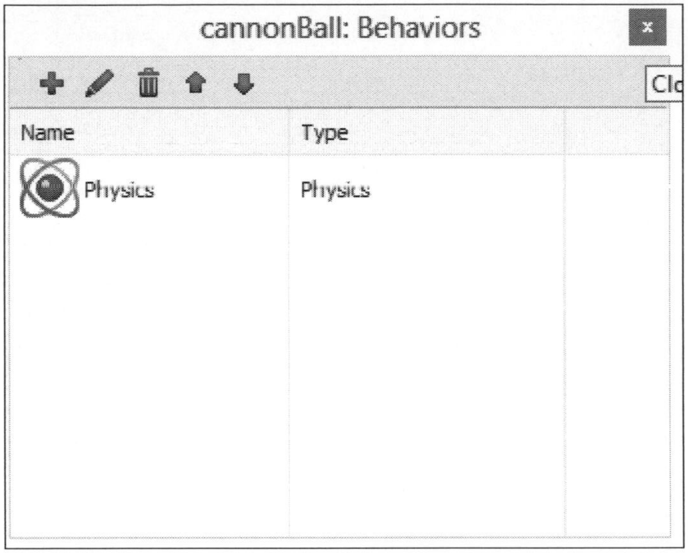

Applying force at an angle

Run the game again.

You will notice that the ball just falls down! Now that we have added physics, we can add a force to the cannonball to make it shoot like real cannon. Add an action to the **Mouse click** event. The action will be **Apply force at angle**, as shown in the following screenshot:

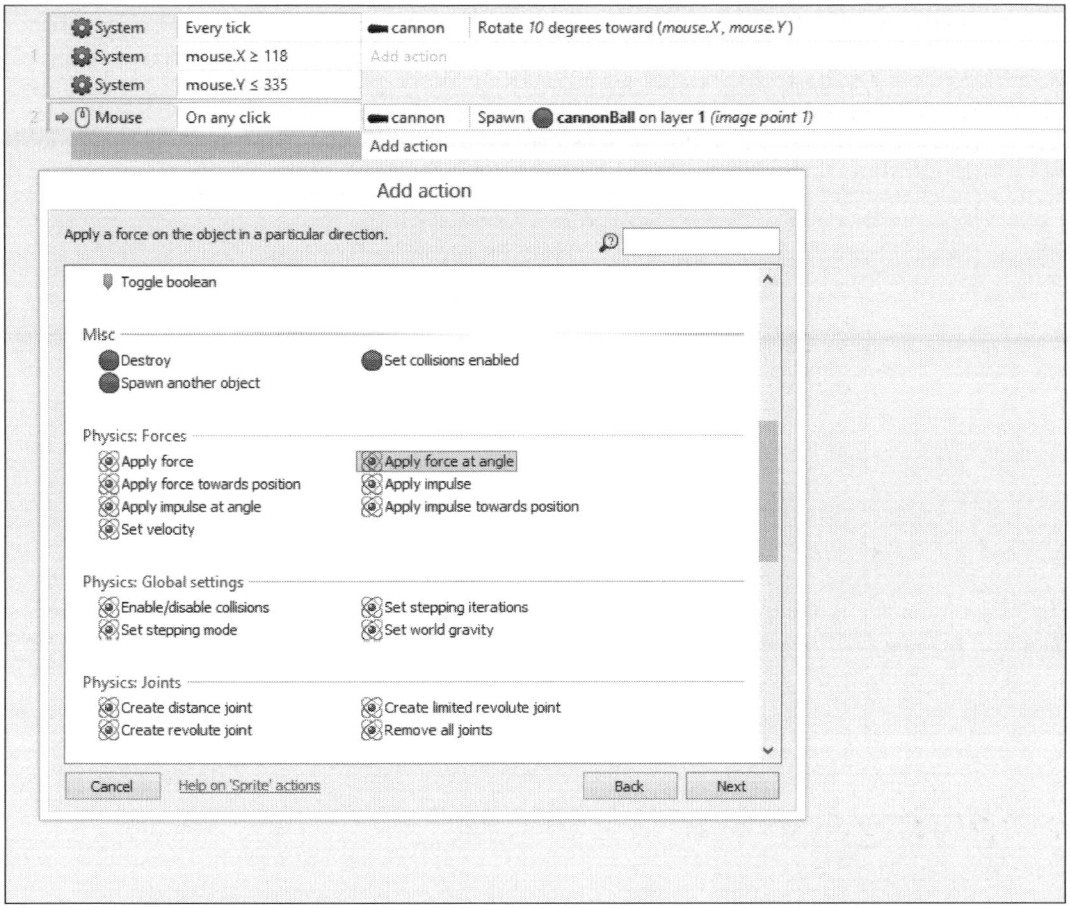

Set the force to around `200`. The bigger the number, the further the cannonball travels. For the angle, type in `cannon.Angle` as shown in the following screenshot. This will ensure that the cannonball is shot in the same direction as the cannon.

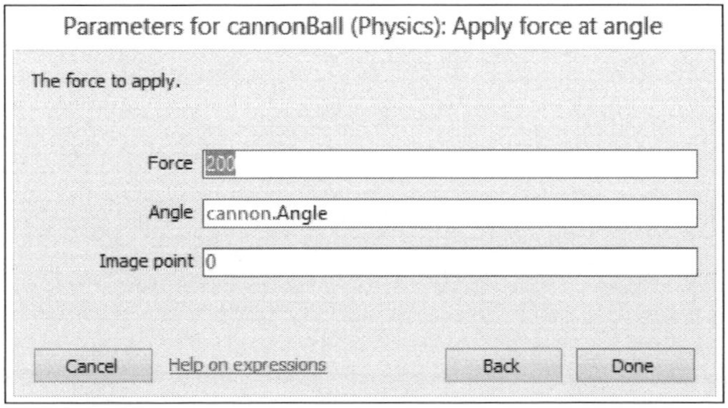

Setting cannonballs to fire one at a time

If you run the game, you will notice that we can fire as many cannonballs as we want. We should limit the cannonballs to make them fire only one at a time. In order to do this, we need to add a global variable. Let's name this variable `canFire` and set its initial value to `0`, as shown in the following screenshot:

New global variable

Name	canFire
Type	Number
Initial value	0
Description (optional)	

Static

Constant

Help OK Cancel

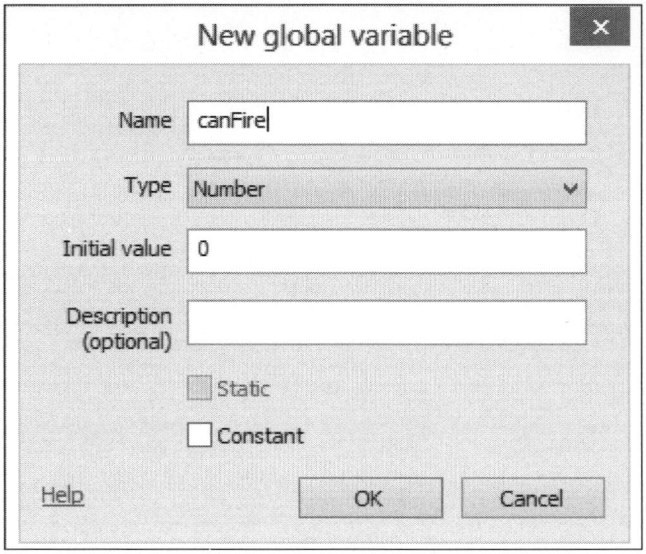

Click on the **On any click** mouse event and press *C* to add another condition. Navigate to **System** | **Compare variable**. Set the `canFire` variable to be equal to `0` (using the **Equal to** condition). This is shown in the following screenshot:

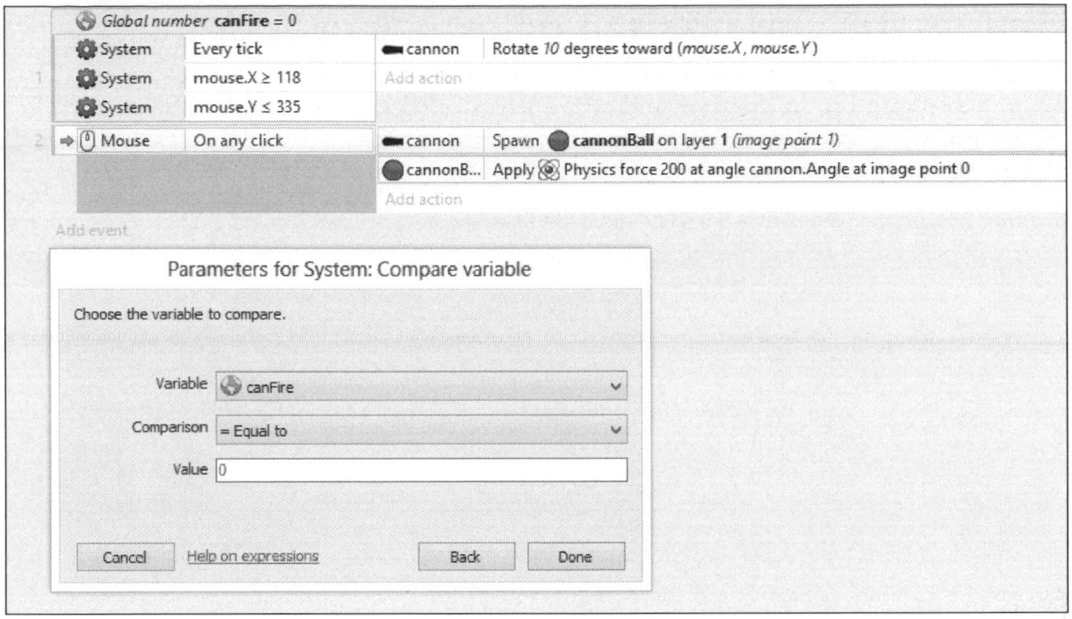

Once you've done that, add a **System** action to the **On any click** mouse event that sets `canFire` to be equal to 1. This will make the cannon fire only one at a time. If you run the game now, you will only be able to fire one cannonball. We will add the "reloading" functionality in a moment. The event sheet should look like the following screenshot:

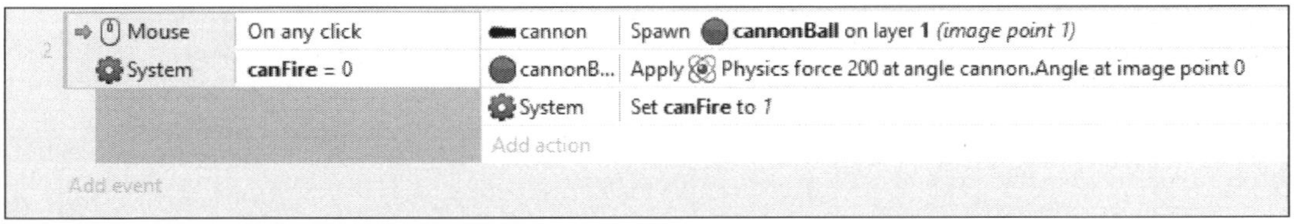

Setting the viewpoint to follow the cannonball

You will notice that the viewpoint or camera does not follow the cannonball. Double-click on the cannonball and add a **ScrollTo** behavior, as shown in the following screenshot:

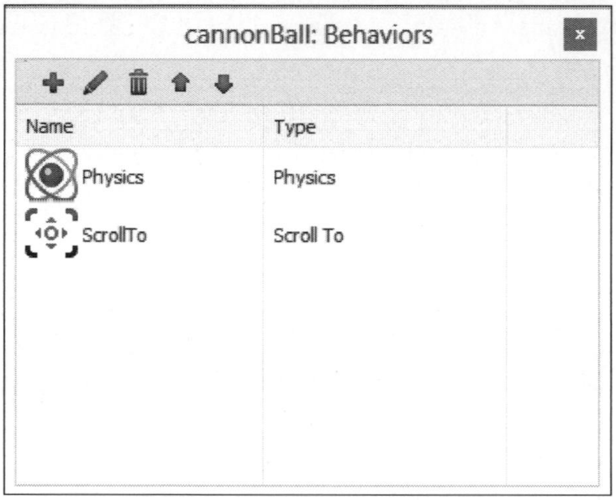

Also, add a **Destroy outside layout** behavior, as shown in the following screenshot:

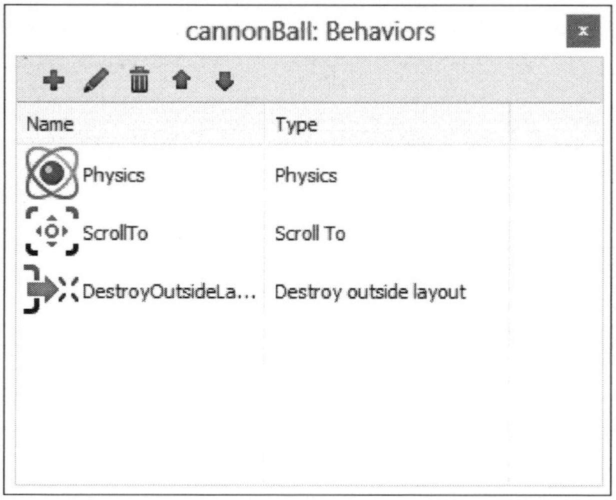

Making an immovable ground

When running the game, you will see that the camera now does indeed follow the cannonball. However, there is only one problem—there is no "ground" and the cannonball just falls to the bottom of the screen. So, let's make a "ground"! Add another sprite and resize it to `1500` by `250`. Put this on a background layer. Let's give the background a blue color—something that stands out. Check the following screenshot:

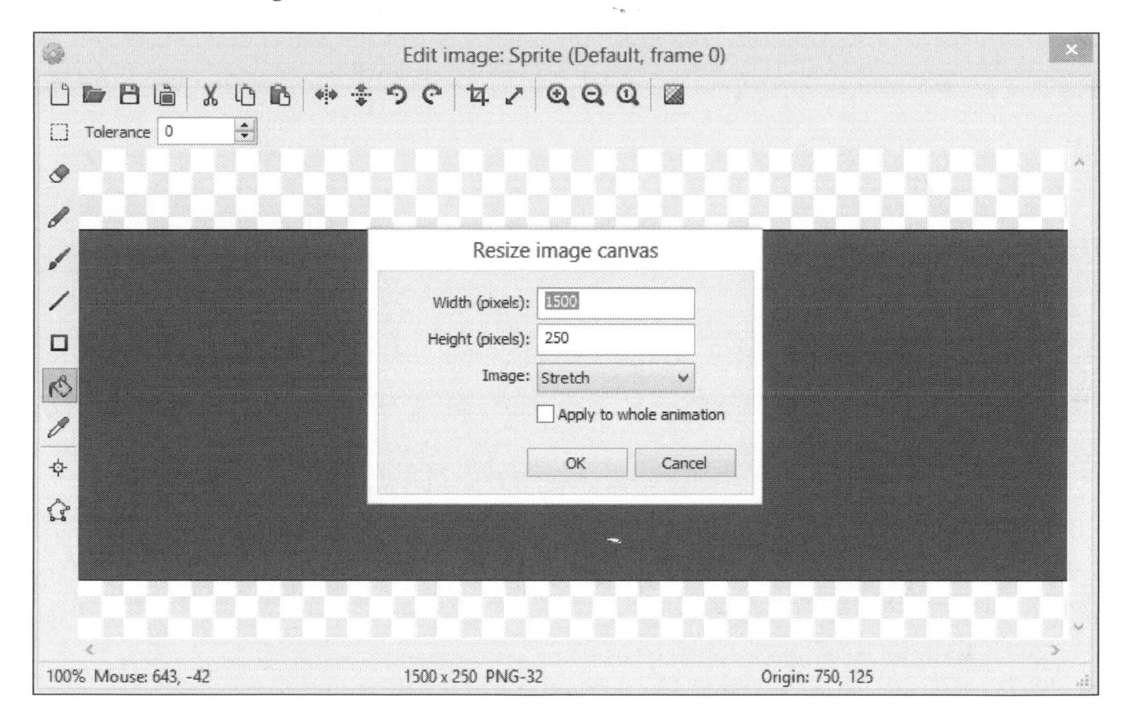

Add a **Physics** behavior to the ground sprite. Set **Immovable** to **Yes** and **Prevent rotation** to **Yes**, as shown in the following screenshot. This will make this sprite immoveable.

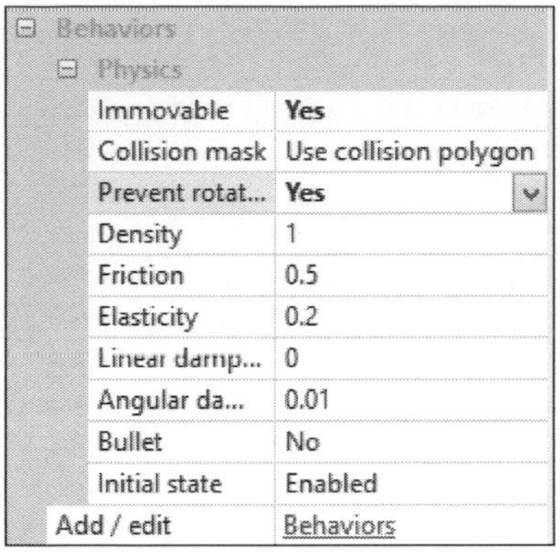

Once you have done this, place the sprite near the bottom of the screen and set **Opacity** to `0` so that it's transparent. This is shown in the following screenshot:

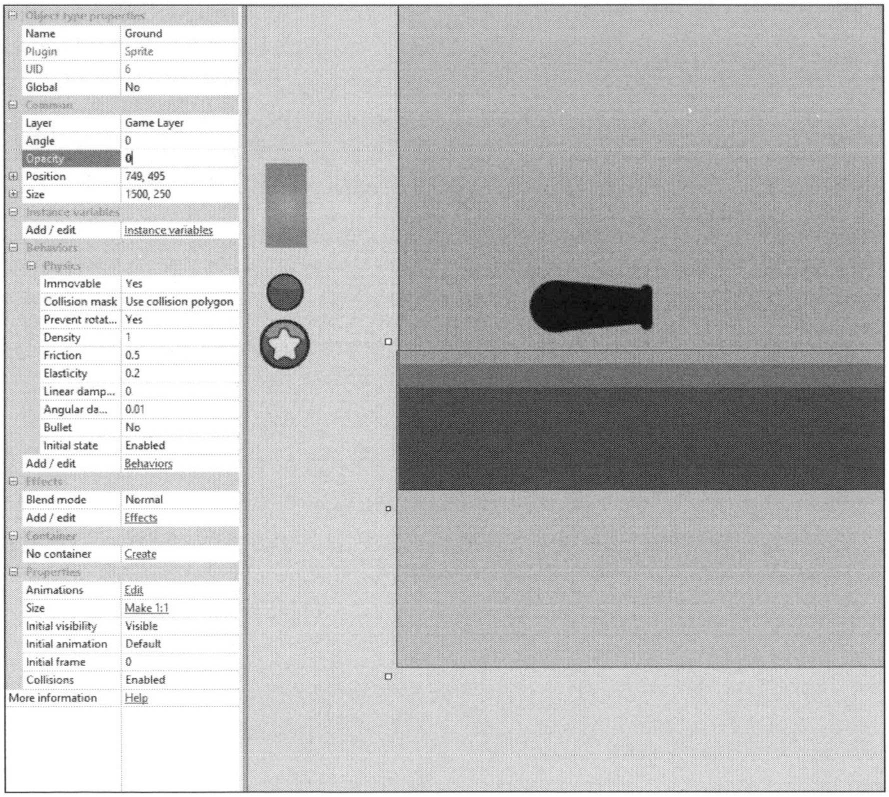

Reloading the cannon

We need to set `canFire` back to `0` so that the cannon can reload and fire another cannonball. Add an **On destroyed** event to our `cannonBall` sprite, as shown in the following screenshot:

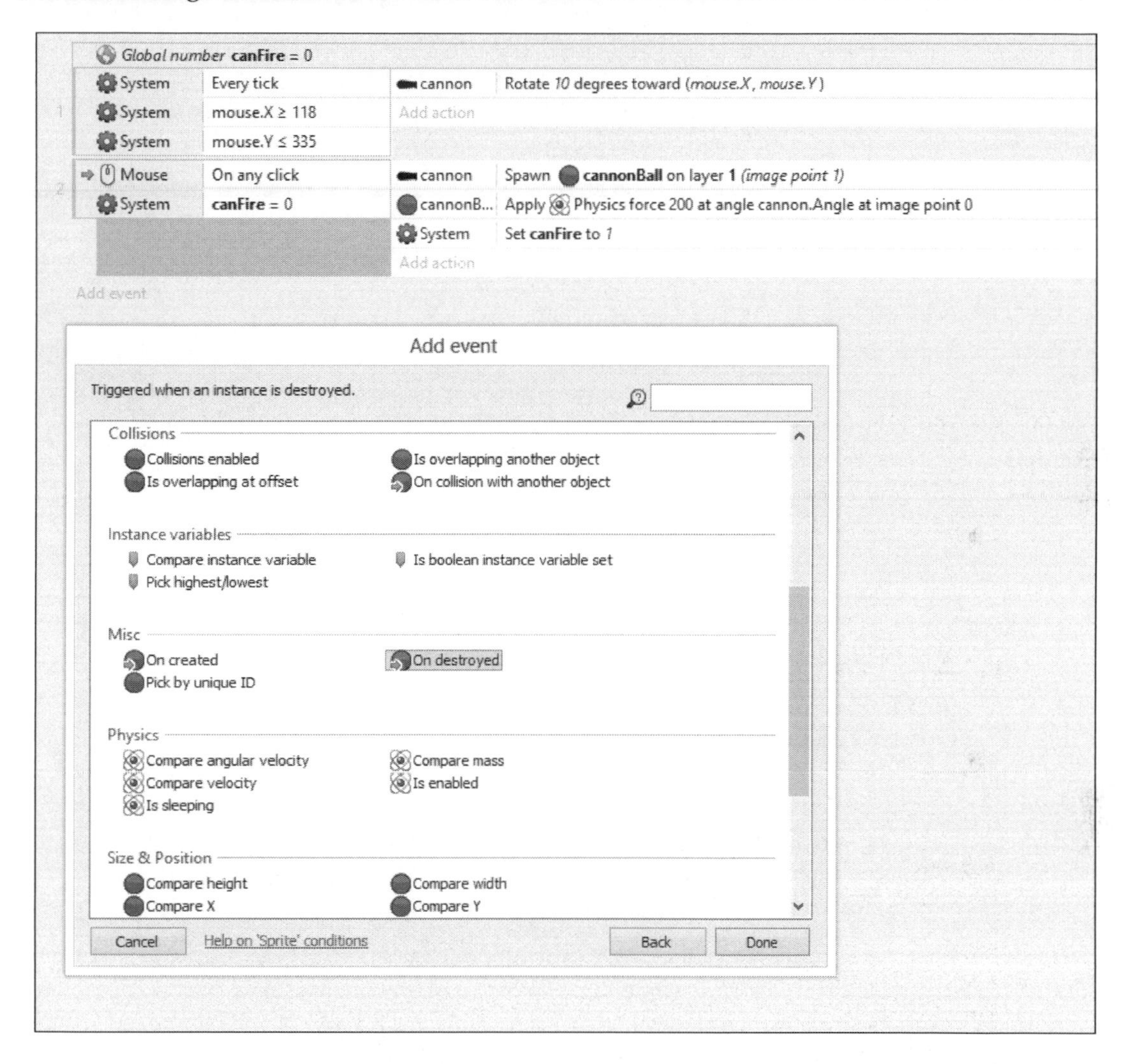

Create the **On destroyed** event and set `canFire` to `0` by adding in a **System** set value of a variable.

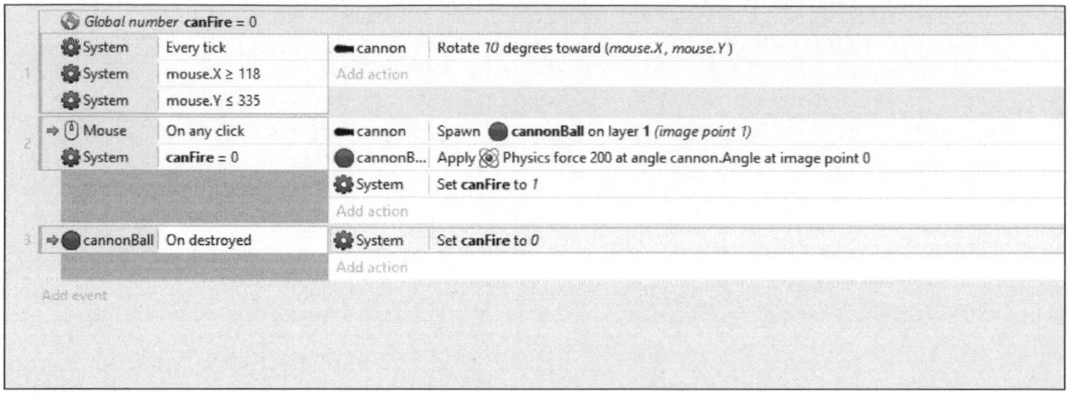

After that, we need to scroll back to the cannon so that the next cannonball will be fired from there. To do this, we need to set in a **Scroll to object** event for the **System**, as shown in the following screenshot:

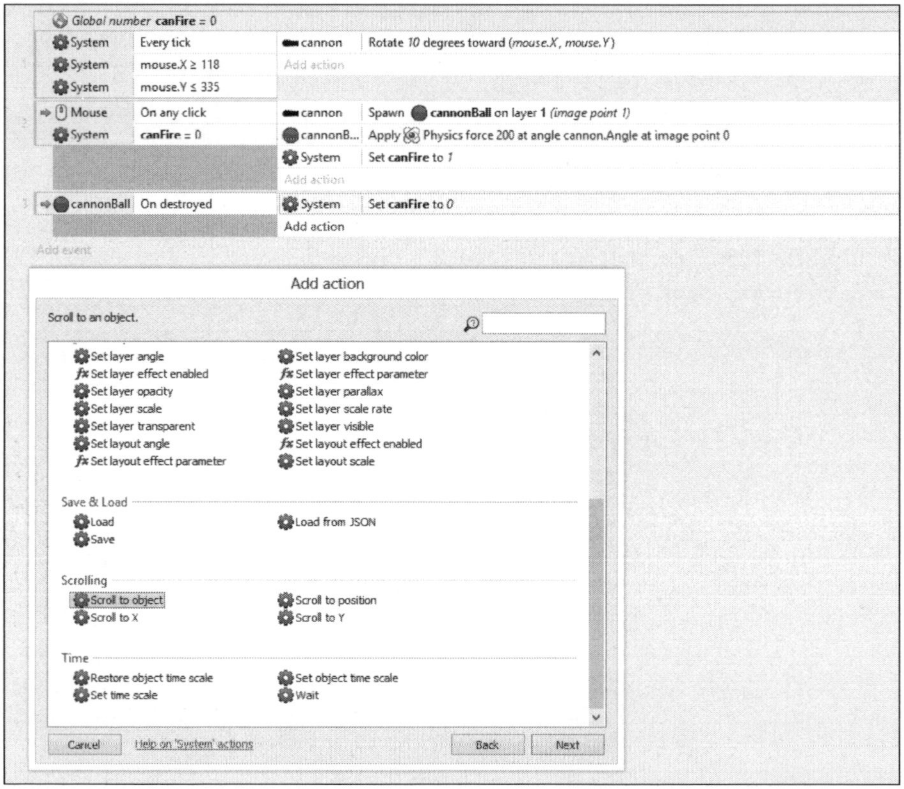

The object for this event is going to be the **cannon**, as shown in the following screenshot:

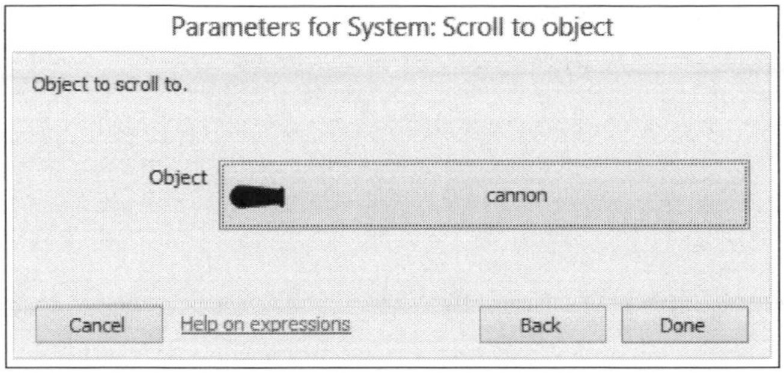

Your event should look like the following screenshot. Run the game. You will notice that when the cannonball goes off of the screen, it gets destroyed. When this happens, the camera scrolls back to the cannon and you can fire again! The event sheet now looks like the following screenshot:

Adding the blocks

Now, we need to add blocks to the game. Click on the `block` sprite and add a **Physics** behavior.

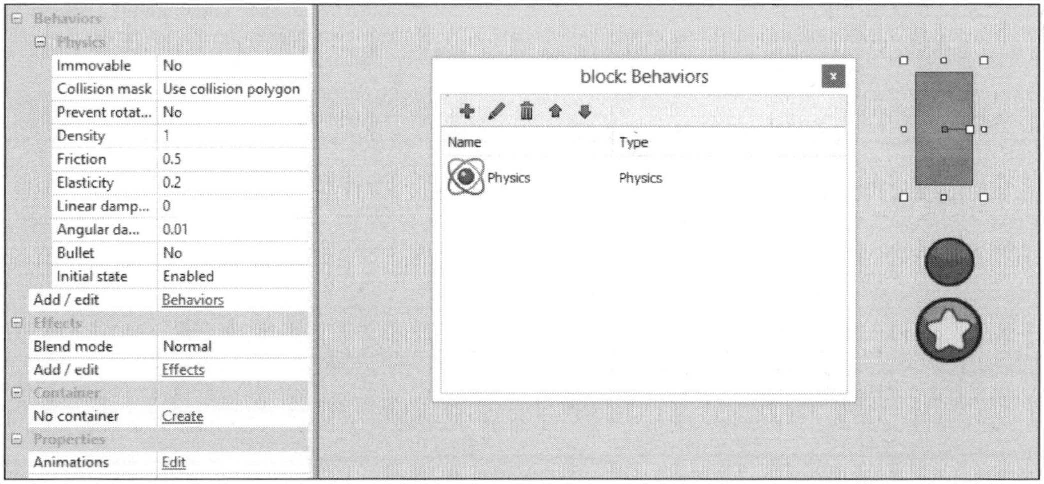

Put the block in front of the cannonball and test it out by firing the cannon! This is shown in the following screenshot:

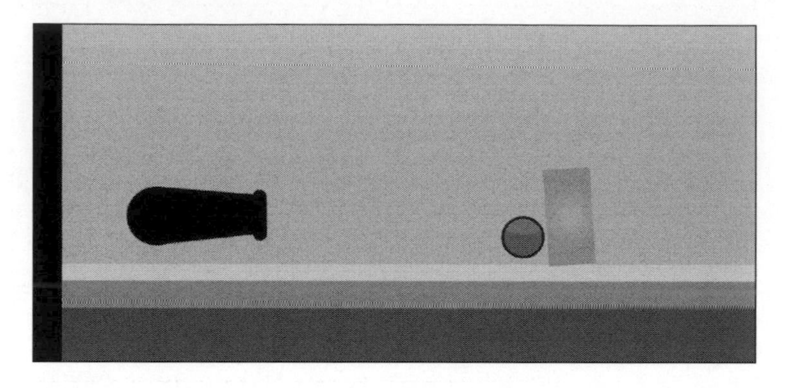

Destroying the cannonball on a complete stop

The cannonball just sits on the screen and doesn't move. We should then add some logic to destroy it after it hits a block. Add a **Compare velocity** event to the `cannonBall` sprite.

The velocity that we are going to compare is **Overall velocity**, and we are going to set **Comparison** to **≤ Less or equal** with value `0.1`. This is shown in the following screenshot. The reason we don't want to set the value to zero is that our object may still have a tiny amount of velocity (for instance, of value 0.00001); but as it has not quite made it to zero, the event would not be activated.

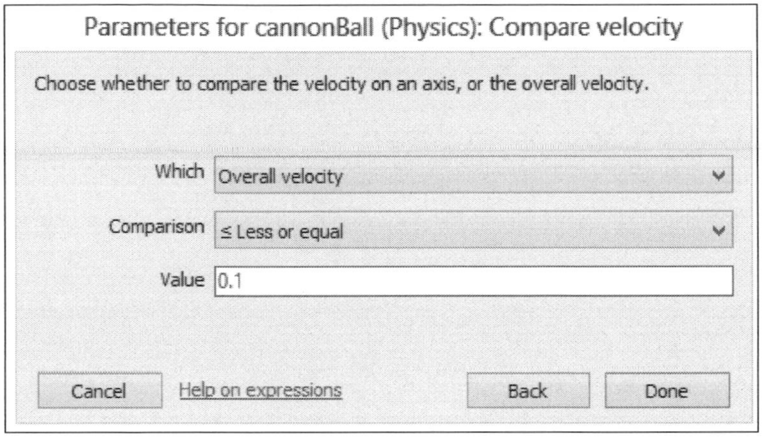

When the cannonball almost comes to a complete stop, we want to destroy it. Add a **Destroy object** action to the event, as shown in the following screenshot:

Delaying cannonball destruction

Run the game. When the cannonball stops, it is reset very abruptly. In order to make this easier for the game to handle, we will add a **Wait** action.

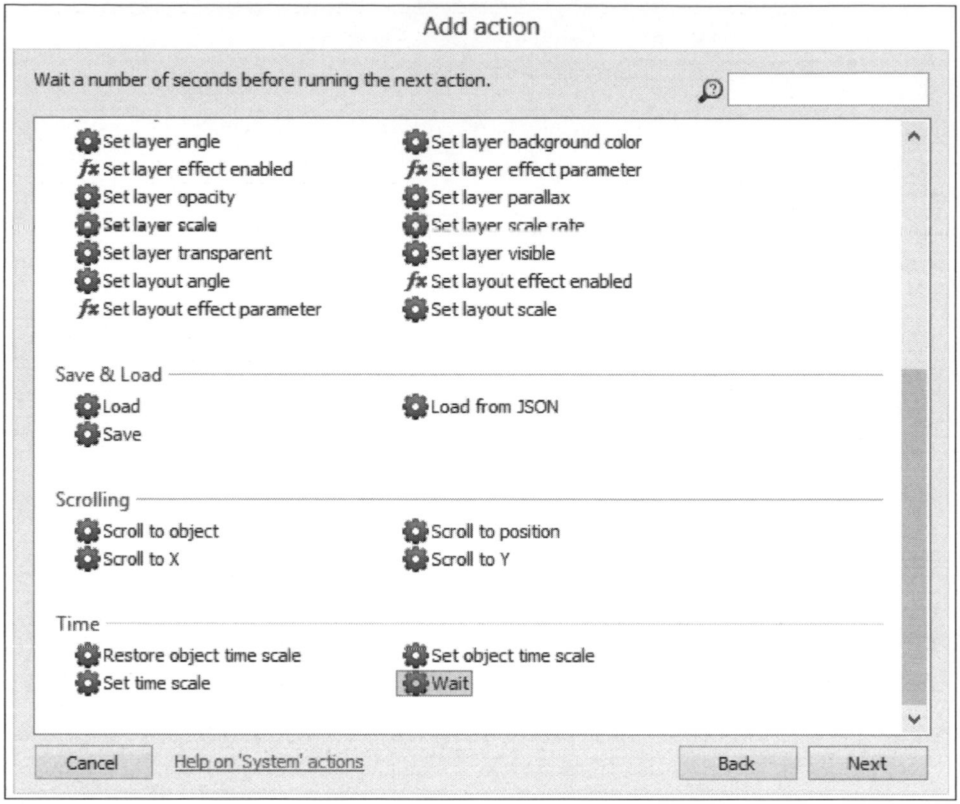

Let's wait for a few seconds; we will set the value of **Seconds** to `2.5` seconds, as shown in the following screenshot:

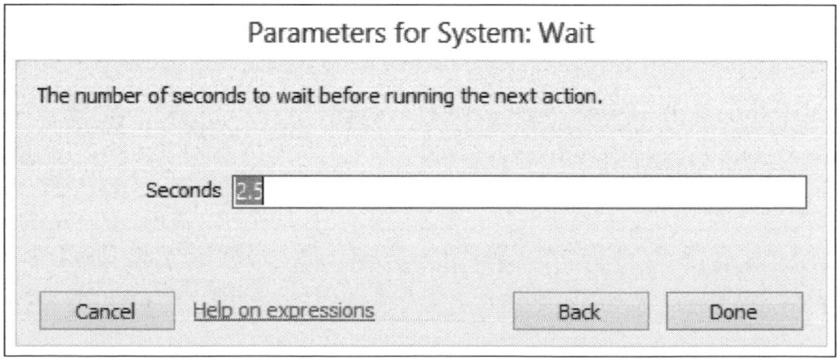

We also need to move the action up in the order of actions. Highlight it and drag it to the top. Remember that the actions are read line by line, which means that the first action will happen first, and so on. In this case, it will wait for 2.5 seconds and then destroy the object. Run the game and try it out.

4	cannonBall	Physics Overall velocity ≤ 0.1	System	Wait **2.5** seconds
			cannonB...	Destroy
			Add action	
Add event				

Designing our level

Let's add some level design. Go to the right area of the layout and add some blocks. As you can see in the following screenshot, we've placed them with a gap between each other. They will fall down; but sometimes if you start a game with an object too close to another, the collision detection can malfunction.

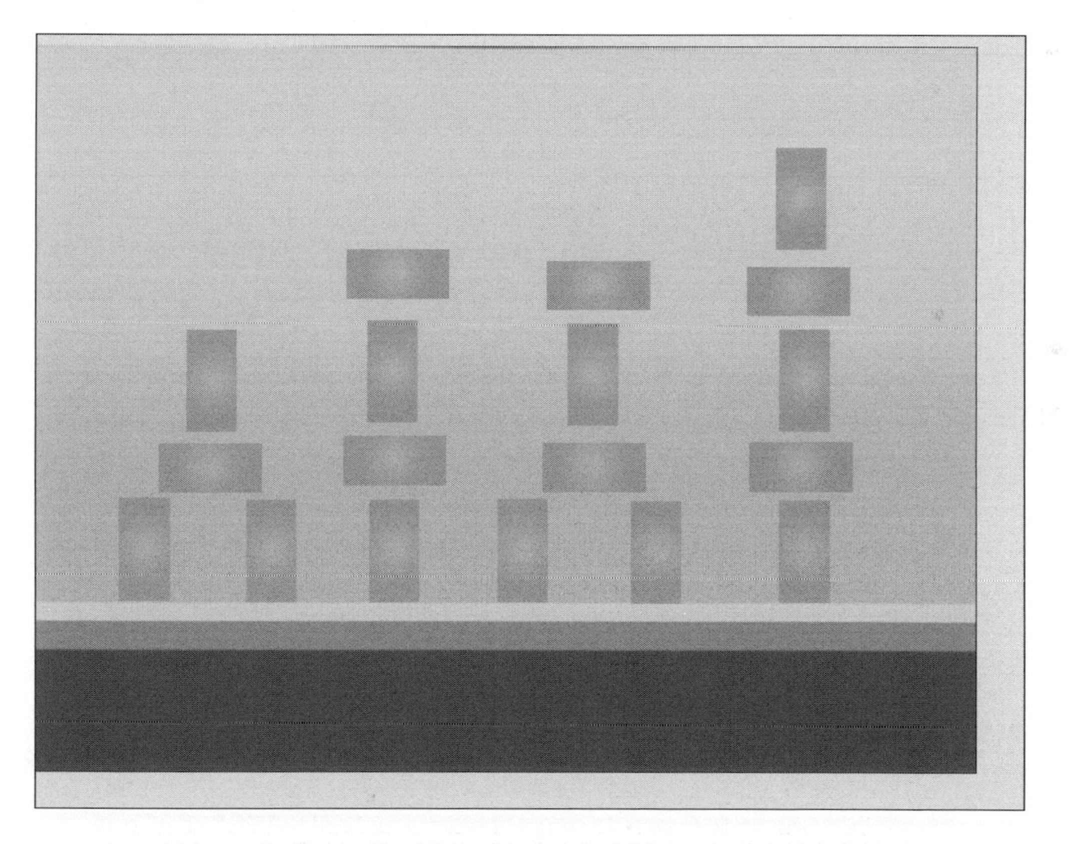

Changing block density

Try out the game. You will notice that the cannonball does not really have a big impact on the blocks. Select them all and change **Density** to `0.2`, or you can change it to whatever value you want. This is shown in the following screenshot:

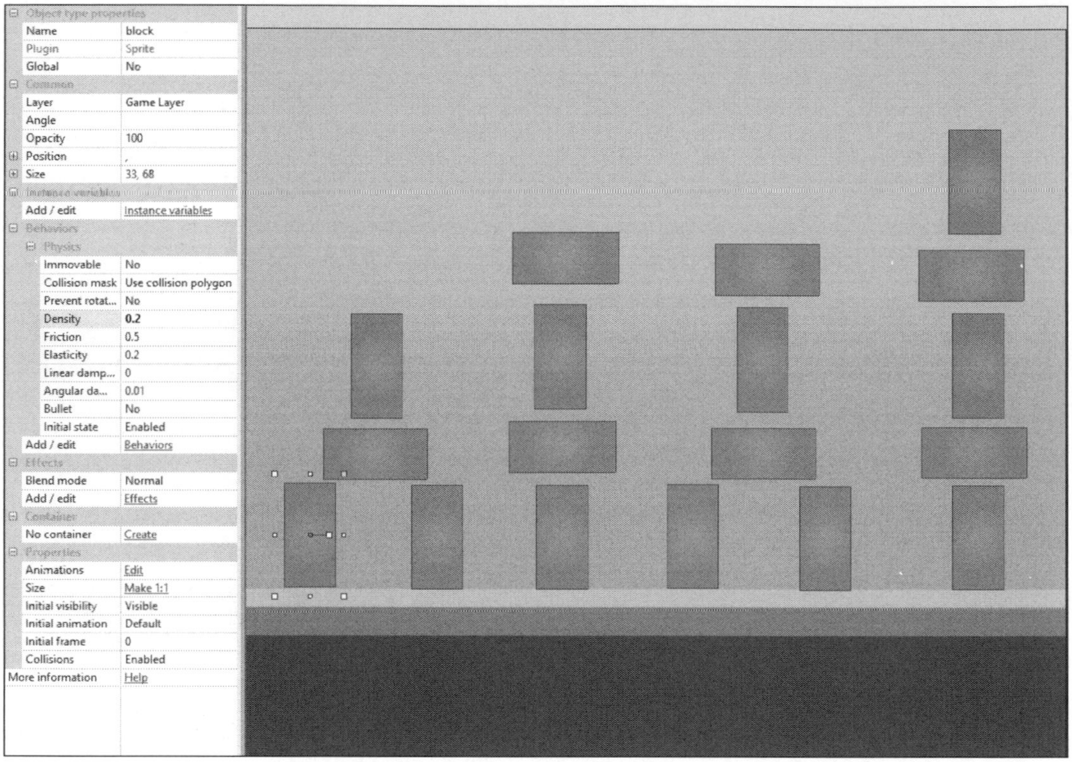

Adding the goal balls

Now, we need to add the `goalBall` sprites. First, add a **Physics** behavior to the `goalBall` sprite, as shown in the following screenshot:

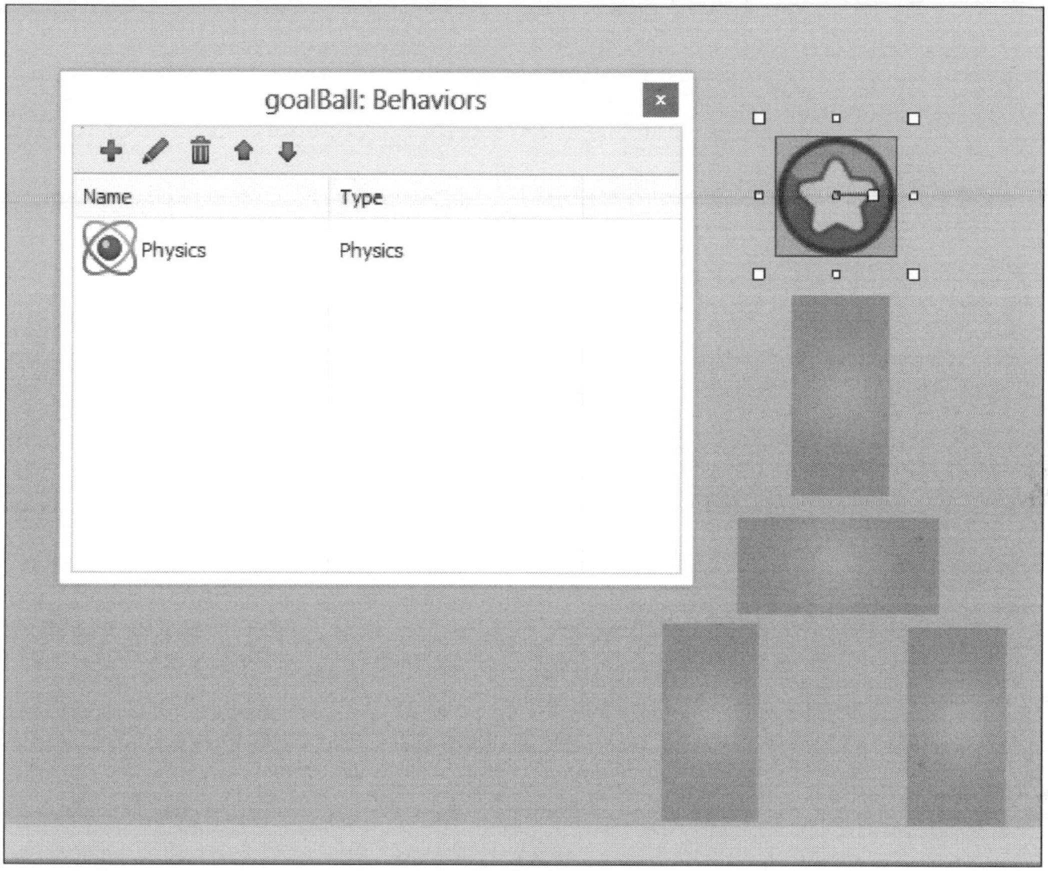

Destroying the goalBall sprite

Next, add more balls to the level and then add an event to the `goalBall` sprite:

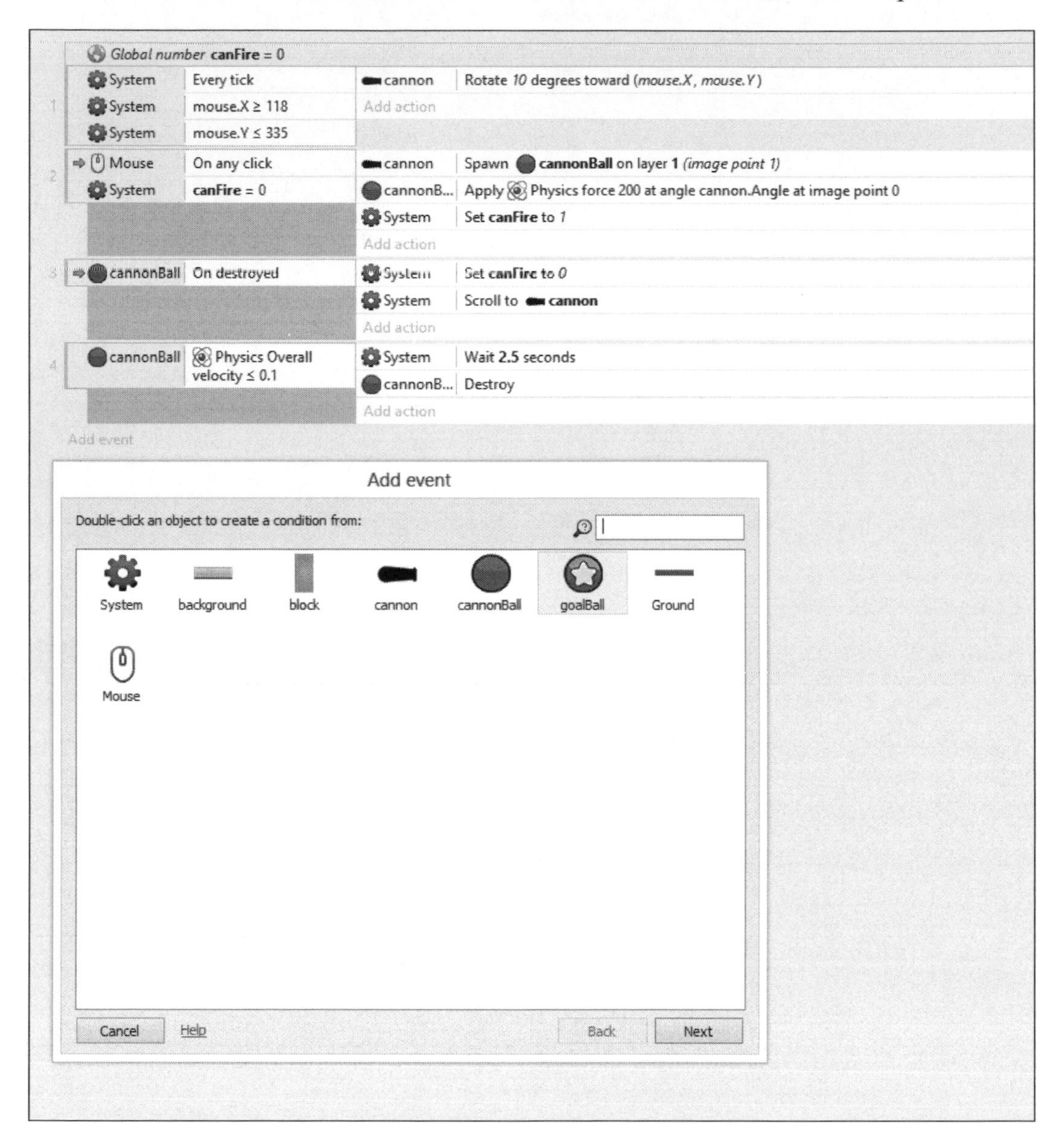
Global number canFire = 0
System | Every tick | cannon | Rotate 10 degrees toward (mouse.X, mouse.Y)
System | mouse.X ≥ 118
System | mouse.Y ≤ 335
Add action
Mouse | On any click | cannon | Spawn cannonBall on layer 1 (image point 1)
System | canFire = 0 | cannonB... | Apply Physics force 200 at angle cannon.Angle at image point 0
System | Set canFire to 1
cannonBall | On destroyed | System | Set canFire to 0
System | Scroll to cannon
cannonBall | Physics Overall velocity ≤ 0.1 | System | Wait 2.5 seconds
cannonB... | Destroy
Add event
Double-click an object to create a condition from:
System
background
block
cannon
cannonBall
goalBall
Ground
Mouse
Cancel
Help
Back
Next

When the `goalBall` sprite touches the ground, we will destroy it, as well as set up some extra functionality.

Add an **On collision with another object** action that checks to see whether the `goalBall` sprite collides with the transparent **Ground** object. This is shown in the following screenshot:

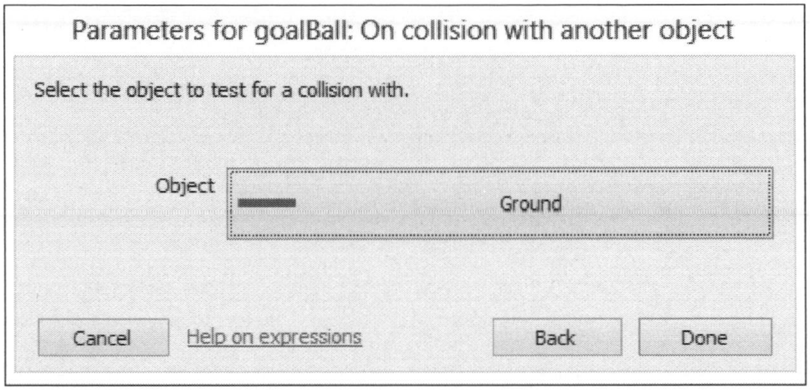

When the `goalBall` sprite touches the **Ground** object, add an action that will destroy the ball. This is shown in the following screenshot:

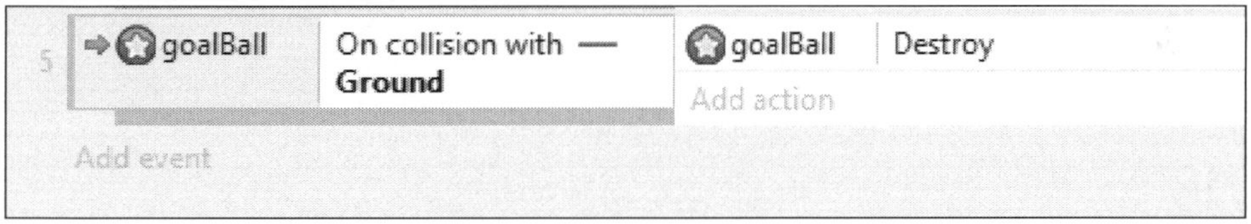

Once you have done this, copy the action by selecting the event and pressing *Ctrl* + *C* and then press *Ctrl* + *V* to paste.

Then, for one of the two actions, change the **On collision with Ground** to **On collision with cannonBall**, as shown in the following screenshot. This will destroy the `goalBall` sprite when the cannonball hits it.

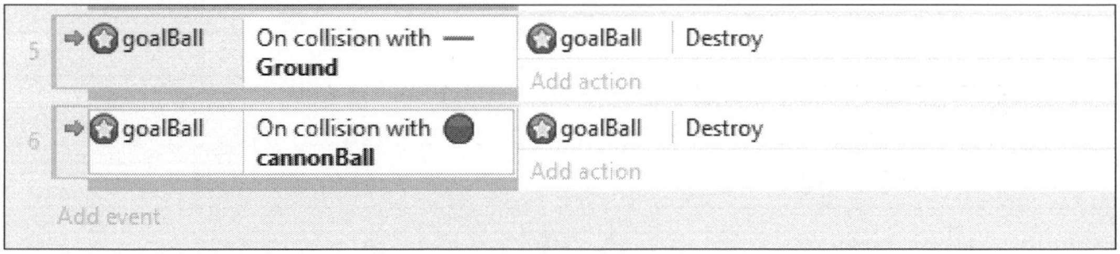

Adding particles

Let's add some particles to make it look better. Go back to the layout, click on **Insert New Object**, and add **Particles**, as shown in the following screenshot:

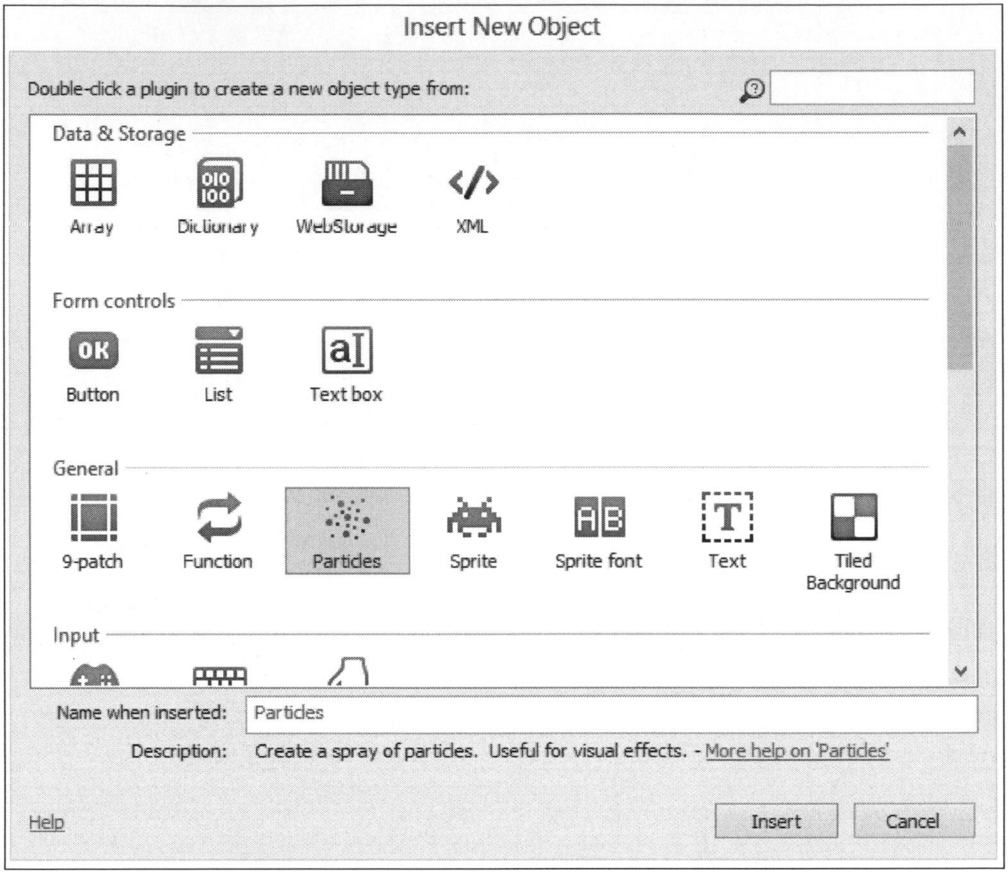

Insert New Object

Double-click a plugin to create a new object type from:

Data & Storage

Array Dictionary WebStorage XML

Form controls

Button List Text box

General

9-patch Function Particles Sprite Sprite font Text Tiled Background

Input

Name when inserted: Particles

Description: Create a spray of particles. Useful for visual effects. - More help on 'Particles'

Help Insert Cancel

When you add a particle emitter, you add an object that spawns lots of two-dimensional images. They are used for things such as explosions, engines, and anything that looks flashy. Double-click on the particles and add a graphic.

Move the particle to the screen and run the game. We want more of an explosion than the way the particles are currently set up.

Adjusting the particle settings

Play around with the settings. We suggest changing **Spray cone** to `360`, **Speed randomizer** to `20` and **Size randomizer** to `20` as well. Also, make sure you change **Type** to `One-shot`. This will make the particles only fire once.

Properties	
Rate	50
Spray cone	360
Type	One-shot
Image	Edit
Initial particle properties	
Speed	200
Size	10
Opacity	100
Grow rate	0
X randomiser	0
Y randomiser	0
Speed randomis...	20
Size randomiser	20
Grow rate rando...	0
Particle lifetime properties	
Acceleration	-150
Gravity	0
Angle randomiser	0
Speed randomiser	800
Opacity random...	0
Destroy mode	Fade to invisible
Timeout	1
More information	Help

Adding particles when goalBall is destroyed

Go back to the event sheet and add an action to the `goalBall` sprite's **On collision with ground**. Add a **Spawn another object** parameter to `goalBall`. Make sure it is spawned at the **Layer** point value `1`, as shown in the following screenshot:

Parameters for goalBall: Spawn another object

The layer name or number to create the instance on.

Object: explosion

Layer: 1

Image point: 0

Cancel | Help on expressions | Back | Done

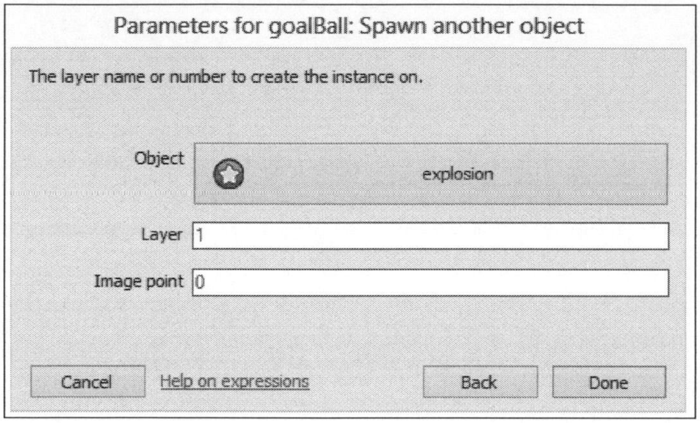

Copy-and-paste this action to the other collision object **On collision with cannonBall** so that there is a particle explosion when the cannonball hits an object. Then, copy the collision object, but change it so that it is activated when this `goalBall` collides with another `goalBall` sprite. Check the following screenshot:

#	Object	Condition	Object	Action
5	goalBall	On collision with Ground	goalBall	Destroy
			goalBall	Spawn explosion on layer 1 *(image point 0)*
			Add action	
6	goalBall	On collision with cannonBall	goalBall	Destroy
			goalBall	Spawn explosion on layer 1 *(image point 0)*
			Add action	
7	goalBall	On collision with goalBall	goalBall	Destroy
			goalBall	Spawn explosion on layer 1 *(image point 0)*
			Add action	

Add event

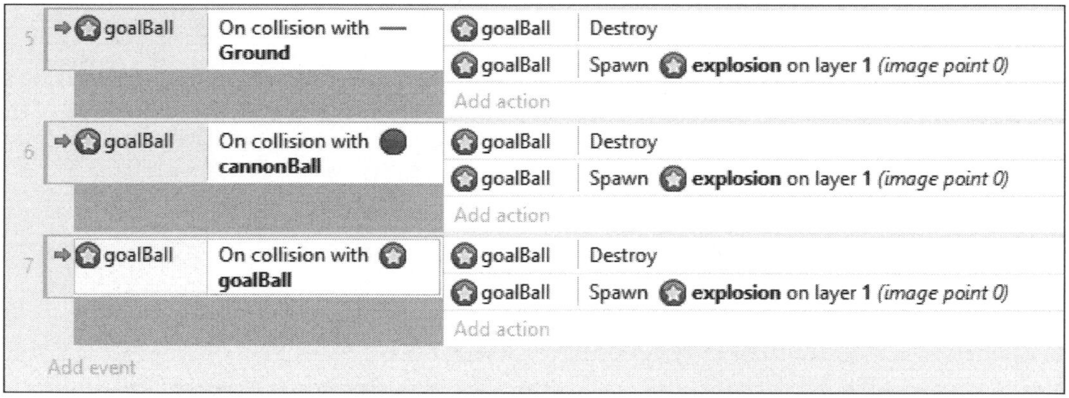

Tracking the score

Let's set things up so that we can track a score for destroying the `goalBall` sprites. Add another global variable and name it `Score`, as shown in the following screenshot:

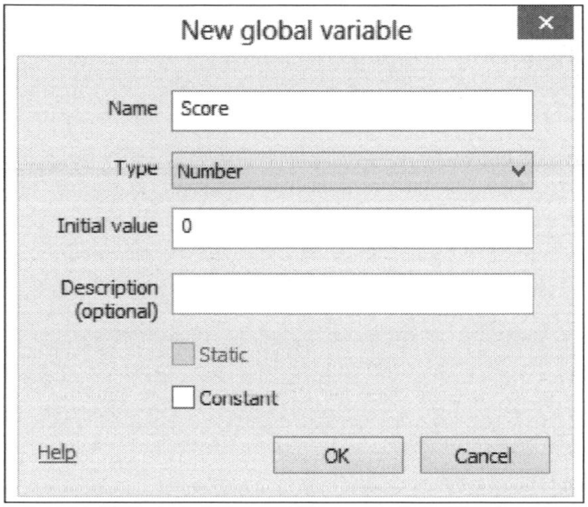

Then, add another `goalBall` action. This time, make it an **Add to** action that adds to the value of **Score**. Let's insert `100` in the **Value** field, as shown in the following screenshot:

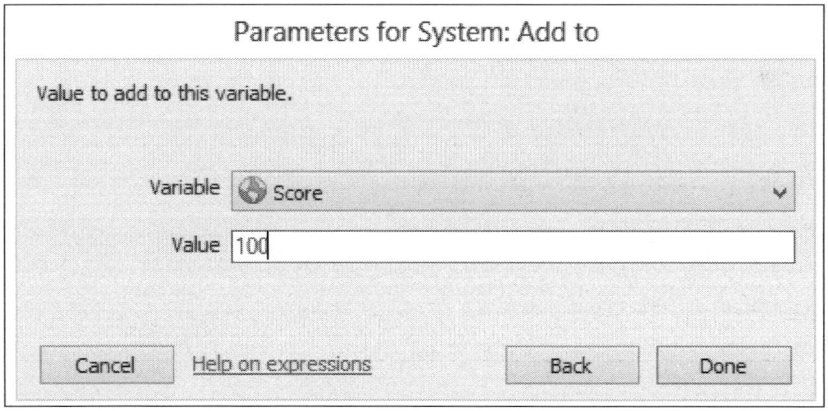

Then, just copy-and-paste this action to all the other `goalBall` collision events. Now, every time a `goalBall` sprite is destroyed, your player's score will increase by 100!

Adding text objects to the HUD

Next, we're going to create a HUD to tell the player what their score is. Let's start by adding a textbox to the screen. Click on **Insert New Object** and select **Text** from the **General** section.

> Our new textbox doesn't look that exciting, so I'd suggest changing the size and font style. I've changed mine to Arial, Narrow Bold Italic, and size 36. It's best to stick to common fonts—Construct 2 draws on the font files available on the player's computer and if they don't have the same file as the one you have, it will substitute for a default that might not look proper.

Spawning the textbox

In order for the textbox to appear, we need to spawn it just like any other game object. Rewrite the text in the textbox to `+100`. This textbox will be spawned when the `goalBall` sprite is destroyed.

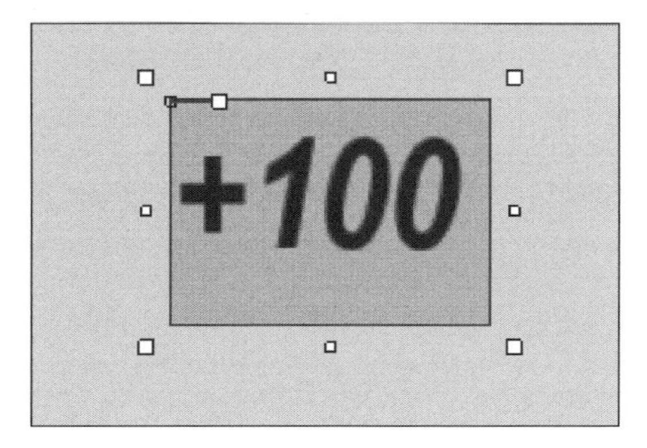

Add a new **On every tick** event, and then add a **Move at angle** action to the new textbox. This is shown in the following screenshot:

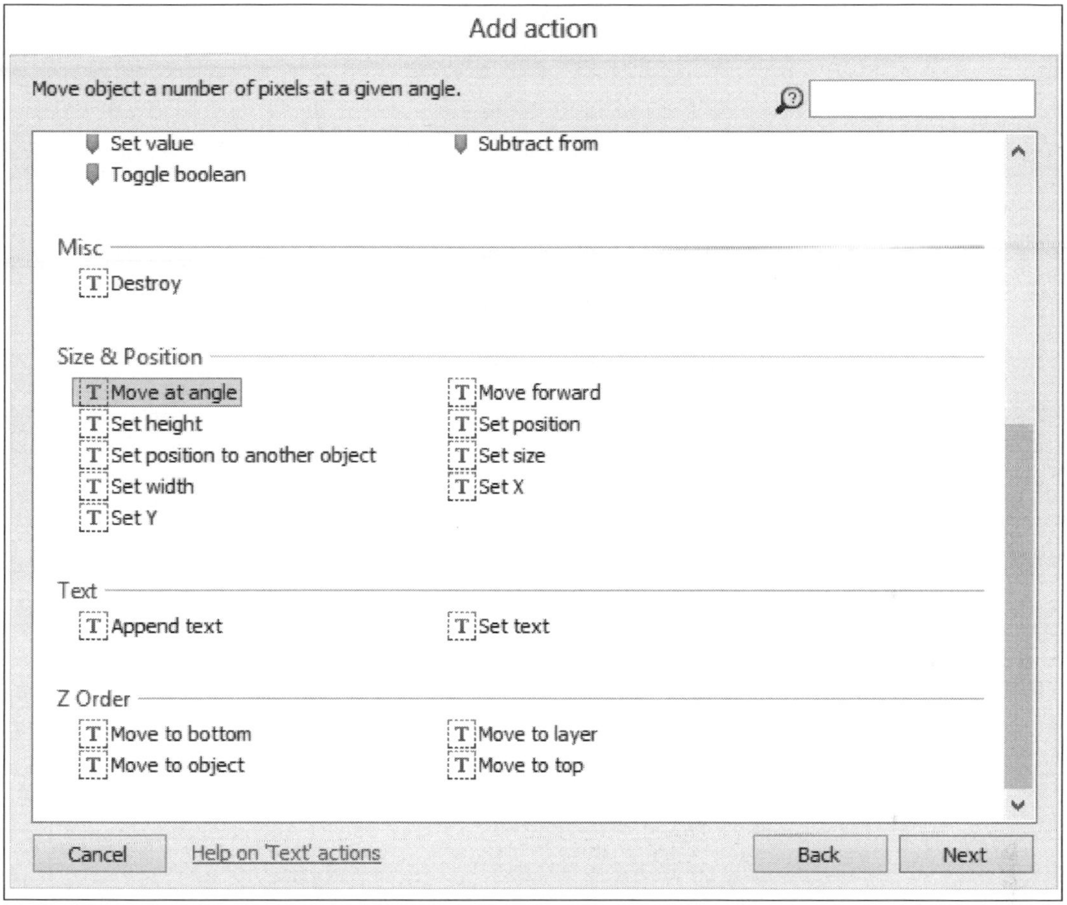

Add action

Move object a number of pixels at a given angle.

Set value
Subtract from
Toggle boolean

Misc
Destroy

Size & Position
Move at angle
Move forward
Set height
Set position
Set position to another object
Set size
Set width
Set X
Set Y

Text
Append text
Set text

Z Order
Move to bottom
Move to layer
Move to object
Move to top

Cancel
Help on 'Text' actions
Back
Next

Set the angle to `270`, which is the angle for directly upwards in the game engine. Set the distance to `8`.

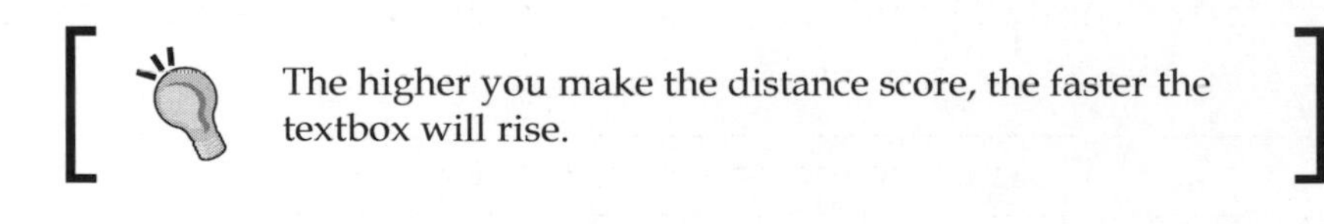

The higher you make the distance score, the faster the textbox will rise.

Parameters for textScore: Move at angle

Angle, in degrees, at which to move the object.

Angle 270

Distance 8

Cancel Help on expressions Back Done

Make a copy of the `goalBall` action that spawns the particle explosion, and then change the settings so that instead of spawning the explosion, it will spawn the textbox.

Parameters for goalBall: Spawn another object

Choose the object type of the new instance to create.

Object textScore

Layer 1

Image point 0

Cancel Help on expressions Back Done

Correcting the spawning angle

When we run the game, we can see that the textbox is spawned at an odd angle. To correct this, we'll add a **Set angle** action to the textbox and set the angle to `0`, as shown in the following screenshot:

Parameters for textScore: Set angle

New object angle, in degrees.

Angle 0

Cancel Help on expressions Back Done

Expanding the HUD

Now, we need to add the rest of the HUD to show the ongoing score and other information we need to give the player. In most cases, it is best to have the HUD as its own layer. Add a new layer and name it `HUD`.

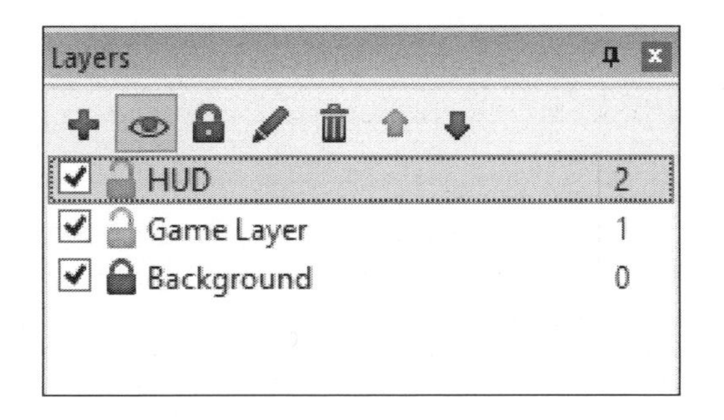

Create a new textbox and move it to the bottom-left corner. Make sure it is outside the game area.

The current size and color of the text isn't great. I'd advise you to change the text to make it bigger, and also change the color to white from the **Properties** panel.

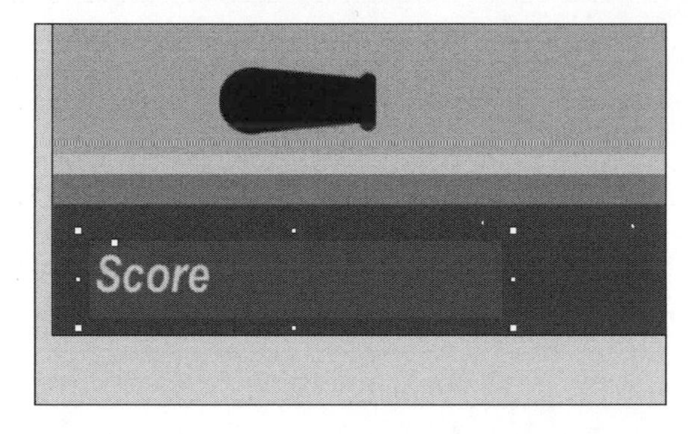

Change the name of the textbox to `HUDscore`, and then add a `HUDscore` action to the **On every tick** event. We're going to add a **Set text** action to `HUDscore`. Set the text to `"Score: "&Score`. This will mean that the HUD textbox will read **Score:**, which we wrote in the quotation marks, and then it will print the exact variable score achieved from `destroy goalBalls`. Make sure you insert a space after the colon of `"Score: "`; otherwise, one won't appear in the game.

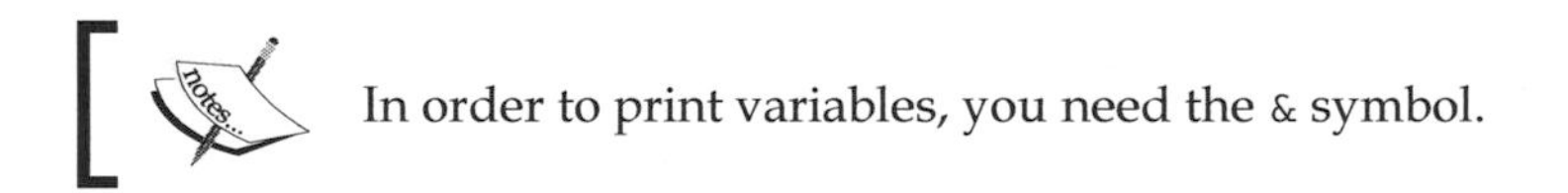

In order to print variables, you need the `&` symbol.

Your event should look like the following screenshot:

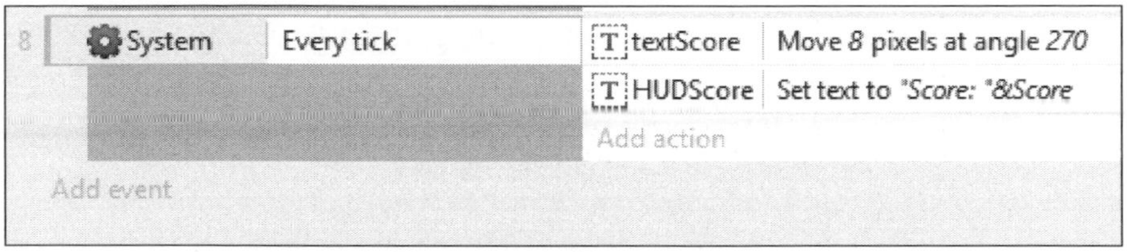

Anchoring the HUD to the camera

If you run the game, you will notice that the score does not follow the camera. This is because we have to anchor it to the screen. Click on the HUD box and add an **Anchor** behavior. This will set the position of the text object to the camera and it will not move.

Setting up an HUD cannonball tracker

Next, we'll set up a tracker for our remaining cannonballs. Right-click on our **Score** textbox and select the `Clone` object type. Change the textbox content to `Balls Left` and add a global variable named `ballsLeft`, as shown in the following screenshot:

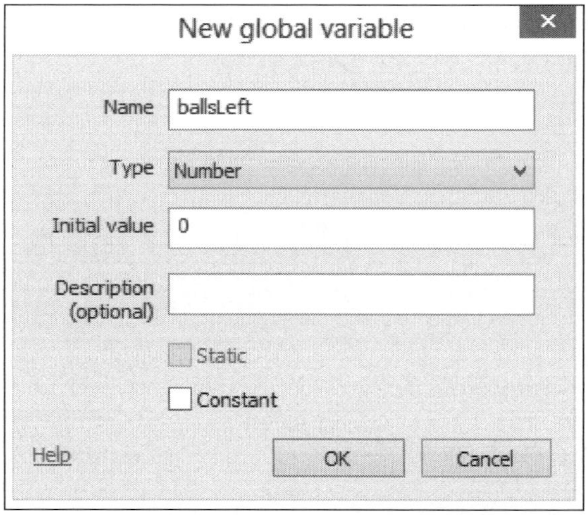

Add another action to the **On destroyed** event for the cannonball and make it a **Subtract from** action. We want to subtract `1` from the `ballsLeft` variable so that the count decreases as each cannonball is fired and destroyed. This is shown in the following screenshot:

Parameters for System: Subtract from
Choose the variable to change.
Variable ballsLeft
Value 1
Cancel Help on expressions Back Done

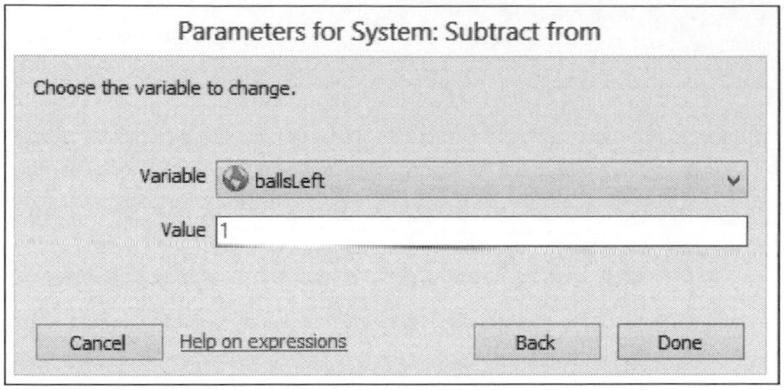

Set the value for the cannonball tracking box to `"Balls Left: "&BallsLeft` so that it will automatically update in the same way as the score tracker.

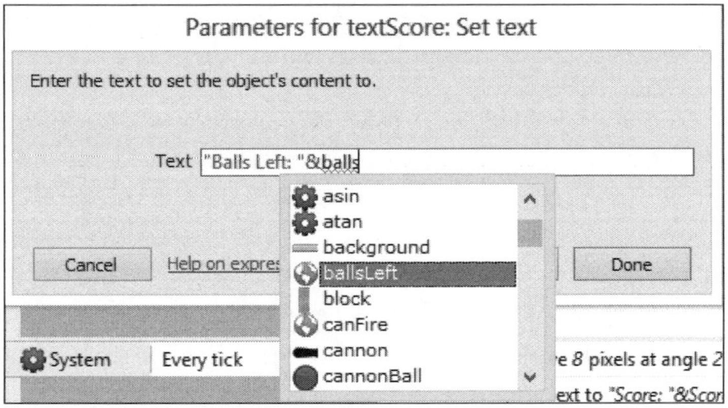

Parameters for textScore: Set text
Enter the text to set the object's content to.
Text "Balls Left: "&balls
asin
atan
background
ballsLeft
block
canFire
cannon
cannonBall
Cancel Help on expres Done
System Every tick e 8 pixels at angle 2
ext to "Score: "&Scor

Your **Every tick** event should therefore look like the following screenshot:

8 System	Every tick	textScore	Move *8* pixels at angle *270*
		HUDScore	Set text to *"Score: "&Score*
		textScore	Set text to *"Balls Left: "&ballsLeft*
		Add action	
Add event			

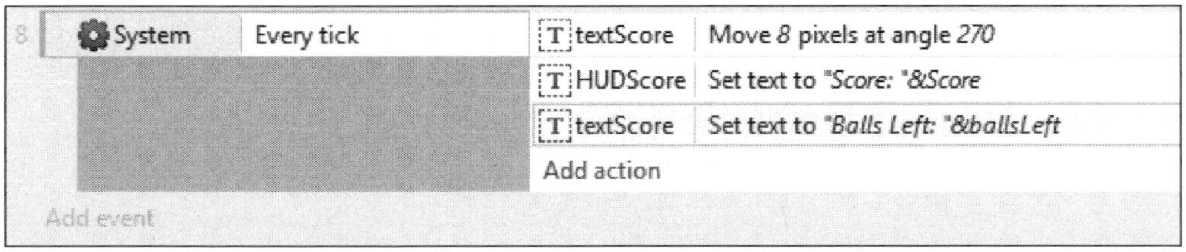

To set the number of cannonballs available, just change the `ballsLeft` global number to whatever you want.

Finalizing the game

Let's add some logic in order to finalize winning and losing our game. Often, the finalization of the game is the hardest part. Most indie developers lose interest and stop producing the game.

Losing the game

Add another textbox, make the text say `"Game Over"`, and change the text size so that it's nice and prominent. Place the textbox somewhere prominent and make note of its position.

Then, we need to add a **Compare variable** event that should compare the variable `ballsLeft` to be **≤ Less than or equal** to `0`. Then, set the position of the `Game Over` text object to the position of the text object noted before.

Make another global variable named `isPlaying`, as shown in the following screenshot:

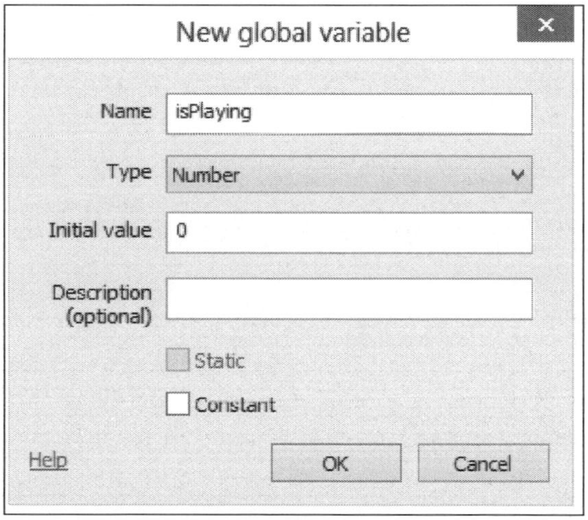

Add an action that sets `isPlaying` to `1` when the `ballsLeft` variable count is equal or less than zero. Then, add a condition (by pressing *C*) to the **On any click** mouse event. The condition is to see whether `isPlaying` is equal to `0`.

Restarting the game on Game Over

When the game is over, we need a way to reset it. Add a **On object clicked** mouse event and set the object to be clicked as **textGameOver**. This is shown in the following screenshot:

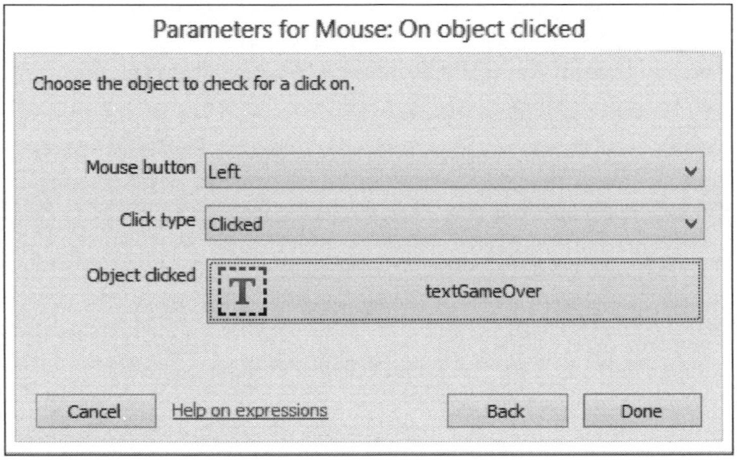

Add a **Restart layout** action and a **Reset global variables to default** action to the **Object clicked** event, as shown in the following screenshot. This will restart the game.

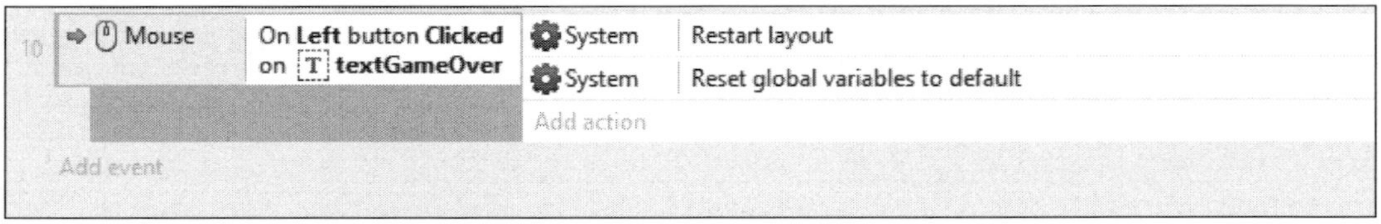

Winning the game

Add two global variables. Name one variable `goalBallCount` and the other one `cannonballCount`. These variables will keep track of the number of `goalBall` and `cannonBall` sprites on the screen, as shown in the following screenshot:

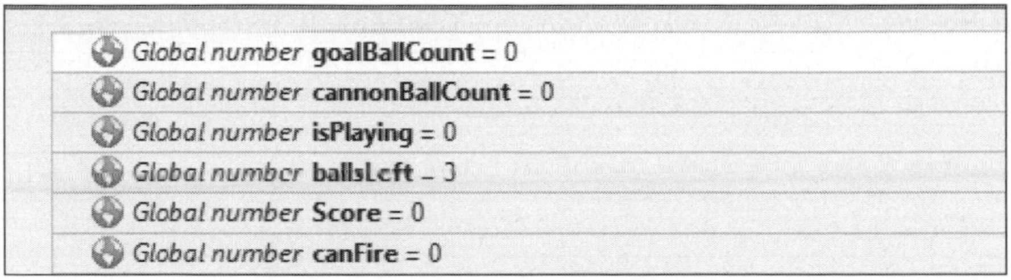

Global number **goalBallCount** = 0
Global number **cannonBallCount** = 0
Global number **isPlaying** = 0
Global number **ballsLeft** = 3
Global number **Score** = 0
Global number **canFire** = 0

Add an **On created** event to `goalBall` and make an **Add 1 to goalBallCount** action, as shown in the following screenshot:

#	Object	Event	Object	Action
11	goalBall	On created	System	Add *1* to **goalBallCount**
				Add action
Add event				

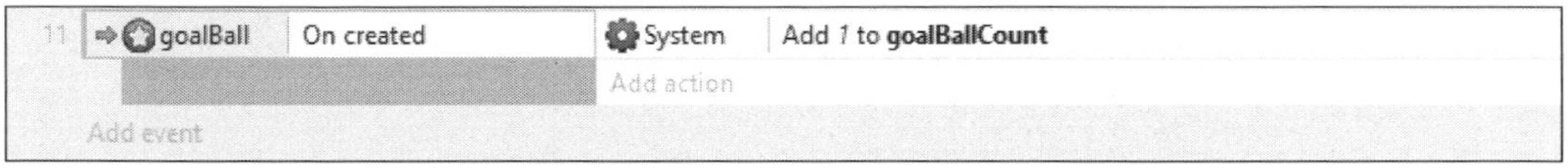

Then, for each **On collision with goalBall** event for our `goalBall` sprites, navigate to **System** and add **Subtract 1 from goalBallCount**. This is shown in the following screenshot:

#	Object	Event	Object	Action
5	goalBall	On collision with **Ground**	goalBall	Destroy
			goalBall	Spawn **explosion** on layer **1** *(image point 0)*
			System	Add *100* to **Score**
			goalBall	Spawn **textScore** on layer **1** *(image point 0)*
			textScore	Set angle to *0* degrees
			System	Subtract *1* from **goalBallCount**
				Add action
6	goalBall	On collision with **cannonBall**	goalBall	Destroy
			goalBall	Spawn **explosion** on layer **1** *(image point 0)*
			System	Add *100* to **Score**
			goalBall	Spawn **textScore** on layer **1** *(image point 0)*
			textScore	Set angle to *0* degrees
			System	Subtract *1* from **goalBallCount**
				Add action
7	goalBall	On collision with **goalBall**	goalBall	Destroy
			goalBall	Spawn **explosion** on layer **1** *(image point 0)*
			System	Add *100* to **Score**
			goalBall	Spawn **textScore** on layer **1** *(image point 0)*
			textScore	Set angle to *0* degrees
			System	Subtract *1* from **goalBallCount**
				Add action

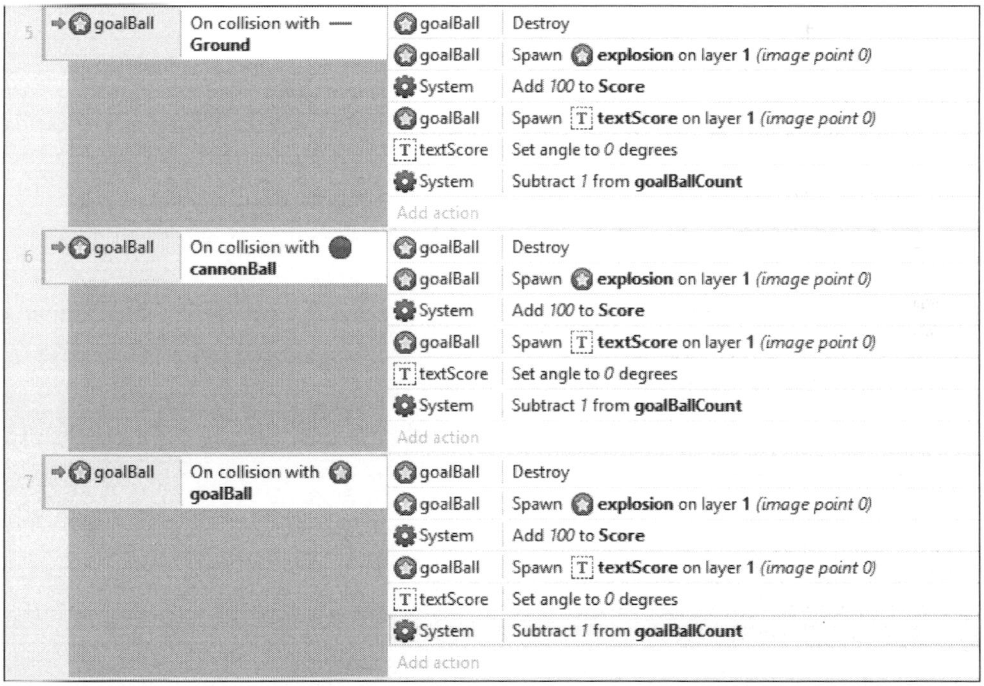

Add an **On created** event to `cannonBall`, and navigate to **System** to add an **Add 1 to cannonBallCount** action.

11	cannonBall	On created	System	Add *1* to **cannonBallCount**
			Add action	

In the **On destroyed** event of the `cannonBall` sprite, add a **Subtract 1 from cannonBallCount** action. This is shown in the following screenshot:

3	cannonBall	On destroyed	System	Set **canFire** to *0*
			System	Scroll to **cannon**
			System	Subtract *1* from **cannonBallCount**
			Add action	

Copy the last two events we made. Add a condition to the **ballsLeft ≤ 0** event by pressing the *C* key. Add a compare variable event to compare whether **cannonBallCount** is less than or equal to zero. Once you have done this, copy the event and change **cannonBallCount** to **goalBallCount**. This will cause the event to activate if there are no `goalBall` or `cannonBall` sprites left on the screen.

9	System	**ballsLeft** ≤ 0	textGam...	Set position to (*1*, *65*)
	System	**cannonBallCount** ≤ 0	System	Set **isPlaying** to *1*
			Add action	
10	System	**ballsLeft** ≤ 0	textGam...	Set position to (*1*, *65*)
	System	**cannonBallCount** ≤ 0	System	Set **isPlaying** to *1*
			Add action	

Add a **Set text** action to **textGameOver**; only this time, make it say **You Win!**. Check the following screenshot:

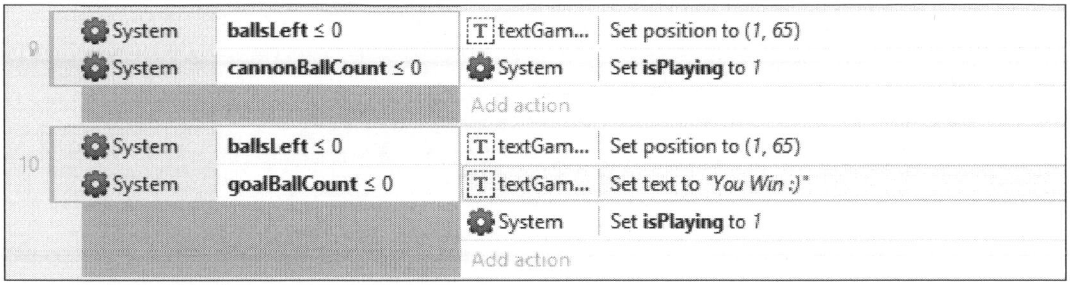

#	Object	Condition	Object	Action
9	System	**ballsLeft** ≤ 0	textGam...	Set position to (*1*, *65*)
	System	**cannonBallCount** ≤ 0	System	Set **isPlaying** to *1*
			Add action	
10	System	**ballsLeft** ≤ 0	textGam...	Set position to (*1*, *65*)
	System	**goalBallCount** ≤ 0	textGam...	Set text to *"You Win :)"*
			System	Set **isPlaying** to *1*
			Add action	

Summary

In this chapter, we learned how to set up a puzzle physics game—setting up physics, particle effects, and adding in the logic to win and lose the game. You can now modify this game and add as many features as you like.

In the next chapter, we will cover how to export your game to multiple locations.

8 Exporting Your Game

In the past, developing a game for multiple systems was tough. Often, developers would have to make the game from scratch for every system they deployed to. In order to get around this problem, they created libraries that could be used across platforms. Luckily, this problem is now solved, and one of the best ways to solve it is HTML5 games.

In this chapter, we will cover the following topics:

- Hosting our game on Dropbox publically
- Exporting our game to an HTML5 website
- Exporting our game to web stores, web arcades, and for mobile devices

Exporting games in Construct 2

One of the best features about Construct 2 is that you can export your games to many locations. If you are new to game development, then this seems normal; most engines try to export to multiple locations. However, this wasn't always the case. In the past, if you wanted to develop a game for two different systems, it meant doing a lot of work behind the scenes. Construct 2 solves this problem by exporting to HTML5.

HTML5 is used in order to have a consistent browser experience between platforms in order to have websites that have the same quality through multiple platforms. This means that if you view your game on a mobile device, it will run the same as on a desktop or any other device.

"But you said websites, and not games!"

I did just say that, but you can also have games on the web. In the past, web games have typically been Flash games. HTML5 games are slowly replacing Flash games, as Flash games cannot run on some mobile devices.

Since HTML5 games can run on a web browser, it stands to reason that they can run everywhere—on a mobile device, console, laptop, or desktop. For the most part, this is true. You can run HTML5 games pretty much everywhere, but it will depend on the hardware provider to support HTML5.

Setting up a Dropbox account

One way to test your game early to see how it performs in a real environment is uploading it to a Dropbox account. You preview the game on your computer, but it isn't the same as uploading it to a website. The reason is that the resources on your computer are much greater than the resources on the server.

If you do not already have one, you can get a free account at `www.dropbox.com`.

Once you have a Dropbox account, you can export the game.

Exporting to an HTML5 website

The most basic form of exporting your game will be to an HTML5 website. This HTML5 website functions much like a website for any other purpose. The main file here is the **index**. However, before you do all of that, you need to click on the export button. You can press *F6* or you can go to **Export Project** under the **File** menu. The following screenshot shows the export window that will come up:

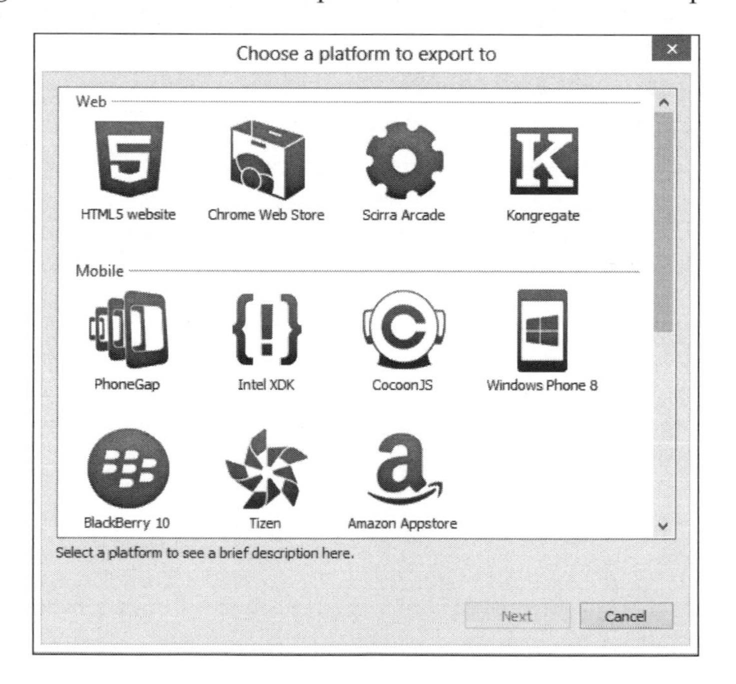

This window is where you can choose the platform you are going to export to. As you can see, there are different areas that you can export to. The most basic one you are going to export to is the HTML5 website. You will probably do this most often. Select the **HTML5 website** and click on the **Next** button, as shown in the preceding screenshot. For most projects, you will need to find a folder to export to. In this case, you will export the folder to the desktop. This way, you can easily drag it to Dropbox or any other website. The contents of the folder will be different, depending on the kind of project you are exporting to. In most cases, if you are uploading to a specific store, there are more specific steps that you have to take to publish on that platform. The following screenshot is of the export window:

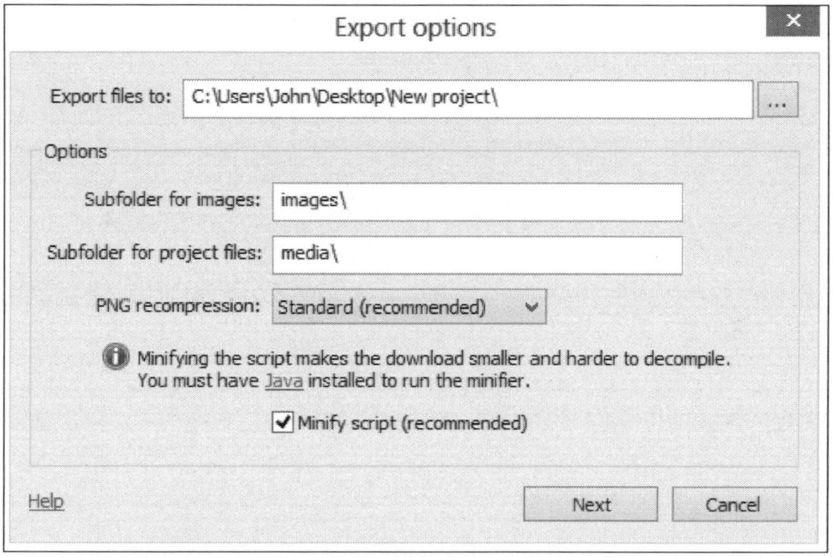

Choosing the template for your HTML5 export

Once we've selected **HTML5 website** and clicked on **Next**, the **HTML5 export options** window will appear, as shown in the following screenshot. As you can see, there are many different options. For most of your games, you want to use the **Normal style**. This is what most of your games will look like. If you want to monetize your game, you can select the **Advert bar style**. If you want to imbed your game in an `iframe` tag, you should choose the **Embed style**. The `iframe` tag is an HTML tag that deals with frames. If you want to export your game to a WordPress blog or website, this is the best option.

Once you have selected a style, click on the **Export** button. You should get the following dialog box when you are finished:

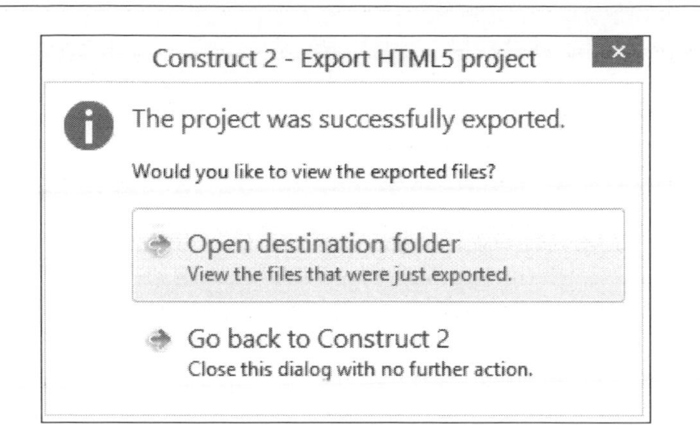

Click on **Open destination folder**. This will open the folder on the computer that has your game.

Assessing the contents of the game folder

Whenever you export a game, it will be contained in a folder of some kind. The following screenshot shows the contents of the destination folder—our new game folder:

images	10/3/2013 15:32	File folder
c2runtime	10/3/2013 15:32	JavaScript File
icon-16	10/3/2013 9:26	PNG image
icon-32	10/3/2013 9:26	PNG image
icon-114	10/3/2013 9:26	PNG image
icon-128	10/3/2013 9:26	PNG image
index	10/3/2013 15:32	Chrome HTML Do...
jquery-2.0.0.min	9/3/2013 13:31	JavaScript File
loading-logo	10/3/2013 9:26	PNG image
offline.appcache	10/3/2013 15:32	APPCACHE File

Here, you can see what an HTML5 game looks like in a folder. You can see that there is an images folder that has all of your images—this contains the various icons associated with your game. If you want to make custom icons, pull up the icons in Photoshop or a similar image editing program and save your new icons over the top of the file. It is important to make the change this way, as most platforms only accept a certain resolution of file.

The main item I want to draw your attention to is the `index` file. This file is the main web page of your game. The functionality of the game comes from the two JavaScript files. If you want, you can take a look at how it is coded in JavaScript. You can simply double-click on the file to view it.

Uploading and sharing a game with Dropbox

Let's upload your game to your Dropbox account. From there, you can share it with your friends. Open up your Dropbox folder and then open the `public` folder. The `public` folder will allow everybody to see the game. Drag-and-drop your game folder into the Dropbox folder. Once it has been uploaded, take a look inside. It should look something like the following screenshot:

images	folder	--
c2runtime.js	code js	5 secs ago
icon-16.png	image png	7 secs ago
icon-32.png	image png	9 secs ago
icon-114.png	image png	6 secs ago
icon-128.png	image png	7 secs ago
index.html	code html	9 secs ago
jquery-2.0.0.min.js	code js	10 secs ago
loading-logo.png	image png	10 secs ago
offline.appcache	file appcache	11 secs ago

As you can see, these are the same files you had in the other folder. What you need to do is right-click on the `index.html` file and paste that link into your web browser, as shown in the following screenshot:

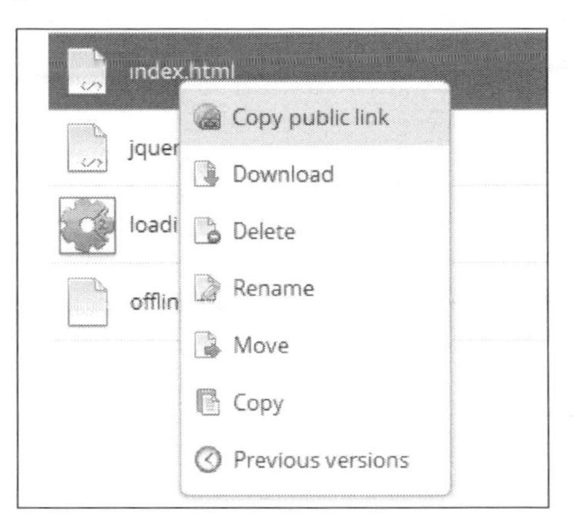

This is what most of your players are going to see when they play your game. Feel free to share the link with all of your friends for feedback. It should look something like the following screenshot that shows one of our games running in the browser:

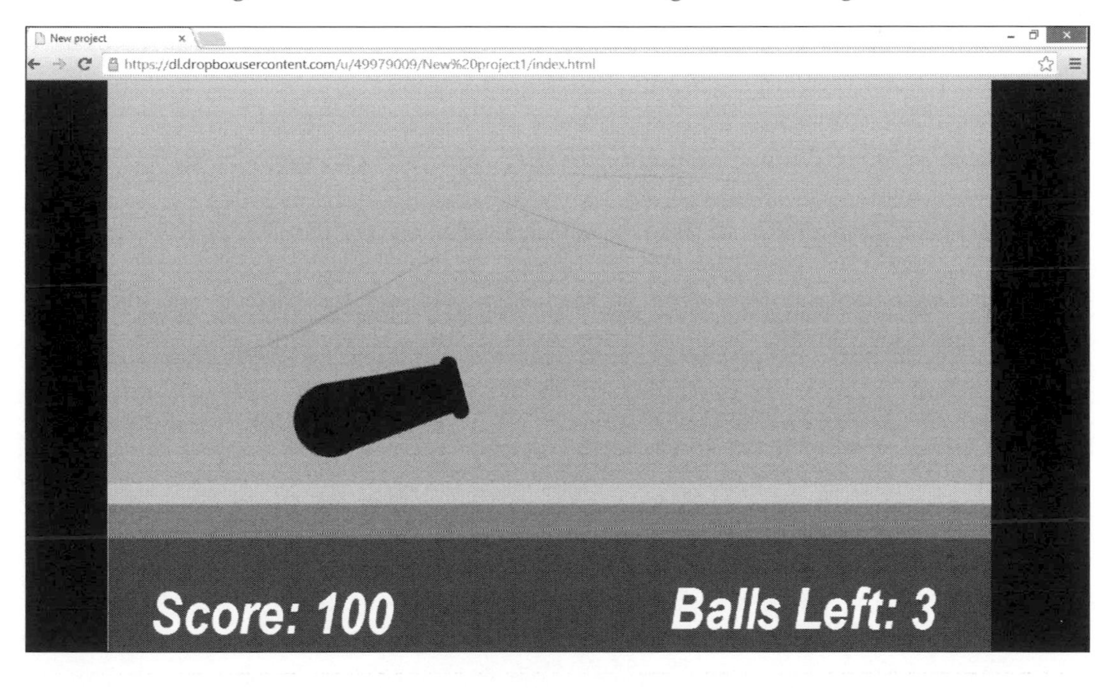

Other places to export your game

There are many more places you can export your game to. Remember that for every platform that you export to, there can be a completely different set of hardware and software that run it. An iPhone is very different from an Android device, and mobile devices are completely different from consoles.

Often, an HTML5 wrapper has to be used for an HTML5 game to run on the hardware.

Exporting to Chrome Web Store

The **Chrome Web Store** is Google's answer to the Mac App Store. The best part about Google is that it is very web friendly. In fact, Chrome is the best browser for HTML5 games. You can export a game to the Chrome Web Store where you can sell it or make it freely available.

In order to export to the Chrome Web Store, you need to perform the following steps:

1. Sign up for a Google Chrome Web Store account.
2. Export your game using the Google Chrome Web Store export in the same way as you exported your game for HTML5.
3. Create some promotional images for the game. They have to be in a specific resolution. These resolutions change all the time. So, make sure that you find out what they are when you log in to the Chrome Web Store and upload your app.
4. Create an app icon.

Once you have these items, you can upload to the Chrome Web Store.

Exporting to Scirra Arcade

Scirra Arcade is made by the people who made Construct 2 and it is a very good arcade for people to publish their games. Publishing to the Scirra Arcade can give you lots of great feedback and exposure. Because it is made by the Construct 2 developers, there should be very few (if any) problems in exporting to this platform. In order to upload to the Scirra Arcade, you need to perform the following steps:

1. Sign up for a Scirra Arcade account at `http://www.scirra.com/arcade`.
2. Export your game to the Scirra Arcade in the same way as you exported your game for HTML5.
3. Upload your game to the Scirra Arcade through your Scirra Arcade account.
4. Make sure you have the necessary promotional images! The following screenshot shows the icon for the Scirra Arcade:

Exporting to Kongregate

Kongregate is an online hosting service that hosts free-to-play games. Kongregate has a lot of web traffic and if you have a good game, you should upload it there. You will need to sign up for a Kongregate account. In order to upload to Kongregate, you need to perform the following steps:

1. Export the game as an HTML5 website.
2. Download Kongregate's JavaScript API located at `http://developers.kongregate.com/docs/api-overview/client-api`.
3. Extract the contents using a file unzipper and drag them over to the game's content folder that was created when you exported the game.
4. Open the `kongregate_shell.html` file and add the following code at the bottom:

```
<div id="contentdiv" style="top:0px; left:0px; width:700px;
  height:500px; borders:none;"></div>
```

5. Place the following code within the content div. You should put the following code before the </div> tag:

```
<iframesrc = "index.html" width = "[gamewidth]" height =
  "[gameheight]">
<p>This Browser does not support the iFrame.</p>
  </iframe>
```

6. Sign up for a Kongregate account.
7. Upload your HTML5 game. The Kongregate icon looks like the following screenshot:

Exporting to PhoneGap

PhoneGap is a wrapper that makes it easy for web applications to be run on native devices such as mobiles. The way it works is that you make your web app, in this case an HTML5 game, and you wrap it with PhoneGap. When you export your HTML5 project to PhoneGap, it has to wrap it in order for it to work. Then, you can deploy your app to multiple platforms. The following screenshot shows the icon of PhoneGap:

Exporting to Intel XDK

Intel XDK is similar to PhoneGap—it acts as a wrapper for your HTML5 web app and makes it deployable to phone devices. The differences between the two will depend on your game as the backend of these apps is completely different. When you are exporting to a mobile device, try these wrappers out. Depending on what is in your game, it could affect the outcome. When you do wrap web apps to native apps, it doesn't always work the way you want it to. It's best to try multiple wrappers and see which one works best. In order to make an Intel XDK, you need to perform the following steps:

1. Export the game to Intel XDK.
2. Use Direct Canvas when you are exporting.
3. Then, make an app at the Intel XDK website. This entails signing up for an account.
4. Create a game so that it can be modified online.
5. Upload the app. The following screenshot shows the icon for Intel XDK:

Exporting to CocoonJS

CocoonJS is another HTML5 wrapper. The only difference is that CocoonJS is tailored towards games. If you want to make games for the Apps Store or Google Play, then try wrapping your game with CocoonJS. In order to make a game for CocoonJS wrapping, you need to perform the following steps:

1. Export the game using CocoonJS.
2. Test your game with the Cocoon JS launcher. This can be found on Ludei's website at `http://wiki.ludei.com/cocoonjs:launcherapp`.

3. Make sure you sign up for a Google Play or an App Store developers account if you want to deploy to these locations.
4. Upload the app to whichever app store you want. The following screenshot shows the icon for CocoonJS:

Exporting for Windows Phone 8

If you want to make a **Windows Phone 8** game, you will have to download Visual Studio from the Microsoft website. Luckily, Microsoft supports HTML5 in their native apps. You will also need to apply for a developer account, which is also on Microsoft's website. In order to make a Windows Phone 8 app, you need to perform the following steps:

1. Make sure your name, description, and author details can be found in the main layout. You need to do this because Visual Studio requires a project name, as shown in the following screenshot:

About	
Name	New project
Version	1.0.0.0
Description	
ID	com.mycompany.myapp
Author	
Email	
Website	http://

2. Export the game using the Windows Phone 8 app.
3. Open up the app in Visual Studio.
4. Double-click on the app manifest, which should be on the right-hand side.
5. Choose **Create a test certificate**. This creates a certificate unique to your game. The certificate is required to upload the game.
6. Sign up for a Microsoft developer's account.

7. Submit it to the Microsoft Dev Store.

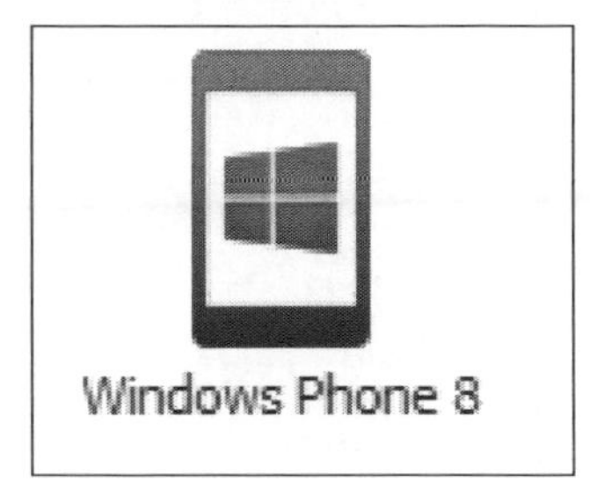

Exporting to Tizen

Tizen is a software platform where you can upload your code once and have it deployed to multiple locations. Like other wrappers, give it a try if you want to export your game to multiple locations. In order to upload to the Tizen Store, you need to perform the following steps:

1. Sign up for a developer account.
2. Export the file to the Tizen exporter.
3. Upload it to the developer account.

Exporting for the Amazon Appstore

Amazon also has an app store. If you want to make a game for the Amazon Appstore, your game has to support multiple screen sizes. (The same is true for any store with devices that have multiple screen sizes.) You also need a developer account at Amazon. There are a few more steps you have to perform with verification keys. Whenever you work with keys, the more secure the platform is, the more in depth the process will be. In order to upload the game to the Amazon Appstore, you need to perform the following steps:

1. Sign up for a developer account.
2. Add a new web app in their interface.
3. Once you are here, go to the app files tab and take a note of the verification key.

> The verification key is a long string of numbers that makes the game unique to the app.

4. Export the file from Construct 2 as a wrapped HTML5 form.
5. Upload it to the developer account, and make sure you copy the verification key. The following screenshot shows the icon for Amazon:

Exporting for Windows 8

If you want to make a **Windows 8** game, such as a Windows Phone 8 game, you have to get Visual Studio and you have to become a developer. You will also have to download the Metro plugin for Construct 2 as well. The process of uploading is very similar for Windows 8 and Windows Phone 8 apps; the only difference is that in the Dev Store, you have to make sure you are uploading a Windows 8 app.

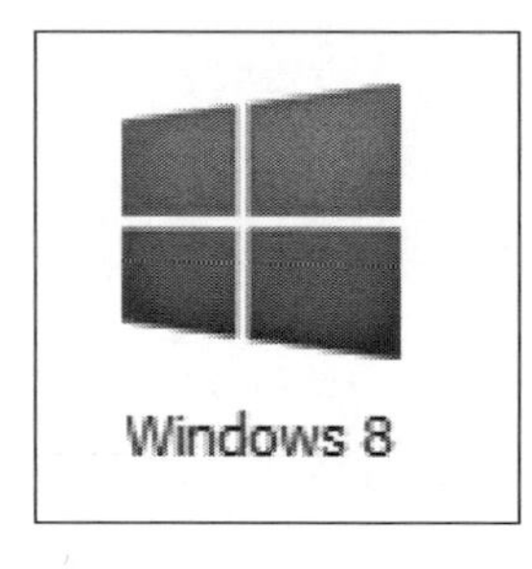

Exporting to Open Web App

The **Open Web App** store is Firefox's answer to the Chrome Web Store. Making a packaged app is very simple. In order to upload to the Firefox Store, you need to perform the following steps:

1. Sign up for a developer account.
2. Export the game using the Firefox exporter.
3. Make sure you set the orientations to what you need them to be. If your game runs in portrait only, then you should select that. You can select these settings in the Firefox Store.

4. Simply submit your app to the Firefox marketplace.

Exporting to Node-Webkit

Node-Webkit is one of my favorite exporters in Construct 2. You can make OSX, Windows, and Linux apps with Node-Webkit. It wraps your game into an `.exe`, `.app`, or `.pak` file and you can see the exported files. From there, all you have to do is run the apps on the respective systems. The following screenshot shows the icon for Node-Webkit:

Just click on **Export to Node-Webkit** and you should see the exported files. From there, all you have to do is run the apps on the respective systems.

linux32	10/3/2013 15:22	File folder
linux64	10/3/2013 15:22	File folder
osx	10/3/2013 15:22	File folder
win32	10/3/2013 15:22	File folder

The best part about this export is that you can start selling from your website immediately.

Summary

In this chapter, we learned how to export our game as an HTML5 file and the details of exporting it to multiple platforms.

In the next appendix, we will wrap up the book and discuss where to go from here when it comes to game design and how you can become a successful developer.

Where to Go from Here

Well, that concludes the book! Thank you for reading it. If you want to see what I and my company, Mammoth Interactive, are up to, you can go to `http://www.mammothinteractive.com`. We are always making new and exciting games as well as other apps and content.

Let's talk about how to really make it big in the gaming industry. Now that you have learned how to make a few games, you probably want to learn more. Learning game development is just like anything else—if you want to get better at it, you have to practice. It is very similar to how a musician gets good at using an instrument, or an athlete gets good at a sport.

Imagine for a second that you were an Olympic weight lifter. The night before the competition, you decide to cram your studies in hopes of competing well the next day. As you probably guessed, this is not the way to become a good weight lifter. It takes years of practice and dedication.

Even though game development is not physical strength but more mental strength, you have to approach it in the same way. It takes a long time to learn how to do everything correctly and efficiently.

People often ask me how they can become good game developers. The answer is actually quite simple—you just have to make lots of games. The more games you make, the better you get. It sounds simple enough but most people never do this. They never make enough games to make them better.

Let me continue with a story. When I was 12, I took a programming class at my local university. It was Visual Basic and when I heard Visual Basic, I thought it meant "making a 3D game". Visual Basic is anything but that. I went home that night and planned out what the game would be like when I completed it. It was a third-person **role-playing game** (**RPG**). I made some sketches and visualized everything I wanted in the game. I wrote a story and wanted to program it. I genuinely thought that I would make an AAA game in my bedroom with my 4/86 processor.

It was then that I was confronted with reality—this was not possible. Flash forward to my early 20s and I still wanted to make a sci-fi game in my bedroom. It still didn't happen. What's the moral of the story? Why am I telling you this?

I am telling you all of this because I don't want you to make the same mistake I did. Instead of making really big games all by yourself or with a small team, you should instead focus on making a lot of really small games.

This is going to go against everything you ever learned in school, but it is something you should do if you want to become good at creating anything. Remember, the more games you make, the better you get. But really, it isn't the game that makes you better—it's how much you improve between the games. Every game you make, you want to try and outdo your last game.

At Mammoth Interactive, we try and make every project 10 percent faster, better, and more profitable. This is a lofty goal but, for every game you make, you should try and do this. It might not happen every time but you should strive for this goal. Let's talk about what you should do in order to make games and get better at them:

1. Make a lot of prototypes.
2. Once you have mastered the basics, make a simple, yet fun game.
3. Release this game. It can be on your website or on the app store.
4. Try hard to release something on the app store or somewhere where people buy it.
5. Repeat the process.

If you look at people who make games or any creative project for a living, they end up spending lots of time on it. Personally, there was a time when I spent all of my days just making games. I recommend this if you want to really excel at designing games.

If you have any questions, you can always e-mail me at `johnbura@mammothinteractive.com`.

Index

Symbols

A

B

C

D

E

G

H

I

K

L

T

V

W

[PACKT] PUBLISHING

Thank you for buying

Construct 2 Game Development by Example

About Packt Publishing

Packt, pronounced 'packed', published its first book "*Mastering phpMyAdmin for Effective MySQL Management*" in April 2004 and subsequently continued to specialize in publishing highly focused books on specific technologies and solutions.

Our books and publications share the experiences of your fellow IT professionals in adapting and customizing today's systems, applications, and frameworks. Our solution based books give you the knowledge and power to customize the software and technologies you're using to get the job done. Packt books are more specific and less general than the IT books you have seen in the past. Our unique business model allows us to bring you more focused information, giving you more of what you need to know, and less of what you don't.

Packt is a modern, yet unique publishing company, which focuses on producing quality, cutting-edge books for communities of developers, administrators, and newbies alike. For more information, please visit our website: `www.packtpub.com`.

Writing for Packt

We welcome all inquiries from people who are interested in authoring. Book proposals should be sent to `author@packtpub.com`. If your book idea is still at an early stage and you would like to discuss it first before writing a formal book proposal, contact us; one of our commissioning editors will get in touch with you.

We're not just looking for published authors; if you have strong technical skills but no writing experience, our experienced editors can help you develop a writing career, or simply get some additional reward for your expertise.

[PACKT]
PUBLISHING

Construct Game Development Beginner's Guide

ISBN: 978-1-84951-660-0 Paperback: 298 pages

A guide to escalate beginners to intermediate game creators through teaching practical game creation using Scirra Construct

1. Learn the skills necessary to make your own games through the creation of three very different sample games.
2. Create animated sprites, use built-in physics and shadow engines of Construct Classic.
3. A wealth of step-by-step instructions and images to lead the way.

GameMaker Game Programming with GML

ISBN: 978-1-78355-944-2 Paperback: 350 pages

Learn GameMaker Language programming concepts and script integration with GameMaker: Studio through hands-on, playable examples

1. Write and utilize scripts to help organize and speed up your game production workflow.
2. Display important user interface components such as score, health, and lives.
3. Play sound effects and music, and create particle effects to add some spice to your projects.
4. Learn how to script common game features: artificial intelligence, collision, reading input, and player feedback.

Please check **www.PacktPub.com** for information on our titles

OUYA Game Development by Example Beginner's Guide

ISBN: 978-1-84969-722-4 Paperback: 268 pages

An all-inclusive, fun guide to making professional 3D games for the OUYA console

1. Create enthralling and unique games for the OUYA console.
2. Learn basic scripting methods in a three-dimensional game engine.
3. Polish and package your games for publishing on the OUYA marketplace.

Starling Game Development Essentials

ISBN: 978-1-78398-354-4 Paperback: 116 pages

Develop and deploy isometric turn-based games using Starling

1. Create a cross-platform Starling Isometric game.
2. Add enemy AI and multiplayer capability.
3. Explore the complete source code for the Web and cross-platform game development.

Printed in Great Britain
by Amazon.co.uk, Ltd.,
Marston Gate.